HUB CITIES IN THE KNOWLEDGE ECONOMY

Transport and Mobility Series

Series Editors: Richard Knowles, University of Salford, UK and Markus Hesse, Université du Luxembourg and on behalf of the Royal Geographical Society (with the Institute of British Geographers) Transport Geography Research Group (TGRG).

The inception of this series marks a major resurgence of geographical research into transport and mobility. Reflecting the dynamic relationships between socio-spatial behaviour and change, it acts as a forum for cutting-edge research into transport and mobility, and for innovative and decisive debates on the formulation and repercussions of transport policy making.

Also in the series

Institutional Barriers to Sustainable Transport
Carey Curtis and Nicholas Low
ISBN 978 0 7546 7692 8

Daily Spatial Mobilities
Physical and Virtual
Aharon Kellerman
ISBN 978 1 4094 2362 1

Territorial Implications of High Speed Rail
A Spanish Perspective
Edited by José M. de Ureña
ISBN 978 1 4094 3052 0

Sustainable Transport, Mobility Management and Travel Plans
Marcus Enoch
ISBN 978 0 7546 7939 4

Transition towards Sustainable Mobility
The Role of Instruments, Individuals and Institutions
Edited by Harry Geerlings, Yoram Shiftan and Dominic Stead
ISBN 978 1 4094 2469 7

Hub Cities in the Knowledge Economy

Seaports, Airports, Brainports

Edited by

SVEN CONVENTZ
Munich University of Technology, Germany

BEN DERUDDER
Ghent University, Belgium

ALAIN THIERSTEIN
Munich University of Technology, Germany

FRANK WITLOX
Ghent University, Belgium

Routledge
Taylor & Francis Group

LONDON AND NEW YORK

First published 2014 by Ashgate Publishing

Published 2016 by Routledge
2 Park Square, Milton Park, Abingdon, Oxfordshire OX14 4RN
711 Third Avenue, New York, NY 10017, USA

First issued in paperback 2016

Routledge is an imprint of the Taylor & Francis Group, an informa business

British Library Cataloguing in Publication Data
A catalogue record for this book is available from the British Library

The Library of Congress has cataloged the printed edition as follows:
Conventz, Sven.
Hub cities in the knowledge economy : seaports, airports, brainports / by Sven Conventz, Ben Derudder, Alain Thierstein and Frank Witlox.
    pages cm. — (Transport and mobility)
Includes bibliographical references and index.
ISBN 978-1-4094-4591-3 (hardback : alk. paper)
1. Knowledge management. 2. Knowledge economy. 3. Information technology.
4. Cities and towns. 5. Regional economics. I. Title.
 HD30.2.C6548 2013
 338.9'26—dc23

                                                                2013023976

ISBN 13: 978-1-138-24702-4 (pbk)
ISBN 13: 978-1-4094-4591-3 (hbk)

Contents

List of Figures

Hub Cities in the Knowledge Economy

List of Tables

Notes on Contributors

Michael Bentlage is research associate at Munich Technical University. He studied Geography at the University of Würzburg and since January 2009 has been working on his doctoral thesis at the chair for spatial and territorial development. He also gives lectures and courses on polycentric Mega-City Regions and scientific work for students of Architecture, landscape design and Geography. He has published on the subject of firm networks, knowledge creation and accessibility; most recently, together with Alain Thierstein, 'Knowledge Creation in German Agglomerations and Accessibility – An Approach involving Non-physical Connectivity', *Cities* 30(1) (2013): 47–58. Furthermore, he works as a consultant in GIS analysis and quantitative methods in social and spatial sciences.

Sven Conventz is research associate at the Chair for Territorial and Spatial Development at Munich Technical University (TUM). Sven received his diploma in Geography, Real Estate Economics and Urban Planning from Bayreuth University and a Master in Urban Affairs and Public Policy with focus on Urban and Regional Planning from the University of Delaware. Before joining TUM, Sven was a research associated at Karlsruhe Institute of Technology, formerly known as University of Karlsruhe. His research interests include urban redevelopment, urban economics, infrastructural planning, airport-linked spatial development and the impacts of the knowledge economy on the spatial structure.

Margaret Cowell, PhD is Assistant Professor of Urban Affairs and Planning at Virginia Tech in Alexandria, Virginia, USA. Her research focuses on economic development with specific interests in local governance, civic capacity, and economic restructuring. Recent research endeavours include several publications on deindustrializing regions across the United States and Europe, regional resilience, and polycentrism. Dr Cowell's research has been funded by the MacArthur Foundation, National Association of Counties, and the United States Economic Development Administration.

Ben Derudder is Professor of Human Geography at Ghent University's Department of Geography, and Associate Director of the Globalization and World Cities research group and network (GaWC). His research focuses on (i) the conceptualization and empirical analysis of transnational urban networks, (ii) polycentric urban development, (iii) the (persisting) importance of business travel in the space economy, and (iv) the potential of new developments in network analysis for geographical research.

Dario Diodato is associated with Utrecht University, The Netherlands. He works on projects concerning interregional European development, skill-relatedness and IO-modelling in collaboration with the Netherlands Environmental Assessment Agency in The Hague.

Teodora Dogaru is assistant professor at "Ioan Slavici" University Timisoara, Romania, and visiting at Utrecht University, The Netherlands and Univesidad de A Coruna, Spain. Her research focus is on regional economic disparities in Europe and European policy implementation, including cross-border development strategies, vocational training strategies and regional socio-economic development.

Anna Growe is Post-Doc Researcher at the Institute of Cultural Geography at the University of Freiburg. She studied and worked in Dortmund and Venice. Her research concentrates on urban systems, challenges of the network economy and the development of metropolitan regions. Most recently she has written the Book *Knoten in Netzwerken wissensintensiver Dienstleistungen. Eine empirische Analyse des polyzentralen deutschen Städtesystems* that was awarded with the dissertation prize of the Faculty of Spatial Planning at the Dortmund University of Technology.

Stefan Lüthi is an economic geographer and professional consultant in the field of urban and regional development at BHP – Brugger and Partners Ltd., Switzerland. His primary area of activity includes spatial development, urban economics, regional economic development, regional innovation systems as well as quantitative and qualitative methods of network analysis. A particular focus lies on the knowledge economy and its impact on polycentric mega-city regions, global cities and world city networks. He is involved in the Globalization and World Cities Research Network (http://www.lboro.ac.uk/gawc/), the leading academic think tank on cities in globalization. Stefan started his career at the Munich University of Technology in Germany, where he completed his Ph.D. and wrote a series of articles on interlocking firm networks and emerging mega-city regions. Stefan serves as an advisor to business, the social sector and the government, especially at the intersection of urban and regional policy, territorial development and sustainability.

Edward J. Malecki is Professor of Geography at The Ohio State University. He has written widely on topics related to technology and economic development, and is the co-author (with Bruno Moriset) most recently of *The Digital Economy* (2008). Ed is Associate Editor of the journal *Entrepreneurship and Regional Development*.

Heike Mayer is professor of economic geography in the Institute of Geography and co-director of the Center for Regional Economic Development at the University of Bern in Switzerland. Her primary area of research is in local and regional economic development with a particular focus on dynamics of innovation and entrepreneurship, place making and sustainability. She is the author of *Entrepreneurship and Innovation in Second Tier Regions* (Edward Elgar) and co-author of *Small Town Sustainability* (with Prof. Paul L. Knox, Birkhäuser Press).

Oli Mould is a lecturer in Human Geography at Royal Holloway, University of London. He has researched and written about all aspects of urban creativity, that which seeks to contribute to capitalist accumulation as well as that which seeks to resist it. His current research focuses on media cities, and how they can be used to foster community-level creative activities as well as economic prosperity.

Zachary Neal is Assistant Professor of Sociology and Global Urban Studies at Michigan State University. He serves on the editorial board of *City and Community* and *Global Networks*, and as co-editor of the *Metropolis and Modern Life* book series. His work focuses on using networks to understand urban phenomena at multiple scales, ranging from micro-level neighbourhood interactions to macro-level world city networks. In addition to numerous articles on cities and networks, he is the author of two books: *Common Ground? Readings and Reflections on Public Space* (Routledge, 2009), and *The Connected City: How Networks are Shaping the Modern Metropolis* (Routledge, 2013).

Peter Nijkamp is professor in regional and urban economics and in economic geography at the VU University, Amsterdam. His main research interests cover quantitative plan evaluation, regional and urban modelling, multicriteria analysis, transport systems analysis, mathematical systems modelling, technological innovation, entrepreneurship, environmental and resource management, and sustainable development. In the past years he has focussed his research in particular on new quantitative methods for policy analysis, as well as on spatial-behavioural analysis of economic agents. He has a broad expertise in the area of public policy, services planning, infrastructure management and environmental protection. In all these fields he has published many books and numerous articles. He is member of editorial/advisory boards of more than 30 journals. He has been visiting professor in many universities all over the world. According to the RePec list he belongs to the top-30 of well-known economists world-wide. He is past president of the European Regional Science Association and of the Regional Science Association International. He is also fellow of the Royal Netherlands Academy of Sciences, and past vice-president of this organization. From 2002 – 2009 he has served as president of the governing board of the Netherlands Research Council (NWO). In addition, he is past president of the European Heads of Research Councils (EUROHORCs). He is also fellow of the Academia Europaea, and member of many international scientific organizations. He has acted regularly as advisor to (inter)national bodies and (local and national) governments. In 1996, he was awarded the most prestigious scientific prize in the Netherlands, the Spinoza award. At present, he is honorary university professor. Detailed information can be found on http://personal.vu.nl/p.nijkamp.

Alain Thierstein. is a full professor for spatial and territorial development at the Munich University of Technology, department of architecture. He at the same time is senior consultant and partner with Ernst Basler Partners Ltd, Zurich, a private engineering and planning consultancy. He holds a Ph.D. in Economics and a master degree in Economics and Business Administration from the University of St. Gallen. Current research interests include impact of the knowledge economy on urban and mega-city regions development, sustainable regional development, innovation and regional policy as well as policy evaluation.

Mark Thissen is senior and coordinating researcher in spatial economics at the Netherlands Environmental Assessment Agency in The Hague, The Netherlands. He publishes frequently on spatial equilibrium modelling in Europe, and works on interregional and longitudinal trade data between European regions.

Emmanouil Tranos is an economic geographer focusing primarily on digital geographies. He has published on issues related with the spatiality of the Internet infrastructure and the economic impacts that this infrastructure can generate on space. His research in this area led in a monograph on "The Geography of the Internet: cities, regions and Internet infrastructure". Recently, he has been researching the use of big, digital data of high spatio-temporal resolution in urban and regional analysis. Regarding research methods, his work combines traditional econometric methods and spatial analysis with tools and concepts from network theory

Elien Van De Vijver is a PhD candidate at the Geography Department of Ghent University, Belgium. She holds a master's degree in Geography (Ghent University). Her research is funded by the Special Research Fund of Ghent University and focuses on the relationship between global air passenger travel, globalized service provisioning and international trade using several quantitative methods, including regression techniques and Granger causality analysis.

Frank van Oort is professor in urban economics at Utrecht University, The Netherlands. He publishes frequently on European regional economic development, knowledge creation and diffusion, urban economics and spatial planning. He is editor of *Regional Studies* and editor-in-chief of the *Journal of Economic and Social Geography*. See: www.frankvanoort.com.

Anne Wiese is an Architect and Urban Designer with an ongoing interest in industrial dynamics. Her experience in practice includes working on large scale urban projects as well as consulting public authorities on spatial development. As a researcher at the TU Munich she has been working with the Nord LB on maritime networks and their resultant spatial implications. She is a lecturer on the course European Megacity Regions. Her research focuses on the multi-scalar development of network dynamics and the special interplay between physical and functional flows in the urban context. Her PhD thesis is entitled 'Does the port anchor the flow? European port cities between spatial ambitions and functional realities'. She has contributed to several books on urban development and published in journals on regional development and urban diversity.

Frank Witlox holds a Ph.D. in Urban Planning (Eindhoven University of Technology), a Master's Degree in Applied Economics and a Master's Degree in Maritime Sciences (both University of Antwerp). Currently, he is Professor of Economic Geography at the Department of Geography of the Ghent University. He is also a visiting professor at ITMMA (Institute of Transport and Maritime Management Antwerp) and an Associate Director of GaWC (Globalization and World Cities, Loughborough University). Since 2010 he is the Director of the Doctoral School of Natural Sciences (UGent). Frank Witlox has hold part-time teaching positions at the Hasselt University (Belgium), University of Antwerp (Belgium), and University of Leuven-Campus Kortrijk (Belgium), and is a guest lecturer at Lund University-Campus Helsingborg (Sweden) and University of Tartu (Estonia). His research focuses on travel behaviour analysis and modelling, travel and land use, sustainable mobility issues, business travel, cross-border mobility, city logistics, global commodity chains, globalization and world city-formation, polycentric urban development, contemporary challenges in agricultural land use, and locational analysis of corporations.

Introduction
Knowledge Hubs: Infrastructure and the Knowledge Economy in City-Regions

Ben Derudder, Sven Conventz, Alain Thierstein and Frank Witlox

The overarching theme addressed in this edited volume is the complex and multifaceted interaction between infrastructural accessibility of city-regions on the one hand, and the knowledge generation taking place in these city-regions on the other hand. To this end, we have brought together contributions broadly analysing how infrastructural accessibility is related to locational patterns of knowledge-intensive industries in city-regions.

The proposed theme in this volume is of course not a new one. There is a longstanding tradition of research addressing the conceptual and empirical relations between infrastructural accessibility and knowledge-intensive production processes (e.g. Andersson et al. 1990, Schmidt and Wolke 2009; for a straightforward overview, see Lakshmanan and Chatterjee 2005). At the same time, however, it is clear that general research questions surrounding these associations are constantly being re-defined and re-coded in the face of evolutions in infrastructural accessibility, knowledge generation, and the multiple ways in which both are related. In this context, the chapters in this volume specifically dwell on *recent* manifestations and developments in the accessibility/knowledge-nexus, with a particular metageographical focus on how this materializes in major city-regions (for a related effort, see Hall and Hesse 2012). In this introductory chapter, we aim to provide more details on the context of the overarching theme of this volume by clarifying our take on some key concepts. In addition, we introduce the most important themes addressed in the different chapters.

Our starting point when dealing with the 'knowledge economy' is the observation that capitalism is undergoing an epochal transformation from a mass production system where the principal source of value was human labour to a new era of 'innovation-mediated production' where the principal component of value creation, productivity and economic growth is knowledge (Florida and Kenney 1993). However, as a concept, the notion of a 'knowledge economy' is both contested and fuzzy. That is, although there seems to be widespread agreement that economic success is indeed increasingly based on upon the effective utilization of intangible assets such as knowledge, skills and innovative potential, Smith (2002: 2) suggests that the 'weakness or even complete absence of a clear-cut definition is actually pervasive in the literature'. Conceding that providing a precise definition may indeed be difficult, in this volume we follow Kok (2004: 19, our emphasis), and assume that the knowledge economy is a concept that 'covers every aspect of the contemporary economy *where knowledge is at the heart of value added* – from high-tech manufacturing and information and telecommunication technologies through knowledge intensive services to overtly creative industries such as media and architecture'. In addition, and as shown in a number of chapters in this volume, the knowledge economy is a 'relational' phenomenon as it is 'part of the economy in which highly specialized knowledge and skills are strategically combined from different parts of the value chain in order to create innovations and to sustain competitive advantage' (Lüthi et al. 2011: 162–163). As a consequence, it is important to stress from the outset that the term 'knowledge economy' refers to an overall economic *structure* rather than more restricted definitions pointing to the rising importance of information technologies and/or research and development in economic output.

Our overall aim in this edited volume, then, is to shed new light on recent territorial manifestations and developments in the accessibility/knowledge economy-nexus, whereby the different chapters predominantly focus on the spatial scale of city-regions. These city-regions are thereby fittingly labelled as *'knowledge hubs'*. The broadly conceived working definition of a 'knowledge hub' adopted in this volume is thereby that of a metropolitan area that is both (1) strongly functionally and physically integrated into networks beyond the metropolitan scale, and at the same time (2) characterized by strong knowledge spill-overs within the metropolitan area (see Bathelt et al. 2004). Although the debate on innovation and city-regional development has a long history (e.g., MacKinnon et al. 2002, Asheim et al. 2007), here we take our cue from the more recent vantage point that an interconnected system of globalized city-regions has emerged (cf. Scott 2001), whereby a limited set of city-regions occupies central places in the global economy because they are the locales where these connections converge (i.e. the knowledge hubs). As a consequence, we thus consider knowledge hubs to be interconnected urban areas characterized by myriad processes of 'vertical' integration and vibrancy that give – to a varying degree – way to 'horizontal' spillovers within the broader urban-regional field (Bentlage et al. this volume; Growe and Blotevogel 2011, Bathelt et al. 2004, Bathelt and Glückler 2011).

The main conceptual link between infrastructural accessibility and the development of a knowledge economy in city-regions is somewhat paradoxically found in the declining marginal costs of transmitting goods, information, services and people across space. This is of course nowhere clearer than in the information technology sector, where the infrastructural ability to manipulate, store and transmit large quantities of information at very low cost has proven to be of key importance for city-regions (see Tranos 2012). However, declining marginal costs of connectivity via other, more tangible forms of infrastructure such as airports and seaports have equally boosted the position of particular city-regions in such networks. It is thereby clear that this conceptual relevance of high-quality infrastructural accessibility is also driven by the rapid globalization of economic activities, emanating from various rounds of reduction of tariff and non-tariff barriers on trade, the reduction of barriers to foreign direct investment and other international capital flows, the lessening of barriers to technology transfers, and the deregulation of product markets in many countries, particularly in terms of the reduction in the power of national monopolies in areas such as telecommunications, air transport and the finance and insurance industries.

The rising importance of knowledge generation within the economy, then, is not a general, 'spaceless' phenomenon: the (rising) centrality of knowledge in economic activity is a key driver for the competitiveness of private companies and the urban and regional economies from which these companies are operating. The spatial concentration of knowledge-intensive economic activity is, for instance, related to firms' need for a set of infrastructural conditions, such as proximity to international gateway infrastructures, including airports, high-speed train nodes, Internet infrastructure with the highest standards in terms of bandwidth connections, shipping networks, etc. One key example of the overall logic the different chapters are describing, then, is that knowledge-intensive firms tend to locate their branches and activities at intersections of physical and intangible flows, as the systematic 'availability' of such infrastructures facilitates the spatial dispersal of different functional elements of firms' value chain to other well-connected city-regions in these infrastructures. The emergence of clusters of international, knowledge-intensive firms around airports (e.g. Schiphol Amsterdam, see Schaafsma et al. 2008) and seaports (e.g. Rotterdam, see Jacobs et al. 2010) is a straightforward example of this. Indeed, the generation and transfer of knowledge require direct face-to-face interactions, and knowledge-intensive activities such as innovation have been shown to be highly concentrated in highly urbanized regions (Simmie 2003). The generation, distribution and transfer of knowledge form a key basis for the development of global city-regions, which can hence be defined as 'knowledge hubs' as they are the 'nodes of the global economy, location of creation of knowledge and also engines of the cultural development' (Goebel et al. 2007: 87).

Against this backdrop, the contributions in this volume present different takes on the infrastructure/knowledge economy-nexus in major city-regions. The different chapters thereby predominantly speak to one of three more specific themes, i.e. (1) the relationships between (air)port infrastructures and knowledge generation in city-regions, (2) the relationships between information and communication technology infrastructures and knowledge generation in city-regions, and (3) alternative considerations of the notion of a 'knowledge hub'. We have therefore opted to use these three overarching themes to organize this volume as a whole.

The first part addresses the debate on the conceptual and empirical inter-relationships between (air)port infrastructures, the flows generated through these infrastructures, and the creation of knowledge within city-regions. Derudder et al. explore the related geographies of producer services and air passenger markets in the global economy to unveil the complex and multifaceted relations between the development of a so-called 'knowledge-intensive service economy' in and the 'physical connectivity' of large-scale metropolitan areas. The overall conclusion is that these relations are indeed sizable, giving further credence to the approach taken in this volume. For instance, given major geographical differences in economic development across the globe, the level of knowledge-intensive services seems to be a much better predictor of airline connectivity than mere population size, which contrasts with the dominant impact of the latter variable at the national scale.

Bentlage et al. present a similar analysis for the German urban system. However, their focus on the national scale allows for a more refined empirical framework: connectivity is defined by the potential to reach as much of the population as possible within a certain area by air, rail and/or road transportation, while the knowledge-intensity of economic activity is broken up by looking at firms providing producer services and firms involved in high-tech production. The overall, strong importance of infrastructural accessibility is thereby corroborated, although there are some differences between both sectors.

In her chapter, Growe analyses the shifting geographies of knowledge hubs in the German urban system. She thus reveals influences of city size as well as path dependency, which in the case of the German urban system also entails the persistence of an east/west divide. As a consequence, and in contrast to the commonly assumed 'polycentricity' of the German urban system, we are seeing a continuing concentration of knowledge-intensive industries in a limited set of city-regions.

Conventz and Thierstein also focus on airports, but their chapter zooms in on how these locales have evolved from pure infrastructure facilities into proper and much sought-after business sites. To this end, the authors scrutinize spatial patterns and process of specialization in and around two major European airports: Amsterdam's Schiphol Airport and Frankfurt's Rhine-Main Airport. They conclude that airports have indeed grown out of their niche as pure infrastructure facilities and morphed into attractive real estate sites.

The chapter by Wiese and Thierstein focuses on ports. Based on an analysis of the maritime economy in Northern Germany, the authors find that contemporary port-city relationships are shaped by spatial and functional interdependencies that stretch well beyond port or city. For instance, in functional terms, the port and its auxiliary functions (formerly an industrial operational site) have extended their operations into other sectors with high knowledge intensity. For instance, Hamburg has developed into a dominant centre for advanced producer service firms providing services to other agents and firms in the maritime economy.

The second part focuses on information and telecommunication infrastructures that collectively facilitate intangible flows. Malecki assesses the position of cities in the context of evolving technical features of the Internet. Based on his analysis of the 'Internet interconnection' taking place in specific locales (so-called 'peering facilities'), he concludes that the presence of this infrastructure not only facilitates flows of data and codified knowledge, but to some degree also of tacit knowledge via e-mail, messaging and teleconferencing. Nonetheless, this rising relevance of 'virtual' flows has by no means resulted in the demise of travel: the Internet is seen as a complement to travel rather than a substitute.

Tranos and Nijkamp equally focus on the city-regional dimensions of digital connectivity. Usefully, they start by noting that the complex technical structure of digital infrastructures makes it hard for spatial scientists to fully comprehend the topology, structure and design principles of such networks. Nonetheless, digital phenomena such as the Internet have spatial reflections that need to be approached from a geographic standpoint, and their chapter corroborates this by providing an overview of a series of hands-on examples.

In the final chapter of this second part, Mould reflects on how urban governance is now focused on trying to create urban environments – in particular by constructing so-called 'media cities' – that help to foster creativity and innovation by making them attractive places to live, work and play. The author shows how urban governments in very different locales have developed extremely expensive media cities to function as 'planned' knowledge hubs in the global creative economy. Based on his critical review, Mould concludes that these policies are certainly innovative as these adhere to a more 'realistic' view of creativity. Nonetheless, their ability to maintain a vibrant and atmosphere of a creative, knowledge-generating cluster should not be overstated, as it is not yet clear whether their planned nature will translate into the stimulation of local creative industry talent and the legacy of a sustainable creative workforce.

The chapters in the third and final part of this volume consider the analytical purchase of the 'knowledge hub' concept in more detail, thereby collectively starting from the observation that knowledge is above all created through personal interaction. For instance, although the use of information and telecommunication technologies clearly facilitates the exchange, storage, and sorting of information, the creation of value out of such information (i.e. *knowledge*) emanates from people getting together to assess, weigh, and decide on the issues at stake in the context of firm and organizational strategies. The concrete way in which infrastructural accessibility leads to knowledge-generation thus depends on a series of contextual factors, and the different chapters tackle this issue from different viewpoints.

The chapter of Dogaru et al. underlines the role of agglomeration and knowledge in European regional growth. Their findings highlights that the spatial scale of 'the region' can only function as a knowledge hub if it is able to 'capture' knowledge and subsequently translate it locally in a productive manner. As a consequence, the spatial diffusion of knowledge and its effect on innovation is of major importance to ensure productivity and employment growth of firms and regions, and to improve the welfare of regions.

Neal provides a more nuanced consideration of the 'knowledge hub' concept by presenting a typology of hub cities based on the effect of airline connectivity on urban creative economies. To his end, he uses data on airline traffic and creative employment in 128 US metropolitan areas to compare the relevance of three different conceptions of hub cities that mirror Freeman's (1979) tripartite treatise of network centrality. The result of his analysis is a new and more precise language for discussing the role of hub cities in the knowledge economy.

In the final chapter, Mayer and Cowell discuss the key features of a particular type of hub city: capital cities. To this end, they examine capital cities in their particular and important role in the formation and consolidation of the cultural, social and political identity of a state. In their contribution, they show this by focusing on Washington D.C., which is characterized by a very specific type of economy that benefits from close interactions between government, administration, and the nonprofit and private sector. The authors thus show that capital cities function as knowledge hubs because they are the centres of political decision-making and the execution of political power.

Given the breadth of the topic addressed here, it is clear that the different chapters offer a partial and specific window into this research domain. For instance, there is a notable unevenness in terms of geographic coverage (e.g., most chapters focus on European cases), while a number of key issues remain unaddressed (e.g. there is only limited reference to the wider literature on regional innovation and growth, see Cooke et al. 2011). Nonetheless, the different chapters in this volume cover a variety of infrastructures (airports, railway stations, ports, Internet infrastructure, etc.), adopt a variety of methodologies (conceptual arguments, large-scale empirical research, case studies, etc.), and focus on different segments of the knowledge economy (knowledge intensive business services, advanced producer services, high-tech industries, etc.). We therefore hope that, collectively, these contributions provide readers with a useful overview of recent research on the nexus between infrastructural accessibility and the knowledge economy in city-regions.

References

Andersson A.E., Anderstig, C. and Hårsman, B. 1990. Knowledge and communications infrastructure and regional economic change. *Regional Science and Urban Economics*, 20(3), 359–76.

Asheim, B.T., Coenen, L., Moodysson, J. and Vang, J. 2007. Constructing knowledge based regional advantage: Implications for regional innovation policy. *International Journal of Entrepreneurship and Innovation Management*, 7(2/3/4/5), 140–55.

Bathelt, H., Malmberg A. and Maskell, P. 2004. Clusters and knowledge: local buzz, global pipelines and the process of knowledge creation. *Progress in Human Geography*, 28(1), 31–56.

Bathelt, H. and Glückler, J. 2011. *The Relational Economy: Geographies of Knowledge and Learning*. Oxford: Oxford University Press.

Cook, P., Asheim, B., Boschma, R., Martin, R., Schwartz, D. and Tödtling, F. 2011. *Handbook of Regional Innovation and Growth*. Cheltenham: Edward Elgar Publishing Limited.

Florida, R. and Kenney, M. 1993. The new age of capitalism: Innovation-mediated production. *Futures*, 25(6), 637–51.

Freeman, L.C. 1979. Centrality in social networks: Conceptual clarification. *Social Networks*, 1, 215–39.

Goebel, V., Thierstein, A. and Lüthi, S. 2007. *Functional Polycentricity in the Mega-City Region of Munich*, Association of European Schools of Planning (AESOP), Napoli, 11–14 July 2007.

Growe, A. and Blotevogel, H.H. 2011. Knowledge hubs in the German urban system: Identifying hubs by combining network and territorial perspectives. *Raumforschung und Raumordnung*, 69(3), 175–85.

Hall, P. and Hesse, M. 2012. *Cities, Regions and Flows*. London: Routledge.

Jacobs, W., Koster, H. and Hall, P. 2010. The location and global network structure of maritime advanced producer services. *Urban Studies*, 21, 2–21.

Kok, W. (2004) *Facing The Challenge. The Lisbon Strategy for Growth and Employment. Report from the High level Group*. Brussels: European Commission.

Lakshmanan, T.R. and Chatterjee, L.R. 2005. Economic consequences of transport improvements. *Access*, 26, 28–33.

Lüthi, S., Thierstein, A. and Bentlage, M. 2011. Interlocking firm networks in the German knowledge economy. On local networks and global connectivity. *Raumforschung und Raumordnung*, 69(3), 161–74.

MacKinnon, D., Cumbers, A. and Chapman, K. 2002. Learning, innovation and regional development: A critical appraisal of recent debates. *Progress in Human Geography*, 26(3), 293–311.

Schaafsma, M., Amkreutz, J. and Güller, M. 2008. *Airport and City – Airport Corridors: Drivers of economic development*. Rotterdam: Schiphol Real Estate.

Schmidt, S. and Wolke, M. 2009. The importance of infrastructures and interaction networks for regional competitiveness in the knowledge economy, in *German Annual of Spatial Research and Policy 2009*, edited by H. Kilper. Berlin: Springer Berlin Heidelberg, 51–66.

Simmie, J. 2003. Innovation and urban regions as national and international nodes for the transfer and sharing of knowledge. *Regional Studies*, 37(6–7), 607–20.

Scott, A.J. 2001. Globalization and the rise of city-regions. *European Planning Studies*, 9(7), 813–26.

Smith, K. 2002. *What is the Knowledge Economy? Knowledge Intensity and Distributed Knowledge Bases, Institute for New Technologies Discussion Paper 2002–2006*. The United Nations University.

Tranos, E. 2012. The causal effect of the Internet infrastructure on the economic development of the European city-regions. *Spatial Economic Analysis*, 7(3), 319–37.

PART I

PART I

Chapter 1

Knowledge Flows and Physical Connectivity in the Global Economy: An Exploration of the Related Geographies of Producer Services and Air Passenger Markets

Ben Derudder, Elien Van De Vijver and Frank Witlox

Introduction

This chapter presents an empirical perspective on the complex and multifaceted spatial relations between the development of a so-called 'knowledge-intensive service economy' in and the 'physical connectivity' of large-scale metropolitan areas. There is a rich empirical literature on the connections between physical infrastructure and the development of knowledge-intensive services at the national scale, especially for the United States. Debbage (1999), for instance, showed that population size, service intensity and airline infrastructure are major covariates in the US urban system. Irwin and Kasarda (1991), in turn, found for a set of 104 US metropolitan areas that changes in airline networks affect the employment growth in business services, while roughly a decade later Brueckner (2003) and Debbage and Delk (2001) obtained similar results.

To date, however, there have been few studies on the association at the level of the *global economy* as a whole. This is undoubtedly in part because of the continued lack of large-scale global urban databases of a high quality (see Short et al. 1996, Taylor 1997). A major exception is the work of Taylor et al. (2007), who assess the impact of airline infrastructure on cities' involvement in the office networks of producer services firms at the global scale. The formative purpose of this chapter is to extend and improve the Taylor et al. (2007) study through the use of a more refined methodological framework. In line with this study, our analysis essentially gauges the spatial parallels between the office networks of globalized business services firms and global air passenger networks. However, here we construct connectivity measures at a more relevant city-regional scale, while we also add some control variables to arrive at a more refined model. These measures are compared through correlation coefficients and a stepwise regression model, whereby the model parameters and the regression residuals are used to explore this specific take on the linkages between the knowledge-intensity of urban economies and their physical infrastructure.

The remainder of this chapter is organized as follows. The next section briefly introduces the conceptual backdrop of our empirical analysis: we discuss the linkages between world city-formation as measured by the presence of globalized producer services firms and air passenger flows, and draw on a literature review to explore which processes can be assumed to further impact these linkages. In the following section, we discuss our data and methodological framework, followed by a section outlining our results. The chapter is concluded with a discussion of the implications for research on the linkages between the knowledge-intensity of urban economies and physical infrastructure networks.

Literature Review

World Cities, Air Transportation, and Producer Services

There is a long tradition of geographical research on the way in which the development of urban systems has been tied up with the development of airline infrastructure (cf. Taaffe 1962, Bird 1973, Warf 1989). This practice has been continued in the research on the emergence of an urban system at the global scale. Keeling's (1995) seminal chapter on 'Transportation and the world city paradigm', for instance, asserts why air transport is a key factor in the rise of a global urban system. The most pertinent factors are: (1) airline networks and their associated infrastructure are perhaps the single most visible manifestation of a city's aspiration towards global prominence (cf. Dubai and Hong Kong); (2) the continued demand for face-to-face relationships in business processes calls for the globalized inter-city movement of people, in spite of the parallel development of (tele)communication networks; and (3) the more general observation that air transportation is the preferred mode of inter-city movement for the transnational capitalist class, migrants, and tourists.

The net result of these straightforward conceptual linkages is that air passenger transportation is clearly tied into the development of a global urban system centered on so-called 'world cities' or 'global cities'. Interestingly for the purposes of this chapter, the latter concepts are in turn often explicitly linked to the increased importance of strategic knowledge generation under conditions of contemporary globalization. For instance, in her well-known book on the globalization of the urban economies of New York, London and Tokyo, Sassen (2001) essentially argues that these cities are strongly associated with contemporary globalization through their development of advanced producer services (APS), offered by firms producing customized financial, professional and creative expertise to corporate clients. The urban disposition of APS rests on the straightforward observation that, to keep ahead in their business, such firms require access to a skilled labour pool, information-rich and prestigious environs, and superior office, transport and telecommunications infrastructures, all of which are primarily found in major cities across the settled world. As the corporate clients of APS firms increasingly begun to globalize from the 1970s onwards, so also did the firms providing APS such as commercial law, wealth management, corporate tax advice and advertising. The result has been that some major cities became simultaneously markets for these services through corporate presences, and production centres of these services through innovative knowledge clusters. It is through the knowledge-generating expertise of APS firms in transnational servicing of their clients that cities became seen as the organizing nodes of economic globalization aka global cities.

Taken together, therefore, one can hypothesize that there will be some parallels and even co-evolution between the globalized urban geographies of knowledge-intensive APS firms and those of airline networks (Neal 2010). In this chapter, we address these parallels at the global scale in more empirical detail.

Empirical Particulars of the Air Transportation/Producer Services Relation

The study by Taylor et al. (2007) explicitly sought to explain cities' airline passenger numbers by their involvement in global APS provisioning. In the event, the authors found that their measure of globalized APS provisioning explains up to 53 per cent of the observed variance in the number of airline passengers associated with major cities. Interestingly, however, Taylor et al. (2007) do not pay much attention to the results of this 'general' relation. This is because they note that US cities seem to have a pattern that is consistently different from that of non-US cities. The authors ascribe this to the sheer size of the deregulated US air passenger market[1] as well as the relatively underdeveloped presence of 'globalized' APS firms because of a strong 'national' APS market (see Taylor and Lang 2005). The net effect is that US cities have generally far more air passenger connectivity than can be expected based on their involvement in the office networks of globalized APS firms. As a consequence, in practice Taylor et al. (2007) assess the relation between the size of the air passenger market and APS presence for US and non-US cities separately. The relevance of this choice is shown by the results, as the explained variance thus rises from 53 per cent to 73 per cent and 61 per cent for US cities and non-US cities respectively.

A first possible factor influencing the relation between cities' airline passenger numbers and their involvement in global APS provisioning is therefore a host of contextual factors at the national level. Taylor et al. (2007) restrict the use of

---

1   This 'sheer size' is also deepened by the fact that alternatives for medium-distance travel, in particular high-speed train links, are quasi-absent in the United States. Ideally, the exercise in this chapter should combine different connectivity modes, including high-speed train links. However, given the very uneven geographies of these high-speed train connections and the paucity of comparative data at the global level, in this chapter we restrict ourselves to the example of air traffic links. For recent research on the transnational geographies of high-speed train connections, see Murayama (1994), Ortega et al. (2012) and a recent special issue of the 'Journal of Transport Geography' on on 'Rail Transit Systems and High Speed Rail'.

'national specificity' in their model to the US because of an assumed 'American exceptionalism' in this context. However, it is likely that the US is not the only case where the relationship between infrastructure networks and the presence of globalized APS firms is driven by national peculiarities. Take the example of China, where a state-processed economy is clearly crucial for understanding cities' involvement in the office networks of globalized APS. For instance, in spite of the country's WTO ascension in 2001, business continues to be tightly regulated in China. The most obvious example, of course, is that of banking in that most of China's financial institutions continue to be state owned and governed, while 75 per cent of state bank loans continue to go to State Owned Enterprises (SOEs). China's entry into the WTO has obviously created opportunities for foreign banks as well. However, there continue to be strict rules regulating foreign financial institutions' possibilities, especially when it comes to doing business in the local currency (Pauly 2011). The key point for this chapter is that, although a high-end service sector is undeniably developing in most Chinese cities, the involvement of firms typically dubbed as global APS firms is restricted by the regulatory context imposed by the Chinese state. Thus in addition to a specific pattern for US cities, one can also suspect a differential pattern for Chinese cities, and perhaps also for cities in other states. In our analysis, we therefore extend the framework of Taylor et al. (2007), not by 'splitting' the analysis in a set of sub-analyses, but by adding dummy control variables in the regression analysis for states with multiple cities in the data.

A second possible factor influencing the relation between cities' involvement in global APS provisioning and their airline passenger numbers is urban population size. For the US, for instance, Debbage (1999) has shown that the most important explanatory variable for understanding cities' airline passenger numbers is simply population size. Short (2004) has shown that metropolitan size is correlated with world city-formation as measured through the presence of globalized APS firms. Although this correlation is small given global differences in economic development, it does suggest that there may be a size effect in that large cities have the tendency to be slightly more connected in the office networks of globalized APS firms and, as a corollary, also in global airline networks. It seems therefore warranted to adopt this indicator in our regression analysis as a potential control variable.

Data and Methodology

The insights derived from this brief literature review have guided our empirical analysis. We consecutively discuss the data we used for our dependent and independent variables, some data transformations, and our modelling approach.

Dependent variable: connectivity in air passenger networks
Although there are quite some data sources detailing the connectivity of cities in global air passenger networks, not all sources are equally pertinent. One major example would be that most airline statistics do not feature origin-destination information, but rather provide evidence of the way in which airlines organize

their networks (Derudder and Witlox 2005). Using such data would, for instance, overvalue the importance of cities such as Amsterdam and Atlanta as these cities function above all as switching points for KLM and Delta Airlines travellers, respectively. To circumvent this problem, here we use 2010 data derived from the Sabre Airport Data Intelligence (ADI) database. ADI is a so-called 'Global Distribution System', which contains worldwide booking information on passenger flights. The database contains information on passenger flows between airports. In contrast to most other statistics, this data source contains information on actual origins and destinations as well as information on the connections of low-cost carriers. This dataset is used to calculate the number of origin and destination passengers for the metropolitan regions in our analysis (on which more below), after which this measurement is used as the dependent variable in our model.

Independent variable: connectivity in the office networks of globalized APS firms
Our data on cities' connectivity in the office networks of globalized APS firms is based on the research of the Globalization and World Cities (GaWC) network. As its conceptual starting point, GaWC uses Sassen's identification of APS firms at the cutting edge of the world economy through enabling transnational commerce and production. However, GaWC extends the argument beyond Sassen's focus on just a small number of select cities (Taylor 2004, Taylor et al. 2012). Typically, leading APS firms operate through office networks across a large number of cities, ranging from a few cities in the case of law firms to thousands of cities in the case of the big accountancy firms. Thus GaWC moves away from an emphasis on a few nodes as 'global cities' to focus on the network relations of many more cities in the servicing of global capital. This is specified as the 'world city network' (WCN), and in this chapter we use a recent operationalization of this concept as an indicator of a city's involvement in globalized APS networks.

In practice, GaWC's measurement of cities' level of globalized APS provision is based on data on the office networks of such firms (Taylor et al. 2012). These data are readily available on firms' websites where they promote their 'global' status as a means of both impressing clients in a competitive services market and recruiting graduates in a competitive jobs market. This information was converted by simple coding to enable cross-firm comparison for analysis. These measures, ranging from 0 to 5, are called service values, and measure the importance of a given city in a given firm's office network. Thus, 0 indicates a city where a firm has no presence, 5 is the firm's headquarter city. Codes 1 to 4 are then allocated as follows: a typical office of a firm scores 2, there must be something deficient to lower to 1, and something extra to rise above 2. For the latter an especially large office scores 3, an office with extra-city jurisdictions (e.g. regional HQ) scores 4. This data collection creates a firm/city service values matrix that provides the basic raw material for GaWC's WCN analysis.

The data used in this chapter were collected in 2010, and provide information on the location strategies of 175 APS firms in cities across the settled world. The firm selection is composed of 75 financial services firms and 25 each of accountancy, advertising, law and management consultancy firms. Firms were chosen using trade information ranking firms by size based upon the latest information available (e.g. on turnover) before the data collection (i.e. for 2009). A city's globalized service intensity (GSI) is then computed by applying an interaction model as detailed in Taylor (2001). To the best of our knowledge, this is the most comprehensive indicator of the involvement of cities in the office networks of APS firms available at the global scale, and here we use it as the independent variable in our model.

Control variables
The population data used as a control variable in our analysis are collected by Brinkhoff (2011), whose website lists up-to-date census data of urban agglomerations with more than 1 million inhabitants. Cities located in countries with at least four cities in the final dataset (on which more below) were brought together in a set of national dummy control variables (e.g. China and the US), after which the remaining cities were brought together in regional dummy control variables (e.g. Latin America and Sub-Sahara Africa).

Data transformations: the initial data were – where necessary – transformed in three consecutive steps to ensure a consistent data framework
The first problem related to the territorial definition of the cities in our analysis. Our population data defines cities primarily in a morphological sense (i.e. urban agglomerations), while airline data entail a functional city-regional approach (i.e. the London airports serve the entire Southeast England), and GaWC data in practice often refer to economic activity contained within specific grids of business activity (e.g. most of the GaWC firms in London are located in 'the City'). To circumvent this problem, we transformed our data so that we adopt a territorial working definition for our 'cities' that is as coherent as possible, after which our data was transformed to fit this operationalization.

In practice, we have chosen to focus on metropolitan regions that are reminiscent of United States CMSAs (Consolidated Metropolitan Statistical Area). As there is no agreed upon global operationalization of this approach, we have tried to devise a list that follows the CMSA logic as closely as possible. For instance, the Dutch cities are combined into a single 'Randstad' measure. However, we concede that this approach is far from clear-cut. For instance, it is hard to make a clear-cut partition of the urban spheres of influence in, say, China's Pearl River Delta (with Hong Kong, Guangzhou, and Shenzhen as major nodes), as airports, urban centrality and morphology in this region exhibit a highly complex and overlapping interaction. In this particular case, we have chosen to retain Hong Kong as a separate metropolitan region, and combine the remainder of the Pearl River Delta as a single metropolitan region because of the 'one state, two systems' logic. We used existing, official designations of CSMA-like metropolitan regions when available.

This territorial working definition implied – where necessary – combining urban populations, retaining APS firms' highest service value of a metropolitan

Table 1.1   Data subset

Metropolitan region	Passengers	GSI	Population size	USA	China
Bangkok Metropolitan Area	17,167,832	45,570	9,550,000	0	0
Greater Rio de Janeiro	8,270,064	32,323	12,600,000	0	0
Greater Tokyo Area	30,348,867	69,525	34,400,000	0	0
Hong Kong	23,273,465	79,352	7,100,000	0	0
London Metropolitan Area	50,796,365	108,912	12,600,000	0	0
Los Angeles-Long Beach-Riverside CSA	44,617,642	62,125	23,110,000	1	0
Melbourne Metropolitan Area	10,012,286	50,063	4,200,000	0	0
Pearl River Delta	23,854,497	43,239	36,510,000	0	1
Randstad	13,689,894	59,915	4,775,000	0	0
Rome Metropolitan Area	14,759,508	41,371	3,300,000	0	0
Yangtze River Delta	37,806,180	69,694	39,225,000	0	1
...	...	...	...	...	...

region's constituent cities, and aggregating origin/destination volumes of the different airports in the metropolitan region.

The second problem relates to the uneven coverage of our datasets. We therefore decided to exclusively focus on metropolitan regions that scored at least 10 per cent of the highest value on each of the (transformed) measures for population (Yangtze River Delta centered on Shanghai), air passenger connectivity (London Metropolitan Area), and GSI (London Metropolitan Area). This resulted in a total of 112 metropolitan regions (see the Appendix at the end of this chapter). And third and finally, as each of the distributions of our continuous datasets is heavily skewed, we logged the data so that the distributions become normally distributed and can be used as the input to standard correlation regression analysis (see Table 1.1, for a sample of the data used in the analysis).

Correlation analysis and stepwise regression analysis
We analyse our variables in two consecutive steps. First, we calculate the impact on air passenger connectivity for each of the variables *separately* through Pearson correlation coefficients (i.e. for the continuous variables population and GSI) and point biserial correlation coefficients (i.e. for the dichotomous variables for regional affiliation).

Second, as it can be assumed that some of the independent variables co-vary (see Short 2004), we construct a single model through a stepwise *multiple* linear regression. This is a systematic method for adding and removing variables from a multi-linear model based on their statistical significance in the regression. An initial model is stepwise expanded by variables that have the highest statistical significance (i.e. the lowest p-value), but in every step the variables that are no longer significant are removed. This iteration terminates when no single step further improves the model. Only the significant variables (here at the 0.05 significance level) thus remain, which effectively removes variables that are either major covariates of other, more important independent variables and/or outright insignificant. Interestingly, it is also possible that variables that have no significant effect on the dependent variable in their own right become significant in the overall model as their source of variation interacts with the other variables. For our purposes, two sets of relevant information are drawn from the stepwise regression model, i.e. (1) the model parameters proper, such as the degree of explained variance (R^2) and the relative importance of each of the variables (standardized β-coefficients); but also (2) the deviations from the model predictions (standardized residuals), which can be used for exploring processes not captured in the model.

Results

Table 1.2 lists the correlation coefficients between our measure of airline connectivity on the one hand and the GSI variable and the envisaged control variables on the other hand. In line with the hypothesis explored in this volume in general and this chapter in particular, the correlation between airline connectivity and GSI boasts by far the largest value for the 112 metropolitan regions studied here. Population size also impacts air passenger connectivity, but the strength of this correlation is far weaker than reported at the national scale (e.g. Debbage 1999) because of global differences in economic development: it is clear that in spite of their comparable sheer size, Dhaka and London Metropolitan Area connect very different numbers of airline passengers. The latter is also corroborated by the instances in which regional affiliation systematically impacts airline passenger numbers: US metropolitan regions have significantly more passengers than the average non-US metropolitan regions; Sub-Sahara African and Latin American metropolitan regions, in contrast, have significantly fewer passengers than the average metropolitan region in our dataset. However, it is only via a multiple regression model that the relative and exclusive impact of each of these variables is exposed.

The model derived from the stepwise regression analysis is:

Ln_passengers = 2.560 +1.258 Ln_GSI +0.742 USA −1.339 Sub-Sahara Africa −0.943 Latin America −0.504 Middle East/North Africa +0.843 China +0.754 Japan

Table 1.2   Bivariate correlations between passenger flows and independent variables

Independent variable	Correlation with Ln_passengers	Significance (2-tailed)
Ln_GSI	0.679	0.000*
Ln_Population	0.199	0.036*
Australasia	0.039	0.686
Europe	0.120	0.207
Germany	0.099	0.300
UK	0.107	0.262
Latin America	-0.273	0.004*
Brazil	-0.146	0.123
Middle East / North Africa	-0.238	0.011*
USA	0.382	0.000*
Canada	0.006	0.953
Pacific Asia	0.151	0.112
China	0.115	0.228
Japan	0.067	0.483
South Asia	-0.184	0.052
India	-0.093	0.330
Sub-Sahara Africa	-0.444	0.000*

Note: * indicates significance at the 0,005 level

Table 1.3 lists the main model parameters. The first and most straightforward result of our analysis is that, together with a host of control variables, metropolitan regions' involvement in the office networks of globalized APS firms is indeed a strong predictor of global airline connectivity: the model as a whole explains a sizable 83% of the variance, whereby GSI has by far the largest β-coefficient. The relevance of including the control variables and/or paying attention to a more coherent demarcation of the metropolitan regions is shown by their statistical significance, as well as the fact that the explanatory power of the model is much higher than for the simple correlation between GSI and airline connectivity in Table 1.2 as well as the one reported in Taylor et al. (2007). In general terms, therefore, the model confirms that the complex web of interrelations between knowledge-intensive services and airline connectivity in metropolitan areas at the national scale (especially in the USA) is also apparent at the global level.

An appraisal of the control variables informs our understanding of the *specific* way in which the dependence of global airline connectivity on GSI is influenced by other variables. Perhaps the most surprising result is that population size is no longer a significant variable: the combined effect of GSI and regional specifics absorbs the relevant level of variance suggested in Table 1.2. In contrast to the US case, therefore, our global model suggests that the interrelations between knowledge-intensive services and airline connectivity in metropolitan areas are not influenced by population size.

However, the global pattern is influenced by national/regional tendencies. Three national dummies have positive and statistically significant β-coefficients (especially the USA, followed by China and Japan, which were not significant in explaining the relative size of airline flows in their own right). This implies that metropolitan areas in these countries have higher levels of global airline connectivity than expected in the 'global' pattern sketched above. For the USA this is explained by the combined effect of a major 'national' market for APS firms and a well-developed airline market (Taylor and Lang 2005), while for China and also Japan the main reason seems to lie in the (continued) tight regulation of the economy, which results in – on average – higher levels of airline flows than expected on the basis of GSI. Latin American, Middle Eastern, and Sub-Saharan African metropolitan areas, in contrast, have lower levels of global airline connectivity than can be expected based on their level of GSI. This can possibly be attributed to the fact that we are dealing here with a set of metropolitan areas that typically function as the sole attractors of virtually *all* of the globalized APS firms in their regions, so that their level of global airline connectivity is somewhat lower than expected: metropolitan areas such as Greater Buenos Aires, Greater Sao Paulo, Tschwane Metropolitan Area (Johannesburg – Pretoria) function as the service gateways for entire regions (in contrast to more dense urban APS

Table 1.3   Results from the stepwise regression model (parameters are ordered by their relative statistical importance)

	Unstandardized coefficients		Standardized coefficients		
	B	Std. Error	Beta	t	p-value
Constant	2.560	0.871	-	2.939	0.004
Ln_GSI	1.258	0.082	0.648	15.339	0.000
USA	0.742	0.098	0.322	7.561	0.000
Sub-Sahara Africa	- 1.339	0.190	- 0.297	- 7.040	0.000
Latin America	- 0.943	0.150	- 0.261	- 6.285	0.000
Middle East / North Africa	- 0.504	0.144	- 0.147	- 3.504	0.001
China	0.843	0.207	0.168	4.072	0.000
Japan	0.754	0.208	0.150	3.619	0.000

Table 1.4   Main residuals from the stepwise regression model

Metropolitan region	Residual	Metropolitan region	Residual
Las Vegas	2.969	Jakarta Metropolitan Area	-2.285
Pearl River Delta (Shenzhen, Guanhzgou,..)	2.508	Pune	-2.155
Greater Orlando	2.318	Karachi Metropolitan Area	-1.958
Guadalajara	2.105	Lahore	-1.754
Jeddah	1.552	Alexandria	-1.708
Fukuoka	1.527	Delaware Valley (Philadelphia)	-1.480
Bangkok Metropolitan Area	1.516	Metropolitan Area of Bogota	-1.469
London Metropolitan Area	1.488	Nagoya	-1.369
Rome Metropolitan Area	1.442	St Louis	-1.309
Glasgow-Edinburgh	1.415	Caracas Metropolitan Region	-1.293
Mexico City Metropolitan Area	1.232	Kuala Lumpur Metropolitan Area	-1.280
Seoul National Capital Area	1.155	Ho Chi Minh City Metropolitan Area	-1.181
Greater Taipei	1.118	Greater Casablanca Region	-1.140
Los Angeles-Long Beach-Riverside CSA	1.072	Kansas City Metropolitan Area	-1.075
Phoenix-Tucson	1.048	Flemish Diamond (Brussels, Antwerp)	-1.074

office networks in Europe and Northern America), which turns the major cities in these regions into major sites of GSI relative to slightly more dispersed airline connectivity geographies in their regions.

Another set of results that can be derived from our stepwise regression analysis stems from the observation that about 17 per cent of this variance in airline connectivity levels is not being accounted for. This can, of course, in part be related to the transformations we had to make to make our datasets comparable, as well as lingering data deficiencies at the global level (Short et al. 1996, Taylor 1997). However, above all this suggests that some of the processes explaining airline connectivity at the metropolitan scale are outside of the model. To aid in exploring these processes, we make use of Table 1.4, listing the major deviations from the model (i.e. all cities with a standardized residual above 1 or below -1). Large positive (negative) values signify that a metropolitan area has a high (low) level of global airline connectivity when considering the combined size of their GSI and – if relevant – national/regional status. Three observations can be made.

First, the large positive residuals for Las Vegas and Greater Orlando (but also, to a lesser degree, Bangkok Metropolitan Area and Rome Metropolitan Area) are very probably due to tourism (in the broadest sense). Tourism is an ancillary function of globalizing cities, and in some cases even comes to dominate the functional tissue of these city-regions (as is clearly the case for Las Vegas). GSI is obviously related to a narrower conceptualization of globalized urbanization (Grant and Nijman 2002, Robinson 2002), and it is therefore no surprise that metropolitan regions in which the tourism function equals or even dominates that of GSI-related business activities attract far more air passengers than predicted by the metropolitan region's GSI.

Second, there is a diverse category of metropolitan areas that have large positive or negative residuals because of national peculiarities. This includes, for instance, Rome Metropolitan area's positive residual because of the well-documented domination of Milan Metropolitan Area. In spite of its smaller size, the latter metropolitan area serves as the de facto leading city region in Italy for global business, which results in the choice for Milan Metropolitan Area over Rome Metropolitan Area for a lot of global APS firms that might otherwise open an office in Rome Metropolitan Area. Thus in addition to the large(r) number of tourists at Rome's airport(s), the metropolitan region also has more passengers than could otherwise be expected based on its GSI. The Pearl River Delta probably also falls within this category, with nearby Hong Kong assuming some or even a lot of the region's GSI potential, resulting in higher-than-expected passenger numbers.

Third, although population size is not a significant variable in the final model, Short's identification (2004) of 'black holes' – cities with very limited levels of GSI given their population size – re-emerges. However, this designation of 'black holes' can here be extended beyond its implicit Third World connotation: Fukuoka in Japan and Guadalajara in Mexico can also be dubbed black holes in that Greater Tokyo Area and Mexico City Metropolitan Area exercise a major shadow effect: these metropolitan areas are so dominant in their GSI that other cities in their countries attract very little such firms, despite having sizable airports.

Conclusions

In this chapter, we have tried to extend previous, predominantly *national* research on the complex impact of the level of knowledge-intensive services in metropolitan regions on their level of (airline) connectivity to the *global* scale. An important conclusion of this analysis is that this impact is indeed sizable. Additionally, given major geographical differences in economic development, the level of knowledge-intensive services seems to be a much better predictor of airline connectivity than mere population size, which contrasts with the dominant impact of the latter variable at the national scale. Furthermore, these interrelations are geographically specific in that they often depend on national/regional particulars (e.g. the US dummy variable, and the relative large connectivity of Rome Metropolitan Area and the Pearl River Delta in airline flows compared to their GSI).

Readers need to bear in mind that the 'knowledge-intensity' of metropolitan economies is of course a much richer concept than captured by the mere presence of globalized APS firms (e.g. Conventz and Thierstein, this volume) just as 'physical infrastructure' is much more than air passenger networks (for an example of the global urban geographies of Internet backbone geographies, see Malecki 2002 and this volume, Malecki and Wei 2009, Tranos 2011). This implies that this analysis represents a very specific take on the more general issues explored in this book, and even on its own terms the hypothesized parallels between globalized APS provision and global air passenger networks requires further conceptual and empirical specification. This conceptual specification has been spelled out in more detail in a number of publications on this topic, such as Bowen (2002), O'Connor (2003), Matsumoto (2004), Grubesic et al. (2011). In this chapter, we have begun exploring on some of the empirical issues. Although we have managed to identify some of the major empirical dimensions of the impact of GSI on airline connectivity, it is clear that our analysis is still fraught with the continued lack of comprehensive urban datasets at the global scale. Although recent research efforts have tackled the data deficiencies involved in studying globalized urbanization – long the 'dirty little secret of world cities research' (Short et al. 1996) –, large-scale comparative datasets of a high quality remain an exception. Put differently: analyzing the regionalized relationships between indicators such as population size, service intensity, and airline infrastructure remains much easier at the national scale because of superior data. As a consequence, and in spite of the use of some of the best data on globalized urbanization and our subsequent transformations to arrive at coherent datasets, there is still much room for improvement.

Some of this room for improvement can be clarified by considering the negative residual of Pune, a major city in West India. The city's large negative residual can essentially be explained by its modest airline connectivity, which is in turn an artifact of the relative proximity of Mumbai Metropolitan Area: Mumbai Metropolitan Area's international airport acts as main gateway for Pune passengers, although globalized APS firms do tend to set up offices there. As a consequence, in spite of our data transformations, there clearly remains a degree of overlap and fuzziness when defining metropolitan areas, especially at the global scale: adding Pune to Mumbai's metropolitan region would have been justifiable, just as retaining both metropolitan areas as separate entities seemed justifiable (see also our treatise of the Pearl River Delta). Future research could focus on more bespoke (and therefore meaningful) territorial definitions of metropolitan regions, as well as the way in which the different data apply to these metropolitan regions.

In addition to refining and developing new datasets, a further avenue for future research lies in the interpretation of the residuals. There seems to be a fair degree of overlap that is hard to disentangle. For instance, Rome Metropolitan Area's positive residual is probably due to both tourism flows and the peculiar role of what is theoretically the 'second city' in Italy (Milan Metropolitan Area), but the model obviously does not allow distinguishing between both. Future research could provide 'interpretation keys' by including extra variables in the model, albeit that the well-known data problems re-emerge here.

References

Bird, J.H. 1973. Central places, cities and seaports. *Geography*, 58 (259), 105–18.

Bowen, J. 2002. Network change, deregulation, and access in the global airline industry. *Economic Geography*, 78(4), 425–39.

Brinkhoff, T. 2011. *The Principal Agglomerations of the World*. [Online]. Available at: http://www.citypopulation.de [accessed: October 2011].

Brueckner, J.K. 2003. Airline traffic and economic development. *Urban Studies*, 40(8), 1455–69.

Debbage, K. 1999. Air transportation and urban-economic restructuring: Competitive advantage in the US Carolinas. *Journal of Air Transport Management*, 5(4), 211–21.

Debbage, K. and Delk, D. 2001. The geography of air passenger volume and local employment patterns by US metropolitan core area: 1973–1996. *Journal of Air Transport Management*, 7(3), 159–67.

Derudder, B. and Witlox, F. 2005. An appraisal of the use of airline data in assessing the world city network: A research note on data. *Urban Studies*, 42(13), 2371–88.

Grant, R. and Nijman, J. 2002. Globalization and the corporate geography of cities in the less-developed world. *Annals of the Association of American Geographers*, 92(2), 320–40.

Grubesic, T.H., and Matisziw, T.C. 2011. World cities and airline networks, in *The International Handbook of Globalization and Global Cities*, edited by B. Derudder, M. Hoyler, P.J. Taylor and F. Witlox. Cheltenham: Edward Elgar Publishing, 97–116.

Irwin, M.D. and Kasarda, J.D. 1991. Air passenger linkages and employment growth in U.S. metropolitan areas. *American Sociological Review*, 56(4), 524–37.

Keeling, D.J. 1995. Transport and the world city paradigm, in *World Cities in a World-System*, edited by P.L. Knox and P.J. Taylor. Cambridge: Cambridge University Press, 115–31.

Malecki, E.J. 2002. The economic geography of the Internet's infrastructure. *Economic Geography*, 78(4), 399–424.

Malecki, E.J. and Wei, H. 2009. A wired world: the evolving geography of submarine cables and the shift to Asia. *Annals of the Association of American Geographers*, 99(2), 360–82.

Matsumoto, H. 2004. International urban systems and air passenger and cargo flows: some calculations. *Journal of Air Transport Management*, 10(4), 239–47.

Murayama, Y. (1994) The impact of railways on accessibility in the Japanese urban system. *Journal of Transport Geography*, 2, 87–100.

Neal, Z.P. 2010. Refining the air traffic approach: An analysis of the US city network. *Urban Studies*, 47(10), 2195–215.

O'Connor, K. 2003. Global air travel: Toward concentration or dispersal? *Journal of Transport Geography*, 11(2), 83–92.

Ortega, E., Lopez, E. and Monzon, A. (2012) Territorial cohesion impacts of high-speed rail at different planning levels. *Journal of Transport Geography*, 24, 130-41.

Pauly, L.W. 2011. Hong Kong's financial center in a regional and global context. *Hong Kong Journal* [Online], 22. Available at: http://www.hkjournal.org/archive/2011_fall/2.htm [accessed: 5 January 2012].

Robinson, J. 2002. Global and world cities: A view from off the map. *International Journal of Urban and Regional Research*, 26(3), 531–34.

Sassen, S. 2001. *The Global City: New York, London, Tokyo*. 2nd edn. Princeton, NJ: Princeton University Press.

Short, J.R. 2004. Black holes and loose connections in a global urban network. *The Professional Geographer*, 56(2), 295–302.

Short, J.R., Kim, Y., Kuus, M. and Wells, H. 1996. The dirty little secret of world cities research: Data problems in comparative analysis. *International Journal of Urban and Regional Research*, 20(4), 697–717.

Taaffe, E.J. 1962. The urban hierarchy: An air passenger definition. *Economic Geography*, 38(1), 1–14.

Taylor, P.J. 1997. Hierarchical tendencies amongst world cities: a global research proposal. *Cities*, 14(6), 323–32.

Taylor, P.J. 2001. Specification of the world city network. *Geographical Analysis*, 33(2), 181–94.

Taylor, P.J. 2004. *World City Network: A Global Urban Analysis*. London: Routledge.

Taylor, P.J., Derudder, B., Hoyler, M. and Ni, P. 2012. New regional geographies of the world as practised by leading advanced producer service firms in 2010. *GaWC Research Bulletin 392*. Available at: http://www.lboro.ac.uk/gawc/rb/rb392.html.

Taylor, P.J., Derudder, B. and Witlox, F. 2007. Comparing airline passenger destinations with global service connectivities: A worldwide empirical study of 214 cities. *Urban Geography*, 28(3), 232–48.

Taylor, P.J., and Lang R.E. 2005. US cities in the world city network. *Metropolitan Policy Program Survey Series*, Brookings Institution, 1–14.

Tranos, E. 2011. The topology and the emerging urban geographies of the Internet backbone and aviation networks in Europe: A comparative study. *Environment and Planning A*, 43(2), 378–92.

Warf, B. 1989. Telecommunications and the globalization of financial services. *Professional Geographer*, 41(3), 257–71.

Appendix

Metropolitan region	Country
Abidjan	Cote D'Ivoire
Ahmadabad	India
Alexandria	Egypt
Ankara	Turkey
Atlanta-Sandy Springs-Gainesville CSA	USA
Attica Basin	Greece
Bangkok Metropolitan Area	Thailand
Barcelona	Spain
Belo Horizonte	Brazil
Berlin-Brandeburg Metropolitan Area	Germany
Birmingham-Leicester-Nottingham	UK
Boston-Worcester-Manchester CSA	USA
Brazilia	Brazil
Brisbane Metropolitan Area	Australia
Calcutta	India
Cape Town Metropolitan Area	South Africa
Caracas Metropolitan Region	Venezuela
Chengdu	China
Chennai Metropolitan Area	India
Chicago-Naperville-Michigan City CSA	USA
Dallas-Fort Worth Metroplex	USA
Delaware Valley (Philadelphia)	USA
Delhi National Capital Region	India
Denver-Aurora-Boulder CSA	USA
Dhaka	Bangladesh
Dubai-Sjarjah Metropolitan Region	UAE
European Metropolitan Region of Zurich	Switzerland
Flemish Diamond (Brussels, Antwerp)	Belgium
Frankfurt-Main Region	Germany
Fukuoka	Japan
Glasgow-Edinburgh	UK
Grand Montréal	Canada
Greater Bangalore	India

Metropolitan region	Country
Greater Beijing Region	China
Greater Buenos Aires	Argentina
Greater Cairo	Egypt
Greater Casablanca Region	Morocco
Greater Dublin Area	Ireland
Greater Moscow	Russia
Greater Orlando	USA
Greater Rio de Janeiro	Brazil
Greater Sao Paulo	Brazil
Greater Taipei	China
Greater Tokyo Area	Japan
Greater Toronto Area	Canada
Greater Vancouver Regional District	Canada
Guadalajara	Mexico
Gush Dan (Tel Aviv & Central Israël)	Israel
Ho Chi Minh City Metropolitan Area	Vietnam
Hongkong	Hongkong
Houston-Baytown Huntsville CSA	USA
Hyderabad	India
Ile de France (Paris)	France
Istanbul Metropolitan Region	Turkey
Jakarta Metropolitan Area	Indonesia
Jeddah	Saudi Arabia
Kansai Region	Japan
Kansas City Metropolitan Area	USA
Karachi Metropolitan Area	Pakistan
Kuala Lumpur Metropolitan Area	Malaysia
Lagos	Nigeria
Lahore	Pakistan
Las Vegas	USA
Lima Metropolitana	Peru
London Metropolitan Area	UK
Los Angeles-Long Beach-Riverside CSA	USA
Luanda	Angola

Metropolitan region	Country
Madrid Metropolitan Area	Spain
Manchester-Liverpool-Leeds-Sheffield	UK
Melbourne Metropolitan Area	Australia
Metro Detroit	USA
Metro Manila	Philippines
Metropolitan Area of Bogota	Colombia
Metropolregion Hamburg	Germany
Mexico City Metropolitan Area	Mexico
Milan Metropolitan Area	Italy
Minneapolis-St.Paul-St. Cloud CSA	USA
Monterrey	Mexico
Mumbai Metropolitan Area	India
Munich Metropolitan Region	Germany
Nagoya	Japan
Naples	Italy
New York-Newark-Bridgeport CSA	USA
Oresund region (Copenhagen, Malmo)	Denmark/Sweden
Pearl River Delta (Shenzhen, Guangzhou, Macao, ...)	China
Phoenix-Tucson	USA
Portland	USA
Porto Alegre	Brazil
Prague Metropolitan Area	Czech Republic
Pune	India
Qingdao	China
Randstad	The Netherlands
Recife	Brazil
Rhine-Ruhr-Megaplex	Germany
Riyadh	Saudi Arabia
Rome Metropolitan Area	Italy
Salt Lake City Metropolitan Area	USA
San Francisco Bay Area	USA
Santiago Metropolitan Region	Chile
Seattle Metropolitan Area	USA
Seoul National Capital Area	Korea

Metropolitan region	Country
Singapore Extended Metropolitan Region	Singapore
South Florida Metropolitan Area (Miami)	USA
St Louis	USA
St Petersburg	Russia
Stockholm-Mälar Metropolitan Region	Sweden
Sydney Metropolitan Area	Australia
Tampa Bay	USA
Tshwane Metropolitan Area (Johannesburg, Pretoria)	South Africa
Vienna-Bratislava Metropolitan Area	Austria
Washington-Baltimore-Northern Virginia CSA	USA
Yangtze River Delta (Shanghai, ...)	China

Chapter 2

Knowledge Hubs: Poles of Physical Accessibility and Non-physical Connectivity

Michael Bentlage, Alain Thierstein and Stefan Lüthi

Introduction

The production of knowledge takes part in complex networks of firms and individuals. Recent decades have witnessed a period of fundamental change in world-wide economic activities (Dicken 2011). During this period, the use and supply of information and communication technology (ICT) has broadened and transportation costs have declined steeply, thus further accelerating the process of globalization. However, this process evoked a concentration of knowledge and the knowledge economy in global nodes such as global cities (Sassen 1991, Castells 2000, Taylor 2004). Dicken (2011) points out that Advanced Business Services in particular 'continue to be extremely strongly concentrated geographically' (Dicken 2011: 390). Thus, the world is likely to become more and more spiky because population, patents, and a number of scientific citations are located in several urban centres in Northern America, Europe and South-East Asia (Florida 2005). Richard Florida uses these variables as indicators of economic activity and assets of knowledge and hypothesizes that globalization has clearly changed competition, but does not level the 'playing field' (Friedman 2005). Indeed, within knowledge creation and application, spatial proximity and face-to-face contacts still play a crucial role (Storper and Venables 2004). In particular, tacit knowledge, which is mainly based on experience, can only be transferred in learning processes. A new division of labour has resulted from this complex process of knowledge creation and application and has led to a new spatial logic (Sokol et al. 2008: 1143). A system of interconnected world cities has emerged and a few cities are held to be central places in which those connections converge: the knowledge hubs (for a more detailed specification, see Neal, this volume). According to the concept of the *space of places* and *space of flows* (Castells 2000) we consider knowledge hubs as urban areas with vertical integration and vibrancy in a horizontal, that is regional, dimension. Therefore a knowledge hub is an urban area, which is simultaneously vertically integrated into functional networks that reach beyond the metropolitan scale and which generates territorial spill-overs within its urban area (Castells 2000, Bathelt et al. 2004, Growe and Blotevogel 2011).

Knowledge is created in a process where implicit and explicit knowledge are interwoven. This process depends on various factors which can be divided into internal and external factors. Internalities, such as investment in research and development or equipment, are conditions which can be influenced by the firm individually. Externalities are advantages from which firms benefit at no cost to themselves, or disadvantages which they have to pay for but for which they are not responsible. In our analysis we will focus on the positive externalities of network economies and agglomeration economies. Network economies highlight the effects of strategic links between hubs of knowledge. Agglomeration economies enable knowledge spill-overs between individuals. Therefore, knowledge intensive firms require an environment in which two main conditions inhere: access to networks to receive information and critical mass to realize knowledge spill-overs. For both conditions, spatial accessibility and the non-physical connectivity, which is provided by firm networks and which is a *proxy* for hypothetical information flows (Taylor 2004: 61, Lüthi 2011: 106), play a crucial role and foster the economic performance of a region (de Bok and van Oort 2011). Exploiting these economies raises the question of how firms or actors can access these externalities in both ways, i.e. the physical and non-physical.

In this paper we assess the emergence of knowledge hubs in Germany by highlighting the interplay of physical and non-physical accessibility within knowledge production. We combine the concept of spatial accessibility with the theoretical approaches of network economies and agglomeration economies that show how firms exploit these externalities. In addition we differentiate accessibility according to mode (air, rail or road) and dimension (physical and non-physical) (see Knowles, 2006), which provide the potential to either establish links within a network or to access parts of agglomerations. Physical accessibility enables the movement of goods or people and establishes face-to-face contacts; non-physical accessibility facilitates the exchange of information. Furthermore, we show that decision-making in choosing locations of firms in Advanced Producer Services (APS) and high-tech sectors correlates quite strongly with the accessibility of spatial entities. Nevertheless, differences between both sectors are observable. We therefore analyse the locational behaviour of firms, their intra-firm and extra-firm networks and the role of physical accessibility and consider this in relation to the economic performance of Functional Urban Areas (FUA) in Germany. Accessibility is understood as the foundation for entering and establishing networks of knowledge creation and impacts economic performance to a large extent. The question arises how firms access externalities to create knowledge.

This paper is structured as follows: section two defines the knowledge economy and discusses externalities of knowledge production. In section three considers the emergence of knowledge hubs in a process of cumulative causation of knowledge production. Section four introduces a concept of spatial accessibility including non-physical connectivity; in section five the interplay between physical accessibility and non-physical connectivity is illustrated; section six focuses on the relatedness of diversified and non-diversified hubs and their functional importance. Section seven concludes the discussion.

Externalities of Knowledge Creation – Networks, Agglomerations and Accessibility

This section provides an insight into the process of knowledge production and how accessibility enables firms to exploit externalities of agglomerations and networks in order to create knowledge. Knowledge production is based on two key features: Firstly, it is carried out in a complex process where people and firms interact (Cooke et al. 2007: 27). Secondly, knowledge is not only a fundamental resource in the innovation process but also a strategic property fostering the development of firms.

The Knowledge Economy and Knowledge Production

The profit imperative is an important logical principle shared by all knowledge-intensive firms. It is not only the creation of new knowledge that preoccupies their managers, but also the appropriation of surplus value (Sokol et al. 2008: 1143). Furthermore, these features underline the relational character of the knowledge economy. Since, highly specialized knowledge and skills are based on the combination of scientific knowledge and operating experiences, the knowledge economy establishes strategic links between firms and other organizations as a way to acquire specialized knowledge from different parts of the value chain (Lüthi et al. 2011: 163). In terms of economic sectors, the knowledge economy can be understood as an interdependent system of Advanced Producer Services (APS) and high-tech firms. APS can be defined as 'a cluster of activities that provide specialized services, embodying professional knowledge and processing specialized information to other service sectors' (Hall and Pain 2006: 4). The essential common characteristic of these sectors is that they generate, analyze, exchange and trade information, making them spearheads and key intermediaries in the knowledge economy (Sassen 2001: 90). However, APS are not the only determining element in the process of structural change towards the knowledge economy. In order to understand the geography of globalization, one has to account simultaneously for both APS- and high-tech sectors (Castells 2000). Nevertheless, there is no commonly accepted definition of what the knowledge economy is. Therefore we apply the following definition of the knowledge economy:

> the knowledge economy is that part of the economy in which highly specialized knowledge and skills are strategically combined from different parts of the value chain in order to create innovations and to sustain competitive advantage. (Lüthi et al. 2011: 162–3)

We can distinguish between different definitions of knowledge. Depending on the processes researchers focus on, we can concentrate on either the modes in which knowledge can be transferred or communicated to others or the bases on which knowledge is founded. Asheim et al. (2007) distinguish three different knowledge bases: analytical, synthetic and symbolic. This takes the increasing complexity of knowledge into account and makes clear that different economic activities draw from different knowledge bases. For instance activities in high-tech sectors such as biotechnology tend to draw their knowledge from scientific work and use the analytic knowledge base, whereas design or architecture draw from the symbolic knowledge base, where aesthetic considerations have a higher importance.

A broader distinction was developed by Polanyi (1966) in his seminal work 'The tacit dimension'. He focuses on the modes in which knowledge can be communicated and argues that 'we can know more than we can tell' (Polanyi 1966: 4). Therefore, knowledge consists of a tacit and an explicit dimension. Both kinds of knowledge work differently in the way people have to interact. Within the process of knowledge creation a dynamic interplay between tacit and explicit forms of knowledge is required. Regarding accessibility, explicit knowledge can be transferred in a non-physical way via ICT, while implicit knowledge requires strong interaction between people and organizations (Bathelt et al. 2004: 32). Therefore physical accessibility plays an important role (Thierstein et al. 2007: 88).

Since the transfer of tacit knowledge requires direct face-to-face interactions, the findings of Polanyi (1966) are not only important for firms but also for regions. Innovative activities have been shown to be highly concentrated in a minority of urban regions (Simmie 2003). The main reason why these regions play an important role in the supply of knowledge is that firm networks benefit from geographical proximity and local knowledge spill-overs. Malecki (2000) describes this as the 'local nature of knowledge' and highlights the necessity to accept knowledge as a spatial factor in competition:

> If knowledge is not found everywhere, then where it is located becomes a
> particularly significant issue. While codified knowledge is easily replicated,
> assembled and aggregated [...], other knowledge is dependent on the context and
> is difficult to communicate to others. Tacit knowledge is localised in particular
> places and contexts [...]. (Malecki 2000: 110)

The distribution and transfer of explicit and tacit knowledge as well as the interplay between geographical and relational proximity forms a key basis for the development of regions. On the one hand, the concentration of knowledge resources in particular regions influences the roles that they may play in the global economy. On the other hand, the dynamics of knowledge exchange within and between regions contribute to either the maintenance or change in those roles within the functional urban hierarchy. Simmie (2003) shows that knowledge intensive firms combine a strong local knowledge capital base with high levels of connectivity to similar regions in the international economy. In this way they are able to combine and decode both codified and tacit knowledge originating from multiple regional, national and international sources (Simmie 2003) and, therefore, they are considered as hubs.

Exploiting Agglomeration Economies

Agglomeration economies are generic geographical processes mapping the microeconomic logic of knowledge creation and business organization in space. Early theories on agglomeration economies are strongly inspired by Alfred Marshall (1920), who argued that spatial concentration could confer external economies on firms as they concentrate in particular cities. Marshall's concept was taken up by Hoover (1937), who grouped the sources of agglomeration advantages into internal returns of scale, localization and urbanization economies. Localization economies reflect the tendency for firms in closely related industries to locate in the same place; urbanization economies, on the other hand, arise from the diversity and the more general characteristics of a city (Hoover 1937). Based on these early agglomeration theories, a second wave of agglomeration models was developed in the 1980s onwards to explain why local space is still important for newly-developing firms of production. For example: the new industrial district (Becattini 1991), the innovative milieu (Maillat, Quévit and Senn 1993) or the regional innovation system (Cooke 1992).

According to recent publications there is no mutual consensus whether specialization or diversification foster spatial development. These contrary opinions can be ascribed to (Marshall 1920), who stated that specialization and therefore localization economies drive innovations, and Jacobs (1969), who adopts the attitude that diversification enables economic growth. Empirical evidence can be found for both strands of theory (Beaudry and Schiffauerova 2009). However, Duranton and Puga (2000: 534 and 553) state that a coexistence of diversified and specialized cities bring out a sufficient condition for successful economies. This coexistence is embedded in a process of spatial division of labour and specialized cities emerge in the shadow of diversified knowledge hubs. Therefore, Boschma and Iammarino (2009) developed the approach of related varieties and define these as 'sectors that are related in terms of shared or complementary competences' (Boschma and Iammarino 2009: 292–3). An individual city may be assessed as specialized to a high extent but considering the entire network in which it is integrated a balanced diversity is generated by establishing links to those parts of the value chain, which are not located in that city. In other words, a high degree of specialization comes along with intensive network processes in both ways the physical and non-physical and, hence, knowledge hubs emerge where those networks converge again.

The commonality of these approaches is that they acknowledge geographical proximity as an important determinant for the innovation activities of knowledge-intensive firms. A number of authors have demonstrated through econometric methods that knowledge spill-overs are closely related to spatial proximity (Jaffe et al. 1993, Bottazzi and Peri 2002, Breschi and Lissoni 2009). The importance of face-to-face contacts in communication and the tacit nature of much of this communication still make geographical proximity a crucial factor in knowledge creation. Short distances bring people together and enable them to exchange tacit knowledge. This leads to the development of localized knowledge pools, which are in turn characterized by personal contacts and informal information flows, both within and between firms of the knowledge economy. The spatial concentration of these information-flows influences scanning and learning patterns, as well as the sharing of localized knowledge and the innovation capabilities of knowledge-intensive firms (Howells 2000: 58).

Exploiting Network Economies

Codified knowledge can be applied, expressed and standardized. Hence, it is a marketable good that can easily be distributed over time and space. New information and communication technologies offer the opportunity to increasingly codify and commodify knowledge and make it tradable across long distances, which means that codified knowledge becomes more and more de-territorialized. This enables companies to source activities and inputs globally and to benefit from relational proximity and international knowledge spill-overs. Tacit knowledge, in contrast, refers to knowledge, that cannot be easily transferred. It comprises skills based on interactions and experiences. Tacit knowledge and personal experience are necessary in order to make use of codified knowledge in creative and innovative processes (Schamp 2003: 181).

The functional logic of the knowledge economy not only has a significant impact on agglomeration economies, but also on global network economies. Although there is strong evidence that knowledge is highly concentrated in a minority of city-regions, it is unlikely that all the knowledge required by a firm for innovation can be found within a single region. Companies have to spread activities globally to source inputs and to gain access to new markets. High-tech industries, for example, use global sourcing to improve existing assets or to create new technological assets by locating R&D facilities abroad (OECD 2008: 10). In order to realize global sourcing strategies successfully, relational proximity – especially organizational and time proximity – is important. Organizational proximity is needed to control uncertainty and opportunism in the knowledge creation process (Boschma 2005: 65). It creates a sense of belonging, which facilitates interaction and offers a powerful mechanism for long-distance coordination (Torre and Rallet 2005: 54). Therefore trust plays a crucial role (Amin and Roberts 2008). Time proximity, on the other hand, is supported by a rich and diversified infrastructure of global travel and communication, such as rapid and frequent trains and flights, and easy access to interactive communication facilities. It covers important aspects of 'being there', but it does not demand enduring co-location and local embedding (Amin and Cohendet 2004: 105).

All in all, the spatio-economic behaviour of knowledge-intensive firms has led to the emergence of a globalised city network. Two major world city network approaches are of particular importance for this paper. The first approach is John Friedmann's (1986) 'world city' concept, which focuses on the decision-making activities and power of TNCs in the context of the international division of labour. He argues that 'key cities throughout the world are [...] 'basing points' in the spatial organization and articulation of production and markets' (Friedmann 1986: 71).

The second approach is Saskia Sassen's 'Global City' concept, which associates cities with their propensity to engage with the internationalization and concentration of APS firms in the world economy (Sassen 2001: 90). Sassen (1994) defines global cities as 'strategic sites in the global economy because of their concentration of command functions and high-level producer-services firms oriented to world markets' (Sassen 1994: 145).

The empirical part of this book chapter applies Taylor's 'world city network' approach to analyse global connectivity (Taylor 2004). This approach provides an empirical instrument for analysing inter-city relations in terms of the organizational structure of knowledge-intensive firms and complements the approach of physical accessibility.

Knowledge Hubs: Result of or Precondition for Knowledge Creation?

As shown above the process of knowledge creation is a key driver for innovation and economic development. However, knowledge is generated in networks where people and organizations interact. Castells (2000: 442) argues 'that our society is constructed around flows' and these 'Flows are not just one element of the social organization: they are the expression of processes dominating our economic, political, and symbolic life [...].' According to this statement, knowledge hubs emerge from the process of knowledge creation by a convergence of global flows of information and regional knowledge spill-overs. Thus, knowledge hubs are considered as a precondition for accessing information and partners along the value chain and, therefore, enable knowledge production. In general, accessibility is an externality that enables firms to reduce costs (de Bok and van Oort 2011: 9) and enlarge their market areas and, therefore, to realize economies of scale and economies of scope, which in turn generate economic growth (Axhausen 2008: 7–10). Specifically, accessibility enables firms to source knowledge from different parts of the world and from the urban area they are located in. Hence, a circular cumulative causation (Myrdal 1957, Hirschman 1958) is initialized because the gains from economic growth usually are reinvested in technological infrastructure, human capital and the knowledge base, which lead to further improvement of accessibility in both the physical and non-physical dimensions.

To conclude, we define knowledge hubs as urban areas with a vertical integration in functional networks. At the same time they have vibrancy in a horizontal dimension, which we refer to as the regional dimension. Therefore a knowledge hub is an urban area, which is simultaneously vertically integrated into functional networks that reach beyond the metropolitan scale and generates territorial spill-overs within its urban area (Castells 2000, Bathelt et al. 2004, Growe and Blotevogel 2011).

The notion of hubs derives from transportation and network analysis. Whereas O'Kelly (1998) analyses the hub-and-spoke system of transportation networks, Barabási and Albert (1999) develop the analytical-mathematical approach. They showed that networks such as the World Wide Web tend to have a few actors with a large number of connections. Based on this finding these actors were defined as hubs (Barabási and Albert 1999). Derived from this method publications in urban geography treated cities as hubs to understand their position and importance within a system (Schmidt 2005, Hesse 2010, Blotevogel and Growe 2011, Redondi et al. 2011). Two main strands exist in considering cities as hubs: first, the integration in networks of physical and, second, non-physical interactions. The physical interactions are given by passenger travel or trade of goods, the non-physical connections are enabled by ICT or internal and external firm networks.

Since studies of relations between world cities were carried out, the interrelation between physical and non-physical has become evident. Derudder (2006) stressed this interplay with a comparison of infrastructural and organizational approaches to assess the world city network. On the global scale of world cities much effort was made to investigate the network structures of airline passengers (O'Connor 2003, Mahutga et al. 2010). Derudder and Witlox (2005) have shown that these data are prime source in order to figure out the central cities within a network. In a further analysis Derudder et al. (2007) state that the network structure of air connections reflects the patterns of the world city system according to the studies of Taylor (2004), however, the strategic thinking of airlines might lead to a change of this system (Derudder and Witlox 2008). Therefore, the 'hub-and-spoke model as a whole may become somewhat dissociated from the major origin/destination nodes in the network, hence the appropriate designation of these hubs as 'new network cities" (Derudder et al. 2007: 318). This finding raises the question to which extent passenger travel will affect the regional economy.

Droß and Thierstein (2011) as well as Goebel et al. (2007) discussed these effects of airline networks. Airports attract knowledge intensive firms, which in turn drive spatial development (Button and Taylor 2000, Goebel et al. 2007, Haas and Wallisch 2008, Kramar and Suitner 2008, Schaafsma 2008, Schaafsma et al. 2008, Schaafsma 2009, Droß and Thierstein 2011; Conventz and Thierstein, this volume). Such firms demand both diverse pools of labour, which are to be found in agglomerations, and high access to global markets provided by airports and strategic links between firms on the other hand. Beyond these analyses, which indicate a strong interrelation between network structures and the effects on spatial development, they further imply that there is a strong dependency between the physical and the non-physical interrelations. For example, Tranos (2011) shows that there is a strong relation between Internet backbones and aviation networks (Tranos 2011). Derudder and Witlox (2005) analyse aspects of the World City Network given by the Interlocking Network Model and its interrelation with air travel – although the direction of causality remains somewhat open (Tranos 2011, Tranos and Gillespie 2011). Nevertheless, network economies and agglomeration economies give a strong theoretical background for this relationship since both concepts provide elements for cumulative causation.

Accessibility: An Approach with Non-physical Connectivity

As mentioned above, accessibility plays a crucial role for the exploitation of externalities and is considered in a physical and non-physical dimension. Physical accessibility is given by the potential to reach a population via air, rail or road traffic. Non-physical accessibility is defined by the Interlocking Network Model (Taylor 2004). This model conceptualizes hypothetical information flows between cities and reflects the degree of integration in global information flows, which is also referred to as the connectivity of a city. Furthermore, physical accessibility can be associated with network economies and agglomeration economies. Whereas rail and road accessibility work on the scale of agglomerations, accessibility by air enables network links to worldwide locations.

Physical Accessibility

Data on physical accessibility was originally calculated by the European Spatial Planning and Observation Network (ESPON) for NUTS 3 level. Here, accessibility is defined by 'how easily people in one region can reach people in another region' (ESPON 2009: 4). This calculation indicates the potential for activities and enterprises in the region to access markets and activities in other regions. It was calculated by reckoning the population in all other European Regions, weighted by the travel time (ESPON 2009: 7). This so called potential measure was introduced by Hansen to indicate opportunities for interaction (Hansen 1959). The potential measure is considered useful for exploiting network and agglomeration externalities. Geurs and van Eck (2001) compiled a detailed catalogue of further accessibility measures, which also take production functions of consumers and activity based approaches into account.

The accessibility values used here are indexes calculated for 27 members of the European Union. A value below 100 indicates an accessibility factor which is lower than the European average. In contrast, values above 100 represent accessibility above the European average. These data from NUTS 3 regions were converted to the spatial units of Functional Urban Areas (FUA) to combine them with data from intra-firm networks. Hence, accessibility data of FUAs reflect an area weighted average of data from NUTS 3 regions. FUAs are agglomerations, which are defined by an average commuting time of 60 min around a defined centre (ESPON 2004).

Figure 2.1 shows a comparison of multimodal accessibility of NUTS 3 entities on the left hand side and FUAs on the right hand side. Multimodal accessibility includes potential accessibility by road, rail and air traffic. The regions with highest accessibility are concentrated around metropolitan areas and reach values of 150

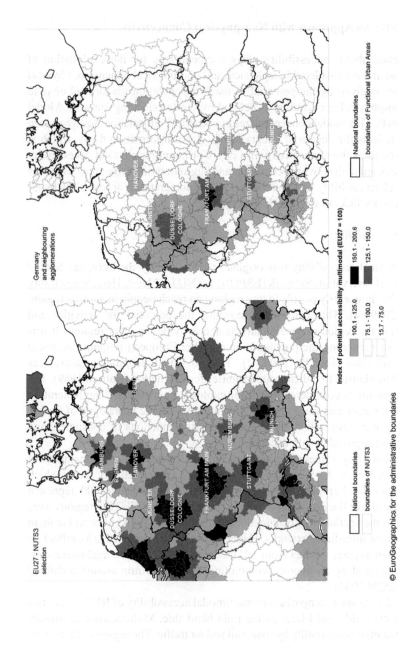

Figure 2.1 Calculation of accessibility for Functional Urban Areas

Source: own calculation based on ESPON (2009)

and more. Regions with low accessibility can be found in the region between Berlin, Hamburg, and Hanover, as well as next to the national borders in the east and north. However, these regions still yield values that are just slightly below the European average.

It can be assumed that Germany, due to its dense population distribution, is well served with physical infrastructure on the one hand and provides good access to several modes of traffic on the other. Whereas road and rail offer a ubiquitous supply and tend to improve accessibility on the regional scale. Data on rail access include regional and supra regional connections. Therefore this mode seems to be ubiquitous. Taking the development of high speed rail in recent years into account might evoke greater regional disparities. Airports and their accessibility are concentrated in metropolitan areas in the western part of Germany. In order to define hubs of physical accessibility air access plays a crucial role, because it is a unique selling position.

Defining Non-physical Connectivity

The analysis of intra-firm networks is based on the methodology of the Globalisation and World Cities Study Group (GaWC) at Loughborough University (Taylor 2004). This approach estimates city connectivities from the office networks of multi-city enterprises. Intra-firm networks are spatially distributed branches of one individual corporation. The basic premise of this method is that the more important the office, the greater its flow of information to other office locations. The empirical work comprises three steps. In the first stage of the empirical work, we had to create a reliable company database in identifying the biggest APS and high-tech firms which operate in Germany and collected information about the importance of their locations worldwide within the firm network from the websites, the so called service values which a location has. The result of this process was a basic set of 270 APS firms and 210 high-tech enterprises.

In the second stage, we developed a so called 'service activity matrix'. This matrix is defined by FUAs in the lines structured along the regional, national, European and global scale, and knowledge-intensive firms in the columns. Each cell in the matrix shows a service value (v_{ij}) that indicates the importance of a FUA (i) to a firm (j). The importance is defined by the size of an office location and its function. By analysing the firms' websites, all office locations are rated on a scale of 0 to 5. The standard value for a cell in the matrix is 0 (no presence) or 2 (presence). If there is a clear indication that a location has a special relevance within the firm network (e.g. regional headquarter, supra-office functions) its value is upgraded to 3 or, in the case of even greater importance, to 4. The enterprise headquarters was valued at 5. If the overall importance of a location in the firm-network is very low (e.g. small agency in a small town) the value is downgraded to 1.

In the third stage, we used Taylor's interlocking network model to estimate connectivities of FUAs (Taylor 2004). Network connectivities are the primary output from the interlocking network analysis. The measure is an estimation of

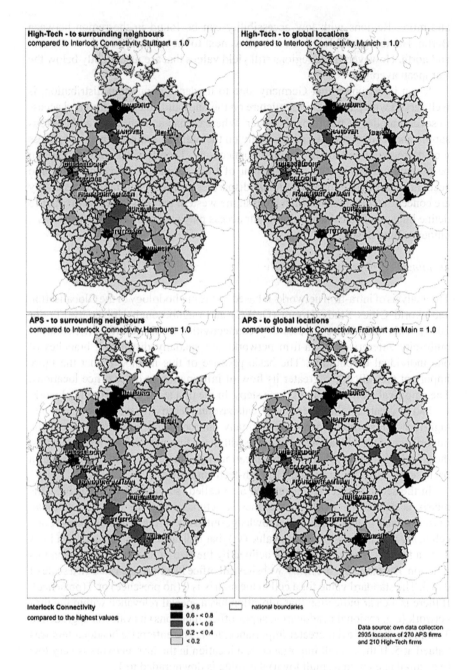

Figure 2.2   Interlock connectivity of APS and high-tech sectors on the regional and global scale (own calculation)

how well connected a city is within the overall intra-firm network. There are different kinds of connectivity values. The connectivity between two FUAs (a, b) of a certain firm (j) is analysed by multiplying their service values (v) representing the so called elemental interlock (r_{abj}) between two FUAs for one firm:

$$r_{abj} = v_{aj} * v_{bj} \quad (1)$$

To calculate the total connectivity between two FUAs, the elemental interlock for all firms located in these two FUAs is summarized. This leads to the city interlock (r_{ab}):

$$r_{ab} = \sum r_{abj} \quad (2)$$

Aggregating the city interlocks for a single FUA produces the interlock connectivity (N_a). This describes the importance of a FUA within the overall intra-firm network.

$$N_a = \sum r_{ai} \quad (a \neq i) \quad (3)$$

From this calculation we obtain an indicator of integration within several networks. Figure 2.2 shows the connectivity to surrounding neighbours and to global locations. Surrounding neighbours are defined by the Rook Contiguity of first and second order. Given a certain FUA, rook contiguity includes the first order neighbours by sharing a common border with the given FUA. The second order neighbours are those, which border to these FUAs of first order. The values shown here are the city interlocks normed to highest values on each scale and sector to either the surrounding neighbours or locations outside Europe on the global scale.

Values for some FUAs such as Hamburg, Munich and Stuttgart are always high on both scales and in both the APS and high-tech sectors. APS-firms tend to organize an area-wide distribution. For example banks offer services even in the smallest FUAs, which lead to high connectivities on the regional scale such as in the area between Hamburg, Düsseldorf and Frankfurt. Nevertheless, global activities are concentrated in a small number of centres.

When considering high-tech by itself, such regional/global opposition is not evident. Regions, which have intensive interaction with neighbouring agglomerations also show strong connections to global locations. Some exceptions can be detected in the southern parts of Germany. In particular, regions between Stuttgart, Nuremberg, and Munich have high values on the regional but not on the global scale. This might be explained by a high concentration of suppliers close to automotive sector plants in the southern part of Germany. All in all, hubs for non-physical connectivity for APS are Hamburg, Frankfurt, Munich, Düsseldorf, Stuttgart and Berlin. For high-tech these are Munich, Stuttgart, Hamburg and Berlin.

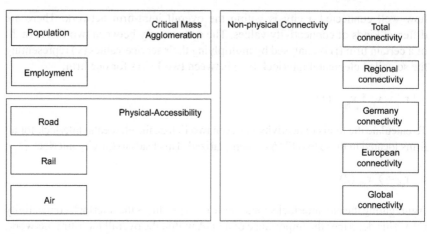

Figure 2.3   Set of variables and methodological proceeding

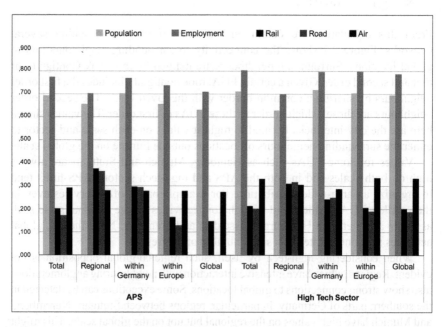

Figure 2.4   Correlation between interlock connectivity on different scales, accessibility by different modes, population, and employment (own calculation)

The Interplay between Physical Accessibility and Non-physical Connectivity

As mentioned above we define knowledge hubs as urban areas at the intersection of physical and non-physical networks, because knowledge creation depends on the interplay between codified and tacit knowledge, since people require experienced based knowledge to understand and adapt codified knowledge. Accordingly, there is also an interplay between physical movement of people and the non-physical exchange of information (Beaverstock et al. 2010). To assess this interplay a correlation analysis is carried out. Figure 2.3 illustrates the set of variables which are used. All variables are grouped thematically. Population and employment are indicators of agglomeration. Road, rail, and air access indicate the potential link-up in physical networks. Finally the group of variables of non-physical networks represents the intra-firm networks on different scales. The regional scale is defined by the interlock connectivity to surrounding neighbours. The national scale is given by the boundaries of Germany. The European scale contains all countries of the European continent and the global scales are all other locations. Since the variables are nearly normally distributed, we employed a bivariate Pearson correlation in order to evaluate interrelations between variables.

There is a strong interdependence between critical mass and integration in networks. This is investigated in the first stage. Simply put, the bigger a region the more companies it hosts. Therefore Figure 2.4 shows a comparison of correlations between interlock connectivity, accessibility, and population as well as employment and population. When calculating the correlations to the latter variables, we excluded all FUAs which are not in Germany because homogenous data for employment is not accessible. Correlation between non-physical interaction and accessibility data are calculated for the whole of Germany and neighbouring agglomerations. Most importantly, correlations are listed when they exhibit significance at or above 95 per cent.

This analysis is carried out on different spatial scales, from the regional to the global scale. These scales do not overlap. As previously mentioned, the strongest correlations are exhibited with population and employment. These results give a reference to the correlations with accessibility modes. With regard to listed spatial scales and their dependency, firstly, the higher accessibility via rail and road, the stronger connections to surrounding neighbours are. This result is attributable to the high values of interlock connectivity within metropolitan regions. We have seen that the Rhine-Ruhr possesses a dense network of rail and road. Above all, especially in high-tech, this area as a whole shows dense non-physical interaction.

Secondly, as expected, correlation coefficients with road and rail decline steadily with increasing distance from the regional to the global scale in both high-tech and APS. In particular, APS correlations lose importance the wider intra-firm networks extend. Similarly, high-tech confirms this trend, but still shows significant interrelations with rail and road access on the global scale, which might be explained by rather high concentration of physical infrastructure such as motorways and railway lines for logistics around production plants than by the actual use of these transport modes for global activities. Basically, firms within this sector operate globally, which collocates with transport infrastructure, and therefore correlation coefficients might be higher on that scale.

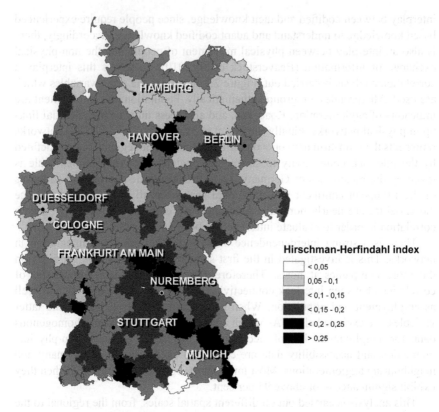

Figure 2.5 **Hirschman-Herfindahl-Index of knowledge intensive employment**

Source: Bundesagentur für Arbeit 2010

Thirdly, correlations to air access do not differ between the several scales. Undoubtedly they are significant but do not confirm the expected impact of growing air access on the European and global scale.

In summary, although ICT have the potential for ubiquitous access to information, localized transportation infrastructure remains important for economic performance because it enables geographical and relational proximity. This in turn leads to different preconditions between regions. As Törnqvist (1968) noted, the 'most important contacts [...] demand direct personal contacts between personal, and thus passenger movement' (Törnqvist 1968: 101). Other modes of interaction, such as telecommunication, are no substitute for face-to-face contacts. The hypothesis that air access remains the most important factor and that air access is a more relevant factor for interactions outside Germany requires clarification. In the case of APS, its influence on connectivity does not change along the spatial scales. Contrastingly, correlations to road and rail decrease uniformly. Hence the relative importance of air access compared to other modes of accessibility increases the wider the scale is. Furthermore, critical mass is slightly less important.

Figure 2.6 Map of value-adding activities in the FUAs of Germany

Source: own calculation

The Spatial Complementary in Knowledge Production

Since physical and non-physical network links converge in knowledge hubs these cities also capture a functional position within this system. Therefore, we analyse, firstly, the coexistence of diversified and specialized FUAs and, secondly, the relations between firms and their external partners along a stylized value chain. Figure 2.6 shows the Hirschman-Herfindahl-Index (HHI) of knowledge intensive branches. The HHI ranges between 0 and 1. Value 1 indicates that knowledge intensive employment is concentrated in one branch and the region is strongly specialized. The opposite is a diversified region, which is indicated by values close to 0. Thus, the HHI is used as an indicator of localization economies (values close to 1) and urbanization economies (values close to 0) (Beaudry and Schiffauerova 2009: 321). According to the HHI the FUAs of Wolfsburg and Ludwigshafen are the most specialized ones in our data sample. Wolfsburg reaches, due to its high concentration of automotive related firms, a value of 0.59 and Ludwigshafen, famous for production in chemistry and pharmaceuticals, has a value of 0.45. The lowest values and, therefore, the most diversified employment are to be found in the FUAs of Munich, Hamburg, Hanover, Dusseldorf and Cologne. At the same time these FUAs have the highest interlock connectivities (see Figure 2.2). Furthermore the specialized FUAs of Ingolstadt, which is located north of Munich, and Wolfsburg located east of Hannover are located quite close to the diversified FUAs of Munich and Hannover. Because of this geographical proximity between specialized and diversified regions we assume that there is a distinct inter-relation between them (Brandt et al. 2008, Thierstein et al. 2011).

A similar investigation was carried out by (Growe 2010) who showed that agglomerations can have either a surplus or deficit of 'functional importance' in employment in advanced producer services, which implies that there might be a spatial division of labour between those agglomerations, which show a surplus and those, which have a deficit in order to complement the value chain of knowledge production (Growe 2010: 12–15). To ground the assumption we compare our analysis of employment with the distribution of the elements of a standardized value chain.

To investigate this assumption we present the results of the web survey in which knowledge intensive firms were asked where their partners are located along a stylized value chain with the elements 'research & development', 'processing', 'financing', 'marketing', 'sales & distribution' and 'customers' (Lüthi et al. 2013). The complete analysis was published in (Lüthi 2011: 136–9). All in all, 331 firms indicated 1346 value-adding activities. In Figure 2.6, a value chain element is mapped only if it reaches the highest LQ within the FUA and – at the same time – if it received at least 4 references in the questionnaire. Hence, the map shows a selection of the questionnaire and it contains the relative functional specialization in the German space economy, with Munich, Stuttgart, Frankfurt and Hamburg having outstanding intensities of high value-added activities such as R&D, financing and marketing. In Nuremberg, Dresden and Mainz, there is a relative concentration of processing, while customers of knowledge-intensive companies are mainly located in Berlin, Hannover and in the Rhine-Ruhr region.

Summing up, we showed that there is a coexistence of specialized and diversified FUAs in Germany. First, the coexistence of diversified and specialized FUAs in a geographical proximity implies a relatedness of those regions. Referring to Duranton and Puga (2000) specialization and diversification are elements of a mutual process. Therefore, knowledge hubs emerge through the relations between those FUAs. Secondly, the analysis of the value chain verifies this finding. We assume that the entire production of goods and services has to combine all elements of the value chain. Since these are distributed unequally in space, firms tend to complement their value chain by interacting with partners.

Conclusion

When taking the non-physical dimension into account there are only a few FUAs in Germany, which can be called a hub. For APS these are Hamburg, Frankfurt, Munich, Dusseldorf, Stuttgart and Berlin and for high-tech these are Munich,

Stuttgart, Hamburg and Berlin. Since the process of knowledge production takes part in a strong interplay between physical and non-physical interaction in order to combine tacit and explicit knowledge. Taking the physical accessibility into account the access by air traffic plays a crucial role for knowledge hubs. Therefore FUAs such as Frankfurt and Munich appear as hubs. Airport cities emerge as a functional spatial configuration from this development (Schaafsma et al. 2008). Nevertheless, APS firms on the whole tend to concentrate and operate intensively on the national scale. In particular, banks and insurance firms are distributed area-wide to supply their services.

Both APS and high-tech firms operate on a global scale to combine the advantages of agglomeration and network economies. Nevertheless, differences between both sectors are observable. High-tech firms on the whole are not fixed to the national markets to offer daily supplies in the way APS firms often do. Our results show that there is relatedness between specialization and diversification of FUAs. The degree of diversification is higher in strongly connected FUAs such as Munich, Hamburg or Dusseldorf, where also a large number of advanced producer services firms are located. Specialization is mainly to be found in less connected FUAs with high employment in high-tech firms. So, high-tech firms and their economic activities concentrate in certain FUAs such as Wolfsburg and Ludwigshafen. Although these FUAs are not equipped with high accessibility by air and, furthermore, they do not capture strong non-physical connectivity, they still assume an important position in a functional and spatial division of labour. Therefore those specialized FUAs obtain a hub-like significance. Both processes – specialization and diversification – seem to complement each other. From a theoretical point of view these findings suggest that urbanized economies benefit from a process of urbanization economies and localization economies.

However, high-tech firms also optimize value chains that have high stakes in production worldwide because the share of physical labour within the production process is supposed to be higher than in APS. Therefore, production is often carried out in locations with lower wages and the co-existence of a highly qualified workforce, such as in India or South-East Asia, and therefore the correlation of air access and interlock connectivity show significant values.

Reflecting Richard Florida's hypothesis that the world is spiky, our results offer an indication of how strongly physical infrastructure influences business operations in the knowledge economy. Indeed, an uneven supply of physical infrastructure, such as airports or other modes of transportation, initializes a cumulative causation. Higher accessibility leads to wider market areas of firms and fosters economic performance, which in turn enables further investment in physical infrastructure. Furthermore, the direction of causation is mutual, because wider market areas in knowledge intensive business activities also require the physical presence of knowledge workers.

50 *Hub Cities in the Knowledge Economy*

References

Amin, A. and Cohendet, P. 2004. *Architectures of Knowledge. Firms, Capabilities, and Communities*. Oxford, New York: Oxford University Press.

Amin, A. and Roberts, J. 2008 Knowing in action: Beyond communities of practice. *Research Policy*, 37(2), 353–69.

Asheim, B.T., Coenen L., Moodysson J. and Vang, J. 2007. Constructing knowledge-based regional advantage: Implications for regional innovation policy. *International Journal of Entrepreneurship and Innovation Management*, 7(2–3–4–5), 140–55.

Axhausen, K. 2008. Accessibility: Long-term perspectives. *Journal of Transport and Land Use*, 1(2), 5–22.

Barabási, A.-L. and Albert, R. 1999. Emergence of scaling in random networks. *Science*, 286(5439), 509–12.

Bathelt, H., Malmberg A. and Maskell, P. 2004. Clusters and knowledge: Local buzz, global pipelines and the process of knowledge creation. *Progress in Human Geography*, 28(1), 31–56.

Beaudry, C. and Schiffauerova A. 2009. Who's right, Marshall or Jacobs? The localization versus urbanization debate. *Research Policy*, 38(2), 318–37.

Beaverstock, J.V., Derudder, B., Faulconbridge, J. and Witlox, F. (2010) *International Business Travel in the Global Economy*. Farnham: Ashgate.

Becattini, G. 1991. Italian industrial districts: Problems and perspectives. *International Studies of Management & Organization*, 21(1), 83–90.

Boschma, R. 2005. Proximity and innovation: A critical assessment. *Regional Studies*, 39(1), 61–74.

Boschma, R. and Iammarino, S. 2009. Related variety, trade linkages, and regional growth in Italy. *Economic Geography*, 85(3), 289–311.

Bottazzi, L. and Peri, G. 2002. Innovation and Spillovers in Regions: Evidence from European Patent Data. Working Paper 215.

Brandt, A., Krätke, S., Hahn, C. and Borts, R. 2008. *Metropolregionen und Wissensvernetzung. Metropolregionen und Wissensvernetzung - Eine Netzwerkanalyse innovationsbezogener Koperationen in der Metropolregion Hannover-Braunschweig-Göttingen. Beiträge zur europäischen Stadt- und Regionalforschung 6.* Münster: LIT Verlag.

Breschi, S. and Lissoni, F. 2009. Mobility of skilled workers and co-invention networks: An anatomy of localized knowledge flows. *Journal of Economic Geography*, 9(4), 439–68.

Bundesagentur für Arbeit 2010. *Knowledge-intensive Employment*. Unpublished Electronic Database.

Button, K. and Taylor, S. 2000. International air transportation and economic development. *Journal of Air Transport Management*, 6(4), 209–22.

Castells, M. 2000. *The rise of the Network Society. The Information Age: Economy, Society and Culture*. Vol. 1. Malden: Blackwell Publishers.

Cooke, P. 1992. Regional innovation systems: Competitive regulation in the New Europe. *Geoforum*, 23(3), 365–82.

Cooke, P., De Laurentis, C., Tödtling, F. and Trippl, M. 2007. *Regional Knowledge Economies. Markets, Clusters and Innovation*. Cheltenham, Northampton: Edward Elgar.

de Bok, M. and van Oort, F. 2011. Agglomeration economies, accessibility, and the spatial choice behavior of relocating firms. *The Journal of Transport and Land Use*, 4(1), 5–24.

Derudder, B. 2006. On conceptual confusion in empirical analyses of a transnational urban network. *Urban Studies*, 43(11), 2027–46.

Derudder, B. and Witlox, F. 2008. Mapping world city networks through airline flows: Context, relevance, and problems. *Journal of Transport Geography*, 16(4), 305–12.

Derudder, B. and Witlox, F. 2005. An appraisal of the use of airline data in assessing the world city network: A research note on data. *Urban Studies*, 42(13), 2371–88.

Derudder, B., Devriendt, L. and Witlox, F. 2007. Flying where you don't want to go: An empirical analysis of hubs in the global airline networks. *Tijdschrift voor Economische en Sociale Geografie*, 98(3), 307–24.

Dicken, P. 2011. *Global Shift. Mapping the Changing Contours of the World Economy. Sixth Edition*. London: SAGE.

Droß, M. and Thierstein, A. 2011. Wissensökonomie als Entwicklungstreiber von Flughafenregionen – das Beispiel München. *Informationen zur Raumentwicklung*. 2011(1), 27–36.

Duranton, G. and Puga, D. 2000. Diversity and specialisation in cities: Why, where and when does it matter? *Urban Studies*, 37(3), 533–55.

ESPON 2004. ESPON Project 1.1.1. *The role, specific situation and potentials for urban areas as nodes of polycentric development. Final report*. Luxemburg: European Spatial Planning Observation Network ESPON.

ESPON 2009. *Territorial Dynamics in Europe. Trends in Accessibility*. [Online: European Spatial Planning Observation Network ESPON]. Available at: http://www.espon.eu/export/sites/default/Documents/Publications/TerritorialObservations/TrendsInAccessibility/to-no2.pdf.

Florida, R. 2005. The world is spiky. The world in numbers. Globalization has changed the economic playing field, but hasn't leveled it. *The Atlantic* [Online], 2005 (296), 48–51.

Friedman, T.L. 2005. *The World is Flat. A Brief History of the Twenty-First Century*. New York: Farrar, Strauss and Giroux.

Friedmann, J. 1986. The world city hypothesis. Development and change, in *The Global Cities Reader*, edited by N. Brenner and R. Kell. Oxon: Routledge, 67–71.

Geurs, K. and van Eck, J.R. 2001. *Accessibility measures: Review and applications. Evaluation of accessibility impacts of land-use transport scenarios, and related social and economic impacts*. Bilthoven: National Institute of Public Health and the Environment.

Goebel, V., Thierstein, A. and Lüthi, S. 2007. *Functional Polycentricity in the Mega-City Region of Munich*, Association of European Schools of Planning (AESOP), Napoli, 11–14 July 2007.

Growe, A. 2010. Human capital in the German urban system – patterns of concentration and specialisation. *European Journal of Spatial Development* [Online], 1–23. Available at: http://www.nordregio.se/EJSD/refereed40.pdf [accessed: 14 January 2012].

Growe, A. and Blotevogel, H.H. 2011. Knowledge hubs in the German urban system: Identifying hubs by combining network and territorial perspectives. *Raumforschung und Raumordnung*, 69(3), 175–85.

Haas, H.-D. and Wallisch, M. 2008. Wandel des Münchner Flughafens zur 'Airport City'. Entwicklungsdeterminanten und raumwirtschaftliche Austrahlungseffekte. *Geographische Rundschau*, 60(10), 32–8.

Hall, P., and Pain, K. 2006. *The Polycentric Metropolis. Learning from Mega-City Regions in Europe*. London: Earthscan.

Hansen, W.G. 1959. How accessibility shapes land use. *Journal of American Institute of Planners*. 25(1), 73–6.

Hesse, M. 2010. Cities, material flows and the geography of spatial interaction: Urban places in the system of chains. *Global Networks*, 10(1), 75–91.

Hirschman, A.O. 1958. *The Strategy of Economic Development*. New Haven: Yale University Press.

Hoover, E.M. 1937. *Location Theory and the Shoe and Leather Industries*. Cambridge, MA: Harvard University Press.

Howells, J. 2000. Knowledge, innovation and location, in *Knowledge, Space, Economy*, edited by J.R. Bryson et al. London, New York: Routledge, 50–62.

Jacobs, J. 1969. *The Economy of Cities*. New York: Random House.

Jaffe, A.B., Trajtenberg, M. and Henderson, R. 1993. Geographic localization of knowledge spillovers as evidenced by patent citations. *The Quarterly Journal of Economics*. 108(3), 577–98.

Knowles, R. (2006) Transport shaping space: Differential collapse in time-space. *Journal of Transport Geography*, 14, 407–25.

Kramar, H. and Suitner, J. 2008. *Verkehrsknotenpunkte als Innovationsstandorte? Die Nähe zu Flughäfen als Standortfaktor wissenschaftlicher und künstlerischer Innovation*, REAL CORP 008, Vienna, Austria, 19–21 May 2008.

Kujath, H.-J. and Schmidt, S. 2010. Wissensökonomie, in *Räume der Wissensökonomie. Implikationen für das deutsche Städtesystem. Serie: Stadt- und Regionalwissenschaften, Urban and Regional Sciences, Bd. 6*, edited by H.-J. Kujath and S. Zillmer. Münster: Lit Verlag, 37–50.

Lüthi, S. 2011. *Interlocking Firm Networks and Emerging Mega-City Regions. The Relational Geography of the Knowledge Economy in Germany*. Munich: Munich University of Technology.

Lüthi, S., Thierstein, A. and Bentlage, M. 2011. Interlocking firm networks in the German knowledge economy. On local networks and global connectivity. *Raumforschung und Raumordnung.* 69(3), 161–74.

Lüthi, S., Thierstein, A. and Bentlage, M. 2013. The Relational Geography of the Knowledge Economy in Germany. On functional urban hierarchies and localised value chain systems. *Urban Studies,* 50(2), 255–75.

Mahutga, M.C., Ma, X., Smith, D.A. and Timberlake, M. 2010. Economic globalisation and the structure of the world city system: The case of airline passenger data. *Urban Studies,* 47(9), 1925–47.

Malecki, E.J. 2000. Creating and sustaining competitiveness. Local knowledge and economic geography, in *Knowledge, Space, Economy,* edited by J. Bryson et al. London, New York, 103–19.

Marshall, A. 1920. Industrial organization continued – The concentration of specialized industries in particular localities, in *Principles of Economics,* A. Marshall. London: Macmillan and Co.

Myrdal, G. 1957. *Economic Theory and Underdeveloped Regions.* London: Duckworth.

O'Connor, K. 2003. Global air travel: toward concentration or dispersal? *Journal of Transport Geography,* 11(2), 83–92.

OECD 2008. *Staying Competitive in the Global Economy.* Paris: OECD.

O'Kelly, M.E. 1998. A geographer's analysis of hub-and-spoke networks. *Journal of Transport Geography,* 6(3), 171–1'86.

Polanyi, M. 1966. *The Tacit Dimension.* London: Routledge & Kegan Paul.

Redondi, R., Malighetti, P. and Paleari, S. 2011. Hub competition and travel times in the world-wide airport network. *Journal of Transport Geography,* 19(6), 1260–71.

Sassen, S. 1991. *The Global City: New York, London, Tokyo.* Princeton, N.J.: Princeton University Press.

Sassen, S. 1994. *Cities in a World Economy.* Thousand Oaks: Pine Forge Press.

Sassen, S. 2001. *The Global City: New York, London, Tokyo.* Oxford: Princeton University Press.

Schaafsma, M. 2008. Accessing global city regions. The airport as a city, in *The Image and the Region – Making Mega-City Regions Visible!,* edited by A. Thierstein and A. Förster. Baden: Lars Müller Publishers, 69–79.

Schaafsma, M. 2009. *Airport Corridors. Drivers of Economic Development.* Standort-Dialog: Ready for take off – Der Flughafen BBI, Berlin, Germany, 25 June 2009.

Schaafsma, M., Amkreutz, J. and Güller, M. 2008. *Airport and City - Airport Corridors: Drivers of Economic Development.* Rotterdam: Schiphol Real Estate.

Schamp, E.W. 2003. Knowledge, innovation and funding in spatial context: The case of Germany, in *Innovation, Finance and Space,* edited by A. Thierstein and E.W. Schamp. Frankfurt: Selbstverlag Institut für Wirtschafts- und Sozialgeografie der Johann Wolfgang Goethe Universität, 179–93.

Schmidt, S. 2005. Metropolregionen als Hubs globaler Kommunikation und Mobilität in einer wissensbasierten Wirtschaft?, in *Knoten im Netz*, edited by H.J. Kujath. Münster: Lit Verlag, 285–320.

Simmie, J. 2003. Innovation and urban regions as national and international nodes for the transfer and sharing of knowledge. *Regional Studies*, 37(6 –7), 607–20.

Sokol, M., van Egeraat, C. and Williams B. 2008. Revisiting the 'informational city': Space of flows, polycentricity and the geography of knowledge-intensive business services in the emerging global city-region of Dublin. *Regional Studies*. 42(8), 1133–46.

Storper, M. and Venables, A.J. 2004. Buzz: face-to-face contact and the urban economy. *Journal of Economic Geography*, 4(4), 351–70.

Taylor, P.J. 2004. *World City Network: A Global Urban Analysis*. London: Routledge.

Thierstein, A., Bentlage, M., Pechlaner, H., Döpfer, B.,Brandt, A., Drangmeister, C., Schrödl, D., Voßen, D., Floeting, H. and Buser, B. 2011. *Wertschöpfungskompetenz der Region Ingolstadt*. München: AUDI AG.

Thierstein, A., Goebel, V. and Lüthi, S. (2007) *Standortverflechtungen der Metropolregion München. Über Konnektivität in der Wissensökonomie*. München: Lehrstuhl für Raumentwicklung, TU München.

Törnqvist, G. 1968. Flows of information and the location of economic activities. *Geografiska Annaler. Series B, Human Geography*. 50(1), 99–107.

Torre, A. and Rallet, A. 2005. Proximity and localization. *Regional Studies*. 39(1), 47–59.

Tranos, E. 2011. The topology and the emerging urban geographies of the Internet backbone and aviation networks in Europe: A comparative study. *Environment and Planning A*. 43(2), 378–92.

Tranos, E. and Gillespie, A. 2011. The urban geography of Internet backbone networks in Europe: Roles and relations. *Journal of Urban Technology*. 18(1), 35–50.

Chapter 3

Knowledge Hubs in the Polycentric German Urban System between Concentration Processes and Conurbation Dynamics

Anna Growe

Introduction

In recent decades the traditional geographical focus on issues of a territorial nature has been complemented by a focus on networks and flows between cities. Networks are discussed as a necessary complement to a territorial perspective, to facilitate the understanding of the processes that produce space (Friedmann 1995, Taylor 2004, Hall and Pain 2006).

The focus on networks can be explained by an increased perception of globalization leading to an intensification of trading and supply networks, resulting in a focus on relational scales (Dicken 2007). Networks, through which input-output relations along the value chain are organized, are discussed as vertical relations (Bathelt and Glückler 2011: 86).

However, all networks and flows are grounded in places. Malmberg and Maskell (2002) have stressed the fact that while firms in spatial cluster formations do not necessarily have input-output relations, spatial proximity still offers the opportunity to observe competitors and share a similar knowledge base (Nooteboom 2002). These processes, which occur between firms of similar goods, form the horizontal dimension.

According to Dicken (2007: 24), who focuses on functional relations, spaces with an intersection of horizontal and vertical dimensions are key points of globalization. This paper seeks to enhance Dickens's statement to the spatial focus. Even if spatial consequences of the horizontal dimension are often associated with spatial clusters, these terms are not to be used synonymously. Horizontal and vertical interactions of firms, this is interactions with competitors and interactions with supplier and customers, may occur locally as well as globally.

Based on assumptions about the necessity of specialization (to enable labour division in vertical dimensions and comparability in horizontal dimensions) and the necessity of diversity (to avoid over-embeddedness) it is supposed in this paper that accessibility of huge labour pools and the integration in inter-regional networks facilitates functional integration in horizontal as well as vertical dimensions. In this context cities are understood as spaces that are determined simultaneously by territorial clusters and by nodes of supra-local networks and that can be described as hubs.

Cities as hubs may be analyzed with regard to different networks, for example with regard to infrastructure networks (Malecki 2002, Zook 2006, Witlox and Derudder 2007, Beaverstock et al. 2009, Jacobs et al. 2011) or to functional economic networks (Hall and Pain 2006, Taylor 2007, Hoyler et al. 2008, Derudder and Witlox 2010, Lüthi et al. 2011). This paper contributes to the latter discussion and focuses on cities as hubs in networks of knowledge-based services in economic networks.

As knowledge is seen as a crucial factor for economic processes in post-industrial societies (Drucker 1969, Bell 1989, Stehr 2001), there is a particular focus on knowledge-based services. The increasing importance of science and technology for economic processes is based on the systematic use and development of knowledge as a resource in all economic processes (Park 2000: 9). However, the immaterial good 'knowledge' cannot be measured directly or identified in space, like material goods of production. It is important to make a distinction between two types of knowledge in this context: implicit and codified knowledge (Polanyi 1967: 64). Implicit knowledge is embodied in people. It allows the creation of temporary monopoly profits based on advances in knowledge and is, therefore, crucial to knowledge-based economic processes (Nonaka and Takeuchi 1995: 33, Amin and Cohendet 2004: 23).

Using knowledge as an input in services and as a product that is sold, knowledge-based services deal with knowledge in two ways. According to Castells (1996: 29), this is the central development that distinguishes the importance of knowledge today from the use of knowledge in economic processes in the past. The focus of this paper is therefore on knowledge-based services, and people and their interaction within organizational networks are used as a proxy to understand the spatial dimension of knowledge.

Analyzing hubs from a spatial background, the research questions discussed in this paper are firstly, whether knowledge hubs are spatially concentrated or equally distributed in a city network and secondly, how these patterns of knowledge hubs change over the course of time. On the basis of theoretical approaches, assumptions can be made about increasing spatial concentration (explained by agglomeration advantages) as well as about increasing spatial de-concentration of economic activities (explained by neoclassical approaches).

However, these theoretical approaches have been developed with regard to industrial production and – mainly – material goods. The exchange of immaterial goods, for example knowledge, in networks of production has not been theorized to the same extent. In this regard the empirical analysis of the changes to certain economic activities in a certain spatial context is of crucial importance.

As it has quite a balanced structure of large cities, the German urban system is used as an example. The analysis of all German cities reveals influences of the city size as well as the historic dependency on the importance of cities as knowledge hubs. Especially the persistence of a west-east divide is remarkable.

The Conceptualization of Hubs as Intersection between Network and Territory

An extensive body of literature discusses cities and their integration into non-local networks (for example Friedmann 1986, Sassen 1991, Scott et al. 2004, Taylor 2004, Hall and Pain 2006). However, the most distinctive new conceptual context was developed by Castells (1996). The basic idea here is the reshaping of space through the emergence of a new network society. In the context of this approach, hubs arise through a definition of the spaces of places through the spaces of flows.

Castells defines space in terms of social practice. Through the introduction of information technologies and the development of a network society, the space of places, in which people are located next to each other, is supplemented by the new space of flows. In this context, places do not disappear but come to be defined additionally by their position within flows (Castells 1996: 412).

Castells (1996: 412–15) differentiates between three layers of flows. The first layer consists of infrastructural support for social practices, for example an information and communication infrastructure such as the Internet. The third layer consists of the spatial organization of economic elites, for example segregated residential and vocational locales as well as certain exclusive restaurants or clubs. Between these, the second layer refers to the space of social practices that forms society, in which agents who use infrastructure networks to link specific places produce functional networks. Castells (1996: 415) uses the terms nodes and hubs in this context and points out that the most direct illustration of hubs and nodes is provided by global cities. Therefore, this paper focuses on processes within the second layer.

To fully understand the processes that determine the functions of cities, Camagni (2004: 103) proposed a combination of two spatial logics: a territorial approach ('cities as cluster') and a network approach ('cities as interconnections'). Hence, the role of cities as hubs cannot be understood simply by analyzing either clusters within cities or interconnections between cities; rather both perspectives must be considered simultaneously (see Figure 3.1).

The conceptualization of knowledge hubs in this paper refers to implicit knowledge. The aim is to understand spatial patterns of implicit knowledge by combining information about territorial clusters and the integration in networks of implicit knowledge.

The territorial approach adopted in this paper focuses on the creation of a critical mass of implicit knowledge by analysts. People who work in knowledge-based professions are assumed to be knowledge-holders in cities and form the labour market of a city. A certain size of the labour market (often described using the term 'critical mass') attracts additional knowledge holders and may create a local buzz (Bathelt et al. 2004). According to Bathelt et al. (2004: 38) the 'buzz' is a new understanding of Alfred Marshall's 'industrial atmosphere', where information is provided through face-to-face contacts, co-presence and co-location. Actors who exchange and participate within the 'buzz' are knowledge-holders, i.e. people who

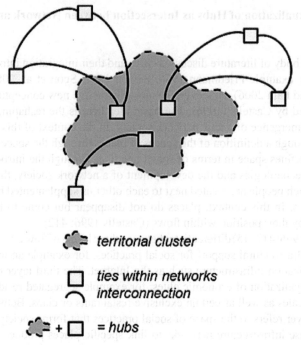

🌸 **territorial cluster**

☐ **ties within networks**

⌒ **interconnection**

🌸 + ☐ = *hubs*

Figure 3.1   Conceptualization of hubs

Source: Author

work in knowledge-based processes. These are people who understand the local buzz and use the information gained in a meaningful and effective way.

Nevertheless, the local buzz is not the only resource for the generation, exchange and use of implicit knowledge, although implicit knowledge is mainly associated with local face-to-face exchange (Bathelt et al. 2004: 32). Firms also create organizational networks by constructing 'global pipelines'. Bathelt et al. (2004) mainly focus on the creation of global pipelines through building up strategic cooperation; however, they also mention the formation of branches. The organizational relationships between the branches and headquarters of a firm are assumed to constitute the basis of knowledge flows within firms (Taylor 2004: 61). Therefore, the network approach adopted in this paper focuses on multi-location firms that produce knowledge-based services.

Changes of Knowledge Hubs in an Urban Network

Changes in economic processes may be accompanied by an altered appreciation of location factors. As the appreciation of location factors can change over time, new spatial patterns of economic activities may develop. This raises the question of whether knowledge-based economic activities, producing knowledge as an immaterial good, are determined by the same location factors as the production of material goods and how patterns of economic activity change in conjunction with a changing appreciation of location factors.

Traditional theoretical approaches base their assumptions and hypotheses mainly on transport costs and neoclassic assumptions that lead to an expectation of spatial de-concentration of economic activities over time (Weber 1909). However, the persistence of city growth and large agglomerations suggest that not only centrifugal but also centripetal effects influence the spatial distribution of economic activities.

Therefore, during the 1960s, a competing strand of theories was developed: the so-called polarization theories. Within these theories, path dependencies in the context of regional and sectoral developments are emphasized. Structures developed in the past shape today's conditions of development by positive or negative backwash effects. Polarization theories assume that circular and cumulative interdependencies lead to distinctive differences of development between spatial units over the course of time (Myrdal 1957, Lasuén 1969, Boudeville 1974).

Considering both strands, theoretical approaches may explain the processes of concentration of economic activities as well as the processes of de-concentration. However, these theoretical approaches have been developed mainly with regard to industrial production processes. Therefore, in the context of knowledge-based services, the question is raised of whether a changed appreciation of location factors, for example the increased importance of the immaterial good knowledge, leads to new spatial patterns of production.

In service production processes, transport costs play a lesser role than in industrial production processes. This leads to the discussion of a possible reduction in importance of geographic space, as information is expected to be exchanged easily via information and communication technologies (Cairncross 1997, Friedman 2006). However, the availability of information and communication technologies is globally very unequal and, furthermore, the use of these technologies is not cost-neutral (Malecki 2002: 404).

Still more important is the distinction between information and knowledge. The latter is a crucial input factor in knowledge-based economic activities like knowledge-based services. It includes interpretation and the processes of making sense of information, and it is the margins of knowledge that lead to monopolization profits. New knowledge only can be gained within interactive learning processes, for which face-to-face-contacts are crucial (Polanyi 1967). After all, knowledge cannot be exchanged easily via information and communication technologies; rather, ways of assuring personal interaction have to be found.

In this context, more recent theoretical approaches focus on the costs of different types of communication and coordination processes. The initiation and coordination of communication processes require transaction costs (Williamson 1981). Transaction costs consist of information costs, adjustment costs and communication costs (Scott 1988, Storper and Walker 1989). According to Scott (1988), spatial proximity facilitates information exchange, adjustment and communication and therefore reduces transaction costs within service production processes.

However, spatial proximity cannot compensate for transaction costs completely. The extent of these costs is also determined by the ease of codifying knowledge. The easier it is to codify knowledge, the lesser the necessity of organizing face-to-face-communication or investing in the means of knowledge exchange, for example business travel or conferences.

Data and Methodology

The paper analyses knowledge-based services through the lens of both a territorial and a network perspective. The basis for the territorial perspective is provided by data about knowledge-based professions. Data on organizational networks of knowledge-based firms by sector provides the basis for the network perspective.

Data

The territorial data used in this paper are extracted from a data set provided by the Federal Employment Office in Germany (*Bundesagentur für Arbeit* (BA)). The data include all employees obliged to pay social insurance contributions, representing about 70% of the total workforce. Employees are differentiated on the basis of their occupations (*sozialversicherungspflichtig Beschäftigte nach Berufsordnungen*), and this in turn is based on the occupational classification of 1988 (KldB 88 BA). The classification of employees by occupation is based on the current type of activity that is performed and not on recent activities or on qualifications. This classification makes it possible to draw conclusions about functional spatial patterns.

The choice of occupational groups is based on the identification of knowledge based professions of Hall (2007). Hall (2007: 46) systemizes occupants according to the research intensity of the labour and according to the share of highly qualified personnel which results in a differentiation of six occupational groups: engineers, technicians, IT-related jobs, consulting, creative and media jobs, and other knowledge intensive jobs.

Following Hall (2007: 8–10), occupational groups with a high share in knowledge-based services and research-intensive industries were chosen and used to select 13 occupational groups: accountancy, advertising, architecture, consulting, consultant engineers, data management, finance, ICT-services, insurance, law, management, media, and real estate. These occupational groups will be used in this analysis as 'knowledge-based professions' (KBP).[1]

---

1   The occupations that are aggregated as 'knowledge-based professions' – the Kldb 88 BA code is shown in brackets: accountancy (753, 771, 772), advertising (703, 833, 834, 835, 837), architecture (603, 604, 623, 624), consulting (752), consultant engineers (611, 612,

To enable the comparison of changes over time, two data sets from 1997 and from 2007 are used. The data set from 1997 covers 2,900,000 knowledge holders. The data set from 2007, which covers 3,100,000 knowledge holders, shows an increase in employment in the knowledge-based professions. The data are provided on NUTS-3 level counties in Germany.

The network data used in this paper are extracted from a data set provided by Hoppenstedt, a commercial data provider in Germany. The database includes all firms that provide information about their locations on a voluntary basis. Hoppenstedt itself claims to include information about the 250,000 largest companies, representing about 85% of added value, in Germany. As this study is interested in processes within organizational corporate networks, only firms with a minimum of two locations are considered. Therefore the database prompts the adoption of a bottom-up approach with a focus on national firm linkages (Hoyler et al. 2008) instead of a top-down approach with a focus on global firm linkages (Taylor 2004).

Firms are differentiated by sector (*Wirtschaftszweige*) based on the classification of economic sectors of 1993 (WZ 93). The classification of firms by sector depends on the similarity of the products or services produced or provided by the firms, the similarity of their production processes or on the use of similar raw materials. The sectors are chosen by two criteria; the sectors have to be classified as knowledge intensive services by Legler and Frietsch (2009: 19) and they have to be comparable to the chosen occupational groups.

A matrix of firms is created on the basis of economic sectors that include advanced producer services. Firms in these sectors are used in aggregate form as 'knowledge-based firms'.[2] Data from 2002 and 2009 are considered to enable the comparison of changes in the city network. The 2002 data set covers around 2,000 knowledge-based firms and the 2009 data set covers around 3,000 firms. Information about firm locations is provided on the NUTS-3 level.

---

626), data management (774), finance (691, 692), ICT-services (602, 622), insurance (693, 694), law (811, 812, 813, 814), management (751), media (821, 822), real estate (704).

2   Firms from the following economic sectors are aggregated as "knowledge-based firms" – the WZ 93 code is shown in brackets: accountancy (74121, 74122, 74123, 74124, 74125), advertising (74401, 74402, 92113), architecture (74201, 74202, 74203, 74204, 74205, 74206, 74207, 74208, 74209), consulting (74131, 74132, 74141, 74142), consultant engineers (74301,74302, 74303, 74304), data management (72100, 72201, 72202, 72203, 72301, 72303, 72304, 72400, 72500, 72601, 72602), finance (65110, 65122, 65124, 65126, 65127, 65128, 65129, 65210, 65220, 65231, 65232, 65233, 67110, 67120, 67130), ICT services (64201, 64202, 64203, 64204, 64205, 64206, 64207), insurance (66011, 66020, 66031, 66032, 66033), law (74111, 74112, 74114, 74115), management (74151, 74152, 74155, 74156), media (22111, 22112, 22121, 22122, 22131, 22132, 22133, 22141, 22142, 22150, 92111, 92112, 92114, 92115, 92116, 92201, 92202, 92401), real estate (70111, 70112, 70113, 70121, 70122, 70201, 70202, 70310, 70320, 74153, 74154).

Preparing Network Data

Firm-based network data are used to enable the identification of cities that are important within flows of knowledge. As there is no direct information about immaterial knowledge flows between different cities, organizational firm networks are used as a proxy. Based on the idea of the firms' different locational strategies, the intercity relations constituted through the multi-local offices represent knowledge flows within the firms. The knowledge flows between different offices mainly consist of electronic communications that include information and knowledge. In the Global and World City (GaWC) model, these flows are seen as constituting the world city network (Taylor 2001: 183, Taylor 2004: 65).

The Global and World City (GaWC) measurement of the city network can be formally represented by a matrix V_{ij} defined by n cities x m firms, where v_{ij} is the 'service value' of city i to firm j. This service value is a standardized measure of the importance of a city to a firm's office network, which depends on the size and functions of an office or offices in a city.

In this study three service values are used (0, 1, and 3). Locations with no offices are valued 0, locations with local offices are valued 1 and locations of firm headquarters are valued 3. The network connectivity NC_a of city a in this interlocking network is defined as follows:

$$NC_a = \sum_{i,j} v_{aj} * v_{ij} \text{ with } (a \neq i)$$

Calculating Changes over the Course of Time

The calculation of changes in the number of persons in employment over the course of time is used in a number of studies to measure changes in economic activities (see for example Südekum (2006) for an analysis of those in employment in all economic sectors in Germany and see for example Boschma and Fritsch (2009) for an analysis of those in employment in creative sectors in seven European countries). Because of the attribution of a specific value x for a space a, the analysis of changes in the numbers in employment is comparatively easy. Changes to the value x can be explained by changes within the spatial unit a.

Changes over the course of time within a network structure are much more difficult to explore, as changes in the connectivity value c of the spatial unit a do not only depend on changes within this spatial unit a. Changes in connectivity can be influenced by two different processes.

- On the one hand, changes in connectivity c in a spatial unit a can arise from a changed number of firms within this space. For example more branches or more headquarters will lead to an increase in connectivity c in the spatial unit a.
- On the other hand the increased number of branches or headquarters in

space *a* may also lead to an increase in connectivity in space *b*, if both spaces are interconnected in one or more firm networks.

Changes within networks must therefore be understood as relative changes and the measurement of changes within networks must refer to the relative nature of these changes. In this paper changes in connectivity from 2002 to 2009 (and in professions from 1997 to 2007) are measured by the (relative) change in the importance of an individual city in the network of cities.

- First, the importance is measured by the percentage share of each city in the overall network at different points in time.
- Second, the change between the percentage shares of each city at both times is calculated.
- Third, z-scores of the percentage change are calculated. This is carried out to show whether the change in importance (CI) is above average or below average. CI values between -1 and 1 are understood as a small change, CI values between -2 and -1 and CI values between 1 and 2 are understood as a medium change, and SC values > +2 or < -2 indicate 'exceptional change' in statistical terms.[3]

Combining Territorial and Network Data

According to Camagni (2004) both a territorial perspective and a network perspective have to be considered when analyzing and understanding cities as hubs (see Figure 3.1). To avoid analyzing territorial and network perspectives in two parallel analyses, in this study an index is used to combine both perspectives: the hub index.

The hub index is an additive index, based on information about the connectivity of each spatial unit and the number of knowledge holders within each spatial unit (Growe and Blotevogel 2011). Two different hub indices are differentiated:

- an index of size that indicates the importance of a certain city as a hub within the German urban system at a given time, and
- an index of change that indicates the relative change in importance of a certain city as a hub within the German urban system between two points of time.

---

3   This approach is based on a method developed by Derudder et al. (2010) to calculate changes within organisational firm networks over the course of time. However, the outline calculation used in this paper has been modified. Instead of calculating z-standardised changes on the basis of z-standardised values in this paper, z-standardised changes on the basis of percentage shares are used to facilitate the understanding of the calculation and the interpretation of data.

Therefore the index of size contains information on the connectivity and on the number of KBPs in each hub at a given time, usually the starting point of the two time points compared subsequently. In this study the earliest connectivity information available is for 2002 and the earliest information about those employed in knowledge-based professions is for 1997. The index of size is calculated by adding z-standardized connectivity values and z-standardized KBP values for the year in question.

The index of change contains information about the changes in connectivity of a hub and about the change in the number of KBPs within the hub between two time points. The change refers to the period between the first and last years for which data are available. With regard to connectivity values, this period covers changes between 2002 and 2009 and for KBP values, this period covers changes between 1997 and 2007. The index of change is calculated by adding CI values for connectivity and KBPs.

Knowledge Hubs in the German Urban System

This paper approaches the discussion of knowledge hubs in Germany in three stages. Firstly, patterns of knowledge-based services are identified by measuring the importance of each county as a place and interconnection in networks. Secondly, changes in these patterns are calculated. Thirdly, the importance of each county as a knowledge hub and the change in each county's importance as a knowledge hub are combined to discuss both the importance and changes at the same time.

Knowledge Hub Patterns

Patterns relating to the importance of counties as a hub are identified on the basis of their importance as a place of knowledge-based services and as a link within networks of knowledge-based services.

Table 3.1 shows the 20 most important knowledge hubs. These are mainly the large cities within the German urban system. The three most important hubs are München, Berlin, and Hamburg, which are, for example, the only three cities with more than a million inhabitants. The smaller of the large cities form the lower ranks of Table 3.1. Erfurt, Wiesbaden, and Chemnitz, for example, have between 200,000 and 300,000 inhabitants. This observation strengthens the frequently-discussed assumption that knowledge-based services show an affinity towards large cities. However, the affinity towards large cities of the two aspects of hubs considered here (KBPs and connectivity) may differ.

Table 3.2 shows the correlation of both of these aspects with structural reference numbers. The correlations indicate a strong positive relation between the importance of a county as a place of knowledge-based services and its connectivity, and the number of inhabitants and the general numbers of persons in employment this county. However, the relationship between the importance of counties as locations

Table 3.1   The 20 most important hub cities in the German urban system

Starting point*			End point**		
Rank	County	Index of size	Rank	County	Index of size
1	München	16.12	1	München	17.25
2	Berlin	15.44	2	Hamburg	15.00
3	Hamburg	15.06	3	Berlin	14.44
4	Frankfurt am Main	12.67	4	Frankfurt am Main	11.70
5	Köln	10.05	5	Düsseldorf	10.32
6	Stuttgart	9.58	6	Köln	9.69
7	Düsseldorf	9.22	7	Stuttgart	9.17
8	Region Hannover	8.37	8	Region Hannover	8.09
9	Nürnberg	5.94	9	Nürnberg	6.16
10	Dresden	5.32	10	Leipzig	4.62
11	Leipzig	4.87	11	Dresden	4.28
12	Dortmund	3.79	12	Bremen	3.84
13	Bremen	3.70	13	Dortmund	3.73
14	Essen	3.65	14	Mannheim	3.38
15	Mannheim	3.32	15	Karlsruhe	3.35
16	Karlsruhe	3.19	16	Essen	3.18
17	Erfurt	3.03	17	LK München	2.91
18	Wiesbaden	2.70	18	Münster	2.62
19	Regionalverband Saarbrücken	2.58	19	Erfurt	2.56
20	Chemnitz	2.50	20	Mainz	2.25
*KBP: 1997; connectivity: 2002			**KBP: 2007; connectivity: 2009		

Source: BA, Hoppenstedt; own calculation

for knowledge-based services and the reference numbers is slightly bigger than the relationship between connectivity and the reference numbers. Also for both the KBPs and the connectivity values, the relationship with the number of persons in employment is bigger than the relationship with the number of inhabitants.

These correlations suggest that the bigger a city is in terms of persons in employment, the more important its role as a hub will be. In this context, the importance of cities as knowledge hubs is unequally distributed in Germany but the distribution is based on the unequal distribution of inhabitants and those in

Table 3.2   Correlation between KBPs and connectivity at the starting point of measurement and structural reference numbers in all 439 counties

Reference number	KBP	Connectivity
Inhabitants	0.825**	0.711**
Total persons in employment	0.942**	0.848**
** The correlation is significant at the level of 0.01.		

Source: BA, Hoppenstedt; own calculation

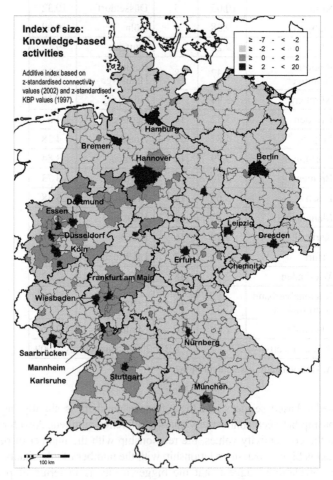

Figure 3.2   Index of size

Source: BA, Hoppenstedt; own calculation

employment. The map in Figure 3.2 shows the geographical pattern of these correlations. It can be seen that hubs of above average size are mainly cities and counties in dense conurbation areas in West German agglomerations.

Relative Changes in Importance as Knowledge Hubs

However, to identify the size of hubs at the starting point is only the first step. The importance of hubs might change during time. In this context it is interesting to see whether large hubs increase their importance more than small hubs and therefore might strengthen a process of concentration or whether a process of alignment can be observed. To discuss processes of concentration and alignment within the urban system, relative changes are observed as they suggest above-average and below-average changes within the interdependent changes in a network structure (see Table 3.3).

Table 3.3   Most positive and most negative relative changes of importance of hubs

County	Index of change* (most positive relative changes)	County	Index of change* (most negative relative changes)
LK München	12.71	Rems-Murr-Kreis	-2.60
Düsseldorf	6.41	Frankfurt (Oder)	-2.79
Rhein-Neckar-Kreis	5.36	Halle (Saale)	-2.81
Erlangen	5.09	Magdeburg	-3.64
LK Heilbronn	5.04	LK Hameln-Pyrmont	-3.68
Hochtaunuskreis	4.08	Region Hannover	-4.06
Regensburg	3.54	Essen	-4.19
LK Freising	3.10	Wuppertal	-4.21
LK Esslingen	3.03	Chemnitz	-4.73
LK Ebersberg	2.93	Berlin	-6.86

*change of KBP: 1997–2007; change of connectivity: 2002–2009

Among the ten counties with the highest positive relative changes only one of the large hubs of knowledge-based services can be found: Düsseldorf. Two more counties (Erlangen and Regensburg) are smaller cities that are hubs of only just above average size. Seven of the ten counties with the most positive relative changes are suburban counties (*Landkreise*, LK) within western or southern German city regions. Three *Landkreise* are close to München (Landkreis München, Landkreis

Freising, and Landkreis Ebersberg). Three other *Landkreise* are located in the urbanized area between Stuttgart and Mannheim in Baden-Württemberg (Rhein-Neckar-Kreis, Landkreis Heilbronn, and Landkreis Esslingen). One further county with exceptional positive relative changes is the county of Hochtaunuskreis, close to the financial centre of Frankfurt am Main.

More core cities can be found among the ten counties with the highest negative relative changes. However, these core cities are mainly located in the eastern part of Germany (Frankfurt (Oder), Halle (Saale), Magdeburg, Chemnitz, and Berlin). Two of the core cities with the highest negative relative change are located in the old industrialized region of the Ruhr (Essen and Wuppertal).

These findings lead to two questions. First, is the finding of few large hubs within the hubs with positive relative changes on the one hand, and the finding of a lot of large hubs within the hubs with negative relative changes a random pattern or an indication of de-concentration processes within the German urban system? Second, is the finding of a lot of East German hubs within the hubs with negative relative changes and the finding of a lot of South-West German hubs within the hubs with positive relative changes a random pattern or an indication of an increasing division within the German urban system?

To discuss the first question, the correlation between the size and relative changes of each hub is analyzed. Table 3.4 shows correlation coefficients of the size and the relative change of the hub index and both of its dimensions for all counties in the German urban system.

Table 3.4   Correlation of size at starting point and relative changes in all 439 counties in Germany

Correlation of	KBPs	Connectivity	Hub index
Size and relative change	-0.008	-0.208**	-0.119*
** The correlation is significant at the level of 0.01. * The correlation is significant at the level of 0.05.			

Source: BA, Hoppenstedt; own calculation

The results of Table 3.4 indicate that no processes of concentration in large hubs can be found. Rather the slight but significant negative correlation of size and relative change suggests the existence of de-concentration processes within the urban system in Germany. However, the most distinctive negative correlation can be found for connectivity values. Relative changes in knowledge-based professions seem to be less influenced by the number of them at the starting point. As the hub index merges both aspects, so the correlation of the size of hubs and the relative change in hubs lies between the correlation coefficients of connectivity values and KBP values.

The negative correlation between the size and relative change in connectivity values has also been found for the changes in connectivity in global networks.

Derudder et al. (2010) discuss this phenomenon as a saturation effect within organizational firm networks. It suggests that the location strategies of firms aim to enlarge the firm network by setting up new branches in cities where the firm has not yet been present. As it can be expected that firms start their branch networks from locations in large cities, in the German urban network this strategy leads to an expansion of firm networks into smaller cities and counties. Therefore, this aspect of hubs is determined by an urban-suburban bias in favour of an increased integration of suburbanized locations. Furthermore, the negative correlation of connectivity values can be an indication of the strategic value of firm networks for easing the exchange of knowledge by reducing transaction costs through organizational proximity. More in-depth research is needed in this context.

The missing correlation between the size and relative change of knowledge-based professions indicates that changes in counties as place of knowledge-based services are not primarily determined by the number of professions that already work in the counties under consideration. This finding reminds one of the observations, developed in the context of Table 3.2, that there might also be an east-west-divide that influences the relative changes in importance as hubs of knowledge-based services.

To discuss the second of the question developed above, Figure 3.3 depicts the geographical pattern of the relative changes in the hub index in all counties in Germany.

Combining Size and Changes in Importance of Knowledge Hubs

Figures 3.2 and 3.3 show two aspects of understanding the spatial organization of knowledge-based services in Germany: the importance of each county as a hub for these activities and the relative changes in importance of each county as a hub. In the following section, both types of information are shown together. Figure 3.4 shows hubs of above-average size and their relative changes.

This map clearly shows that above-average relative changes are not necessarily connected to hubs of great importance. Berlin and Hannover are, on the one hand, hubs of great importance at the starting point of the measurement and show a below-average relative change in importance over time. On the other hand, smaller hubs that are located in counties with conurbations in agglomeration areas, like the surrounding counties in the area of München, Stuttgart, and Frankfurt am Main, show distinctive above average relative changes.

Based on this, one important observation that can be made is that it is not only large hubs of knowledge-based services which increase their importance within the national urban system in Germany, but within dense agglomerations, former suburban counties may also increase in importance as a hub within economic networks.

Another important aspect that can be seen in Figure 3.3 is the gap between the development of counties in the western and eastern parts of Germany. Within the former East German *Länder*, only three hubs with (slightly) above-average changes

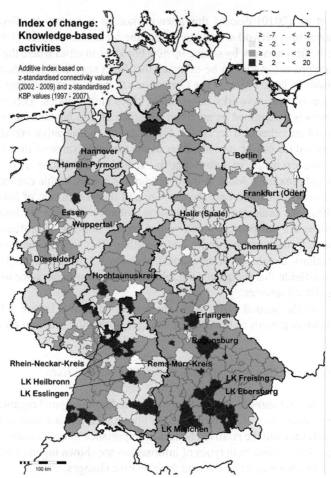

**Index of change:
Knowledge-based
activities**

Additive index based on
z-standardised connectivity values
(2002 - 2009) and z-standardised
KBP values (1997 - 2007).

| ≥ -7 - < -2 |
| ≥ -2 - < 0 |
| ≥ 0 - < 2 |
| ≥ 2 - < 20 |

Hannover
Hameln-Pyrmont
Berlin
Frankfurt (Oder)
Essen
Wuppertal
Halle (Saale)
Chemnitz
Düsseldorf
Hochtaunuskreis
Erlangen
Regensburg
Rhein-Neckar-Kreis
Rems-Murr-Kreis
LK Heilbronn
LK Freising
LK Esslingen
LK Ebersberg
LK München

100 km

Figure 3.3   Index of change

Source: BA, Hoppenstedt; own calculation

can be found. None of the large hubs in the eastern part shows above-average positive changes. Then again, in the western part some of the large hubs show distinctive positive relative changes as well as smaller hubs in suburbanized counties.

Based on this, a second observation can be made on the basis of Figure 3.3. Knowledge-based services may be discussed as a new form of economic activity in terms of using knowledge as a main factor of production and producing new knowledge as immaterial economic goods, and based on this assumption these types of economic activities may have modified their location requirements in comparison to traditional manufacturing and industries, yet they nevertheless still seem to be integrated into the same structures that may facilitate or complicate the economic activity. About 20 years after the reunification of Germany, the eastern part not only

Figure 3.4   Hub index

Source: BA, Hoppenstedt; own calculation

has difficulties in traditional economic activities that may not have caught up or developed during recent decades, but also within new economic activities.

Discussion

This paper has discussed knowledge hubs in the German urban system in line with the idea of spatial hubs in networks of globalised economic activities. The distribution of and changes to knowledge hubs in Germany has been analyzed, having regard to the crucial importance of implicit knowledge for creating new economic processes. Two important questions from a geographical perspective are whether knowledge hubs are equally distributed in Germany or spatially concentrated, and how the spatial distribution changes over the course of time.

Not surprisingly, large core cities have been identified as the most important hubs of knowledge-based services in the German urban system. However, changes within the overall urban system do not tend to be concentrated on large cities alone, but show two considerable variations.

Firstly, a gap between the relative change of north-eastern and south-western hubs can be observed. The relative change to south-western hubs is more positive, whereas the relative change to north-eastern hubs shows a decrease in importance as knowledge hubs in the German urban system. These changes show different development paths between large core cities in the German urban system.

Secondly, even though large cities are the biggest hubs of knowledge-based services, it is not only large core cities that increase their importance in the national urban system. Especially in the south-western parts of Germany, conurbation areas show a significant relative growth in importance as hubs of knowledge-based services within the urban network. These changes show unexpected developments in some of the cities' urban hinterland.

In a nutshell, these observations soften the assumptions of the exclusive advantages of high density in core cities and urban amenities that have led to the expectation of cities as the main hubs of knowledge-based services. The decrease in importance of large East German cities like Berlin, and the increase in importance of suburbanized counties in South and West Germany, like Landkreis München and Main-Taunus-Kreis seem to contradict the well-established expectation of cities as the only knowledge hubs. What factors reasons can enable us to understand these developments?

The relative changes in importance within the national urban system in Germany indicate that a city's size is neither the only nor the most important criterion that influences a city's attractiveness as a hub of knowledge-based services. The decrease in importance in the Eastern part of Germany may be interpreted as a structural deficit. Although knowledge-based services are understood as a new form of production in which knowledge, in particular, is a crucial input and output of the production process, these forms of economic activity do not develop independently from other kinds of economic production. In this context, the relative economic weakness of East German cities impinges on the development of knowledge-based services in these cities. The results for Berlin are especially thought-provoking. Although its size qualifies Berlin as an important hub, and considerable political efforts have been made since the German reunification to strengthen Berlin as a place of knowledge (Growe 2009), the results of this analysis indicate that by the end of the first decade in the new millennium Berlin has a decreasing share within the overall urban system.

Therefore, the persistence of a divide between the north-eastern and the south-western parts of Germany throws new light on concepts and approaches that aim to strengthen economically-challenged cities and regions by focusing on knowledge-based work. The assumption that all cities benefit similarly and increase their knowledge-based labour is proved to be unfounded. Further research is needed on the links between knowledge-based services and other forms of production, and the impact of this interweaving on economic development.

The positive relative change in importance of counties with conurbations may be understood as an indicator of a much more differentiated location strategy on the part of knowledge-based services than is often suggested by studies that focus on core cities and the advantages of urban amenities. However, like the development of cities, the positive relative change of counties with conurbations does not occur everywhere. It is mainly counties in densely-urbanised regions that show positive relative changes in importance in the network of all cities in Germany. These are mainly regions in the south and west of Germany, for example München, Stuttgart and Frankfurt. The increased importance of neighbouring counties to the large core cities may be interpreted as increased functional polycentrism in the three regions. The three regions are prospering economically and are challenged by high location-related costs, especially through high real estate costs. However, these regions enable a compromise to be achieved between easy face-to-face-interaction that is assumed to reduce transaction costs, and the possibility of establishing new locations in more reasonably-priced areas than the heart of the core cities.

In this context, the results confirm assumptions about increasing functional regionalization in prospering regions that are determined by development pressure in core cities. Furthermore, it should be noted that the regions affected by processes of functional regionalization are determined by different economic structures: Frankfurt by services, Stuttgart by the automobile industry and mechanical engineering, and München by services and high-tech industries. In this context, the functional regionalization of knowledge-based services seems to depend more on the economic strength of a region than on a specific economic structure.

To summarize, the size of the hubs indicates the importance of cities for knowledge-based services, whereas the relative change in importance of the hubs clearly shows the impact of history on economic structures and dynamics, and on functional regionalization.

Finally, it should be stated that, on the one hand, intra-firm networks are just one way for cities to be connected to flows of knowledge, and on the other hand, the assumption that two offices of the same firm in two different cities share knowledge with each other is not really verified yet. Further research is needed on (1) the basis of other flows of knowledge and (2) on the sharing of knowledge within companies.

Acknowledgements

The author wishes to thank two referees for their helpful comments on this paper. Financial support from the German Research Foundation (Deutsche Forschungsgemeinschaft, Projekt BL 163/6–1) is gratefully acknowledged.

References

Amin, A. and Cohendet, P. 2004. *Architectures of Knowledge: Firms, Capabilities, and Communities.* Oxford: Oxford University Press.

Bathelt, H. and Glückler, J. 2011. *The Relational Economy: Geographies of Knowing and Learning.* Oxford: Oxford University Press.

Bathelt, H., Malmberg, A. and Maskell, P. 2004. Clusters and knowledge: local buzz, global pipelines and the process of knowledge creation. *Progress in Human Geography*, 82(1), 31–56.

Beaverstock, J.V., Derudder, B., Faulconbridge, J. and Witlox, F. 2009. International business travel: some explorations. *Geografiska Annaler: Series B, Human Geography*, 91(3), 193–202.

Bell, D. 1989. *Die nachindustrielle Gesellschaft.* Frankfurt am Main: Campus.

Boschma, R.A. and Fritsch, M. 2009. Creative class and regional growth. Empirical evidence from seven European countries. *Economic Geography*, 85(4), 391–423.

Boudeville, J.-R. 1974. *Problems of Regional Economic Planning.* Edinburgh: Edinburgh University Press.

Cairncross, F. 1997. *The Death of Distance: How the Communications Revolution will Change our Lives.* Boston, MA: Harvard Business School Press.

Camagni, R. 2004. The economic role and spatial contradictions of global city-regions: The functional, cognitive, and evolutionary context, in *Global City-Regions: Trends, Theory, Policy*, edited by A.J. Scott. Oxford: Oxford University Press, 96–118.

Castells, M. 1996. *The Rise of the Network Society.* Malden, MA: Blackwell.

Derudder, B. and Witlox, F. 2010. World cities and global commodity chains: an introduction. *Global Networks*, 10(1), 1–11.

Derudder, B., Taylor, P.J., Ni, P., De Vos, A., Hoyler, M., Hanssens, H., Bassens, D., Huang, J., Witlox, F., Shen, W. and Yang, X. 2010. Pathways of change: Shifting connectivities in the world city network, 2000–2008. *Urban Studies*, 47(9), 1861–77.

Dicken, P. 2007. *Global Shift: Transforming the World Economy.* 5th edn. London: Chapman.

Drucker, P.F. 1969. *The Age of Discontinuity: Guidelines to our Changing Society.* London: Heinemann.

Friedman, T.L. 2006. *The World is Flat: The Globalized World in the twenty-first Century.* 10th edn. London: Penguin Books.

Friedmann, J. 1986. The world city hypothesis. *Development and Change*, 17, 69–83.

Friedmann, J. 1995. Where we stand: A decade of world city research, in *World Cities in a World-System*, edited by P.L. Knox and P.J. Taylor. Cambridge: Cambridge University Press, 21–47.

Growe, A. 2009. Wissensträger und Wissensvernetzung in Metropolregionen. Raumansprüche von Wissensträgern und die Vernetzung von Politiken. *Raumforschung und Raumordnung*, 67(5/6), 383–94.

Growe, A. and Blotevogel, H.H. 2011. Knowledge hubs in the German urban system: Identifying hubs by combining network and territorial perspectives. *Raumforschung und Raumordnung*, 69(3) 175–85.

Hall, A. 2007. *Tätigkeiten und berufliche Anforderungen in wissensintensiven Berufen: Empirische Befunde auf Basis der BIBB/BAuA-Erwerbstätigenbefragung 2006*. Bonn: Bundesinstitut für Berufsbildung.

Hall, P. and Pain, K. 2006. *The Polycentric Metropolis: Learning from Mega-City Regions in Europe*. London: Earthscan.

Hoyler, M., Freytag, T. and Mager, C. 2008. Connecting Rhine-Main: The production of multi-scalar polycentricities through knowledge-intensive business services. *Regional Studies*, 42(8), 1095–111.

Jacobs, W., Koster, H. and Hall, P. 2011. The location and global network structure of maritime advanced producer services. *Urban Studies*, 48(13), 2749–69.

Lasuén, J.R. 1969. On growth poles. *Urban Studies*, 6(2), 137–61.

Legler, H. and Frietsch, R. 2006. *Neuabgrenzung der Wissenswirtschaft: Forschungsintensive Industrien und wissensintensive Dienstleistungen*. Berlin: Bundesministerium für Bildung und Forschung.

Lüthi, S., Thierstein, A. and Bentlage, M. 2011. Interlocking firm networks in the German knowledge economy. On local networks and global connectivity. *Raumforschung und Raumordnung*, 69(3) 161–74.

Malecki, E.J. 2002. The economic geography of the Internet's infrastructure. *Economic Geography*, 78(4), 399–424.

Malmberg, A. and Maskell, P. 2002. The elusive concept of localization economies: towards a knowledge-based theory of spatial clustering. *Environment and Planning A*, 34(3), 429–49.

Myrdal, G. 1957. *Economic Theory and Under-Developed Regions*. London: Duckworth.

Nonaka, I. and Takeuchi, H. 1995. *The Knowledge Creating Company: How Japanese Companies create the Dynamics of Innovation*. New York: Oxford University Press.

Nooteboom, B. 2002. *Learning and Innovation in Organizations and Economies*. Oxford: Oxford University Press.

Park, S.O. 2000. *Knowledge-based Industry and Regional Growth*. Frankfurt am Main: Institut für Wirtschafts- und Sozialgeographie, Johann Wolfgang Goethe-Universität Frankfurt

Polanyi, M. 1967. *The Tacit Dimension*. Gloucester, MA: Smith.

Sassen, S. 1991. *The Global City: New York, London, Tokyo*. Princeton: University Press.

Scott, A.J. 1988. *New Industrial Spaces: Flexible Production Organization and Regional Development in North America and Western Europe*. London: Pion.

Scott, A.J., Agnew, J., Soja, E.W. and Storper, M. 2004. Global city-regions, in *Global City-Regions: Trends, Theory, Policy*, edited by A.J. Scott. Oxford: Oxford University Press, 11–30.

Stehr, N. 2001. *Wissen und Wirtschaften: Die gesellschaftlichen Grundlagen der modernen Ökonomie*. 1st edn. Frankfurt am Main: Suhrkamp.

Storper, M. and Walker, R.A. 1989. *The Capitalist Imperative: Territory, Technology, and Industrial Growth*. New York, NY: Blackwell.

Taylor, P.J. 2001. Specification of the world city network. *Geographical Analysis*, 33, 181–94.

Taylor, P.J. 2004. *World City Network: A Global Urban Analysis*. London: Routledge.

Taylor, P.J. 2007. Cities within spaces of flows. Theses for a materialist understanding of the external relations of cities, in *Cities in Globalization: Practices, Policies and Theories*, edited by P.J. Taylor, B. Derudder, P. Saey and F. Witlox. London: Routledge, 287–97.

Weber, A. 1909. *Über den Standort der Industrien: Erste Teil: Reine Theorie des Standorts*. Tübingen: Mohr.

Williamson, O.E. 1981. The economics of organization: The transaction cost approach. *American Journal of Sociology*, 87(3), 548–577.

Witlox, F. and Derudder, B. 2007. Airline passenger flows through cities: Some new evidence, in *Cities in Globalization: Practices, Policies and Theories*, edited by P.J. Taylor, B. Derudder, P. Saey and F. Witlox. London: Routledge, 37–51.

Zook, M. 2006. The geographies of the Internet. *Annual Review of Information Science and Technology*, 40(1), 53–78.

Chapter 4

Hub-airports as Cities of Intersections: The Redefined Role of Hub-airports within the Knowledge Economy Context

Sven Conventz and Alain Thierstein

Introduction

Air transportation is gradually creating a completely new spatial pattern, as did other kinds of transportation modes in the past. Within this development process, airports are taking centre stage. Formerly planned as stand-alone facilities in the cities' periphery, airports – particularly those with a hub function – have gone through a morphogenesis into more or less urban-like entities. As Güller and Güller (2003) have stated, today 'airports are not just airports any more'. Far more interactive within the spatial context than in the past, airports have evolved from purely infrastructure facilities into multimodal and multi-layered, spatial poles of growth and centres of competences distinguished by their unique accessibility and connectivity profiles.

In recent years, airports have not only made a contribution to a process sometimes referred to as 'urban restructuring' (Soureli and Youn 2009), but also in reshaping real estate markets (Schubert and Conventz 2011). Today, hub airports are perceived as powerful economic engines capable of having considerable economic and social impact on cities and regions (ACI 2004) by acting as nodes of transnational value-creation chains and hubs of knowledge exchange.

As a consequence, airports are no longer primarily seen as pure infrastructure facilities, but rather as advantageous business sites. The European section of the Airports Council International, taking cues from different studies, considers global accessibility as 'absolutely essential' to businesses making location decisions (ACI 2004: 6; see also Bentlage et al., this volume). According to the ACI survey,

> 31% of companies relocating to the area around Munich Airport cited the airport as the primary factor in their location decision. A survey of businesses in the Hamburg area found that 80% of manufacturing companies reported air service connections as important to getting customers to look at their products. [...] The Île de France Region generates 30% of the French national GDP. Accessibility to Paris CDG Airport is powerful factor in companies' location decision, particularly for the large global companies headquartered in the Paris

area, and to firms engaging in new High-tech and innovation industries. [...]
The attractiveness of airports and their hinterland is particularly strong for high
tech industries as evidenced by Copenhagen und Nice Airports. (ACI 2004: 6)

Regarding German airports, the European Centre for Aviation Development
(ECAD) notes that they, and their key services as international network
infrastructure, are a prerequisite for long-term competitiveness of regional and
national economies (for a discussion of the role of small airports, see Redondi et
al., 2013). Moreover, airports are essential not only for added value but also for the
development of business markets in and outside Europe (ECAD 2007).

Against this backdrop, this chapter scrutinizes spatial patterns and process of
specialization in and around two major European airports: Amsterdam's Schiphol
Airport and Frankfurt's Rhine-Main Airport.

The present chapter thereby analyses the linkages between airports, air transport
and the knowledge economy. In particular, we issue on the following questions:
What are the contributions of the knowledge economy that explain the economic
effects of airports on the spatial structure of cities and regions? What kind of
locational patterns have already emerged around airports that have to be linked with
the presence of firms from the knowledge economy realm? What is their spatial
relationship to more traditional locations, for example within the Central Business
District? Why does an array of knowledge-based companies relocate their business
activities to spaces of highest accessibility such as international airports?

In order to get a deeper understanding of the subject matter, it is helpful to
briefly look at the complex interplay between technological changes in modes of
transportation and their impacts on rewriting the urban and metropolitan geography.
After this, we reflect on the diverse morphogenesis of airports into complex and
multifunctional real estate sites. Situated in this inquisitive background, part three
is our argumentation that changed locational behaviour of the knowledge-economy
and the way new knowledge is created plays an important role in understanding
this newly emerged spatial entity. Part four concretizes these findings by discussing
two selected European case studies. The chapter is concluded with a discussion of
some avenues for further research emerging from the analysis.

The Past as Prologue

Since the emergence of urban systems, advances in transportation technology have
had a distinctive impact on urban forms, built environments and spatial patterns.
The more radical the change, the more has been altered in the spatial structure.
For a long time, traffic junctions and transportation facilities have functioned as
nodes for trade of goods and knowledge, as well as platforms for communication
and social interaction. Whether in ancient times or our contemporary world,
transportation infrastructure is an initiator for supporting and shaping spatial
development, and acting as a catalyst for further economic prosperity (see

Derudder et al., this volume). Prior to the revolutionary nineteenth-, twentieth- and twenty-first-century improvements in transportation, animal-drawn carriages and merchant ships were the only forms of vehicular or maritime transportation that allowed for long-haul movement of commodities and people. Because of this, from a historical standpoint cities tended to be located alongside navigable rivers, canals or shorelines. However with the invention of the railway, streetcars and commuter trains, urban development started to radiate outward alongside of the railway tracks far into the hinterland of the cities. Similar to role played by harbours in the past, train stations soon became centres of urban development and new nodes of trade and communication. The upcoming mass motorization at the beginning of the twentieth century brought a new break in the relationship between transport technology and urban development patterns. New dispersed spatial patterns appeared and highway intersections became highly popularized locations for commercial developments.

Thus, it can be deduced that new forms of transportation create new places and spatial structures. Since World War II, mobility has increased and many activities that were formerly centralized in the Central Business District (CBD), moved from the city centres to the outskirts. With reference to airports, Edward J. Taaffe already stated in the mid 1950s that 'Canals, railroads, and highways, channelling the flows of traffic, have created new urban alignments, hinterlands and nodal points. Now air transportation promises to become a vital force' (Taaffe 1956: 219). How appropriate Taaffe's assumption about interaction between airports and territorial development from the 1950s would turn out to be in contemporary settings is almost astonishing. This new role of airports as anchors of a new peripheral urban-like entity will be discussed in the next section.

Airports Reconsidered: Evolving Urban Patterns At and Around Airports

From a lexical understanding, an airport is a large-scale, infrastructural facility or a point of interchange within the aviation industry where aircrafts, such as airplanes and helicopters, can take off and touchdown. Normally, airports are characterized by five core elements: runways and taxiing areas, the air traffic control building, aircraft maintenance buildings, passenger terminals and car parks, and the freight warehouses (Edwards 2005: 6). However, this very narrow, engineering-related definition falls short because it does not consider the current developments and dynamics that describe airports as a new multi-layered and self-contained spatial entities which they have become: a city or mall-like, multi-functional site and general-purpose public space where interchange takes place for and between a broad group of participants with diverse and flexible connections to local, regional, national and international market areas.

Forced by new general conditions within the international aviation industry, airport operators have started to open new business segments in order to realize additional non-aviation revenues to supplement the traditional core business (e.g. ramp-handling, landing-fees etc.). In this context, airports have started to concentrate their engagement not only on supplying the core aeronautical infrastructure and services, but also on the development of the so-called non-aviation sector where commercial facilities and services play a key factor in terms of future growth (Deimler et al. 2004, Ringbeck et al. 2006). Such non-aviation activities can be comprised of retail developments and the implementation of new retail concepts like shopping arcades and malls, Michelin Star Award-winning restaurants, and other real estate developments such as offices, hotels, conference, exhibition and convention centres, hospitals and beauty facilities, leisure, recreation, museums, fitness facilities, and crematories. This developmental process is very often described by the term 'airport city'. Supposedly, this term was coined for the first time in 1960 when TIME magazine ran a five-page feature called 'Airport Cities, Gateway to the Jet Age' (Time Magazine 1960). Today, the term of airport city principally refers to 'the more or less dense cluster of operational, airport-related activities, plus other commercial and business corners, on and around the airport platform' (Güller and Güller 2003: 70). Already in 2004, the Boston Consulting Group (BCG) foresaw that the non-aviation sector would become a key factor in terms of future growth and profit of airports (BCG 2004: 10). Today, as clearly demonstrated in the cases of Oslo, Copenhagen, Munich or Zurich airports, non-aviation revenues already contribute around 50 per cent to the airport operators' profit (AT Kearney Consulting 2007, 2010). In this context, retail activities and office real estate developments in particular have become important for the airports' financial sustainability (Conventz 2008).

Knowledge, Airports and the Mega-City Region

The Rise of the Knowledge Economy

The concept 'knowledge economy' as defined by Thierstein et al. (2006) refers to an interdependent system of advanced producer service (APS), High-Tech industries and knowledge-creating institutions such as universities and research establishments. Figure 4.1 depicts these three pillars of the knowledge economy. APS provide expertise, knowledge-based services, and process-specialized information for other service sectors and advanced manufacturers. Examples include financial service firms such as Price Waterhouse Coopers or KPMG, management consultancies such as Boston Consulting Group or Bain & Company, engineering firms like HochTief, architectural outfits such as Arup or Skidmore, Owings & Merrill (SOM), and logistics firms like UPS or FedEx (Bowen, 2012). Because these services all generate, analyse, exchange and trade information, they are key intermediaries in the knowledge economy. The service they provide is enabled by internal links between APS offices all over the world as well as by manifold links with related companies and customers along their individual value chain. Additionally, because APS firms

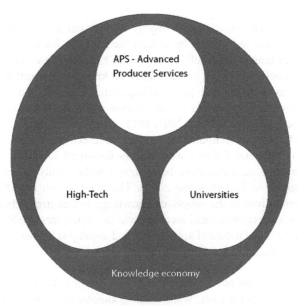

Figure 4.1   The three pillars of the knowledge economy

are expanding everywhere, flows of information within and between firms play a crucial role in linking cities to the global economy.

The High-Tech sector (including manufacturing) is defined by highly skilled employees, of which many are scientists and engineers, a fast rate of growth, a high ratio of R&D expenditures to sales, and a worldwide market for its products.

Advanced producer services and High-Tech firms constitute the main pillars of a knowledge-based economy. Cities are home to these operations, and hub cities play a key role as nodes in global knowledge networks, whether as intra-firm or extra-firm links.

Knowledge is a key driver for the competitiveness of private companies as well as the urban and regional economies from which these companies are operating. Especially for privately held companies, knowledge is an important resource for innovation, which in turn, is a key driver for continued growth. Knowledge is a complex term offering different definitions and approaches, and therefore there is no commonly accepted definition (Lüthi 2011).

Following Polanyi's seminal classification, knowledge can be distinguished into codified or explicit knowledge on the one hand, and tacit knowledge on the other (Polanyi 1967). As opposed to tacit knowledge, explicit knowledge is codifiable, articulable, or storable – verbally, visually, or symbolically. New information and communication technologies offer the opportunity of increasingly codifying and commodifying knowledge and making it tradable across time and long distances, which means that codified knowledge becomes more and more de-territorialized. This enables companies to outsource activities and inputs globally and to benefit from relational proximity and international knowledge spill-overs.

Once again, tacit knowledge is highly contextualized and not effectively transferable between individuals by certain media. With his well-known phrase 'we know more than we can tell' Polanyi (1967: 4) illustrates the fundamental idea of the distinction between explicit and tacit knowledge (Gertler 2003). Tacit knowledge in combination with personal experience is considered as an essential prerequisite in creative processes and innovation, and therefore as a foundation of the knowledge economy (Schamp 2003: 181).

Since the transfer of tacit knowledge requires direct face-to-face interactions, the findings of Michael Polanyi are not only important for firms, but also for regions. Innovative activities have been shown to be highly concentrated in a minority of urban regions (Simmie 2003). The main reason why these regions play an important role in the supply of knowledge is that firm networks benefit from geographical proximity and local knowledge spill-overs. Malecki describes this aspect as the 'local nature of knowledge' and highlights the necessity to accept knowledge as a spatial factor of competition:

> If knowledge is not found everywhere, then where it is located becomes a particularly significant issue. While codified knowledge is easily replicated, assembled and aggregated [...], other knowledge is dependent on the context and is difficult to communicate to others. Tacit knowledge is localized in particular places and context [...]. (Malecki 2000: 110)

Significance of Face-to-Face Activities and Knowledge Economy

The distribution and transfer of codified and tacit knowledge as well as the interplay between geographical and relational proximity forms a key basis for the development of polycentric Mega-City regions. Mega-City regions are the 'nodes of the global economy, location of creation of knowledge and also engines of the cultural development' (Goebel et al. 2007: 87). They bring into spatial proximity, dense spaces and diverse urban neighbourhoods and other opportunities for information exchange. Increasingly, such places have popped up outside the traditional city centres. Following Hall and Pain's (2006) definition, a polycentric Mega-City Region is

> a series of anything between ten and 50 cities and towns physically separate but functionally networked, clustered around one or more larger central cities, and drawing enormous economic strength from a new functional division of labour. These places exist both as separate entities, in which most residents work locally and most workers are local residents, and as part of a wider functional urban region connected by dense flows of people and information carried along motorways, high speed rail lines and telecommunication cables. (Hall and Pain 2006:3)

In recent years airports have continued emerging as another powerful core with discernible impacts on urban structures. Edge Cities (Garreau 1991), City Ports (van

Wijk 2007), Aerotropolis (Kasarda 2001), Airport Corridor (Schaafsma 2008) and Airport City (Güller and Güller 2003) are just a few of the expressions from an array of neologisms (Lang 2000) that attempt to catch the new reality of polycentric spatial configurations. This newly defined spatial structure is based on two different but inter-related processes: agglomeration economies and network economies.

Agglomeration economies result from the clustering of knowledge-intensive firms in certain areas, enabling them to benefit from spatial proximity and local knowledge spillovers. Network economies, on the other hand, result from global sourcing strategies of knowledge-intensive firms leading to relational proximity and international knowledge spillovers. Based on this functional logic, we argue that polycentric Mega-city regions are the outcome of a spatial up-scaling of agglomeration economies and spatial re-concentration process of network economies. Figure 4.2 schematically depicts the inter-relationships between the knowledge economy, which follows a functional logic, and the emergence of Mega-City Regions, which are essentially the effect of a specific spatial logic at work.

On the one hand, the up-scaling process of agglomeration economies is determined by achievements realized in transportation and telecommunication technologies. The costs of certain modes of transport and communication have drastically declined, and, in some cases, speed and reliability have significantly improved. As consequence, polycentric Mega-city Regions are increasingly enabled to achieve agglomeration economies of comparable magnitude to those of large mono-centric cities.

On the other hand, the spatial re-concentration of network economies is determined by the location behaviour of knowledge-intensive companies. In order to optimize their added value, knowledge-based companies need a set of local, supportive business conditions such as proximity to international gateway infrastructures, including airports and high-speed train nodes. In recent years, many international knowledge-intensive enterprises have already recognized the advantage of being located around airports and within the corridors between the airport and the former central city.

The concentration of knowledge resources in particular Mega-city Regions influences the roles that these may play in the global economy. In addition, the dynamics of knowledge exchange within and between Mega-City Regions contribute to either the maintenance or change in roles within the functional urban hierarchy. This raises questions over the relative importance of regional versus international knowledge spill overs. Simmie (2003) shows that knowledge-intensive firms combine a strong local knowledge capital base with high levels of connectivity to similar regions in the international economy. Through this, they are able to combine and translate both codified and tacit knowledge originating from multiple regional, national and international sources.

As previously stated, communicative devices facilitate the transmission of information. Through a cognitive performance new knowledge is generated. This creative process is not readily practicable via data transmission or by telephone. Instead, a common cultural, social or cognitive context and direct interaction are

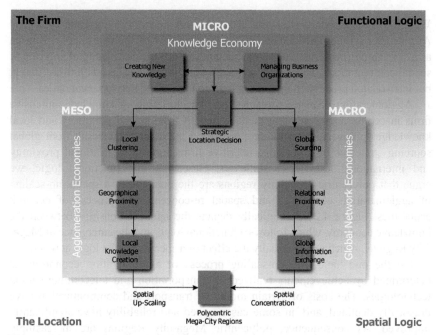

Figure 4.2   Agglomeration and network economies in the context of Mega-City Region development

Source: Lüthi (2011)

required, and very often the best medium is face-to-face communication. This is because the effective transfer of tacit knowledge necessitates the kind of trust built up through face-to-face interactions (Läpple 2001: 23).

> During the past half century, the faster pace of specialization, globalization, and technical change has profoundly altered companies, their customers, the supply chains around them, and, consequently, the nature of work within them and at their borders. The result is a dramatic increase in the volume and value of interaction. (Beardsley et al. 2006: 2)

Research done by the consulting company McKinsey established that tacit interaction is central to economic activity and constitutes approximately 63 per cent of the employees' total work in insurance business, 60 per cent in securities companies, 70 per cent in healthcare, and 45 per cent in retailing.

Airports as Network-infrastructure

Knowledge-intensive enterprises generate new knowledge locally through physical interaction. Generally, individual branches of a company are part of a global corporate network and are efficiently networked among each other.

Short geographical distances between individuals, organizations or towns bring people together and enable them to exchange tacit knowledge, the *je ne sais quoi* of any learning process, which, once more, requires personal contact. The larger the distance between people or cities, the less chance there is of such exchanges occurring. Relational proximity, typified by people in far-flung locations collaborating on a shared project, is supported by a rich and diversified infrastructure of global travel and communication, including rapid and frequent trains and flights, sophisticated logistics networks – nowadays continental high-speed trains and intercontinental hub airports fall under this category – to keep freight and people on the move, and provide easy access to a variety of facilities for real-time and interactive communication. APS and High-Tech firms involve a mix of geographical and relational proximity. Both proximities are counterparts of the knowledge economy and go hand in hand.

In this context, international airports and Mega-City Regions have become crucial for tacit interactions and international knowledge generation. Very often new and decentralized cores of urban activity have emerged close to areas of high accessibility such as high-speed railway stations or international airports.

Airports, especially those with a hub function, have evolved as locations where local, regional, national and global information-exchange overlap. Like no other infrastructure facility, airports integrate two locational qualities: worldwide connectivity by air and multimodal landside accessibility on a local, regional, national and sometimes international scale. With respect to the urbanization of airports and their hinterlands, landside infrastructure investments have become vitally important (Schubert and Conventz 2011). Once planned as simple airport train stations or a terminal stop of a single rail or metro line, the airport railway stations have become interchanges with key positions within the national and international high-speed train systems, railway, and light rail networks (Güller and Güller 2003). According to Güller and Güller (2003: 131), the airport interchange can be defined as follows: 'Airport interchange is the airport railway station's function as node in landside traffic networks: it not only serves air traffic passengers and airports employees, but also uses to interchange between regional and national public transport networks (rail–rail, rail–subway, rail–bus, bus–bus … etc.)'.

The Emergence of a New Airport-linked Office Property Landscape

Under the general framework of the global (time-based) competition, the potential and the locational advantages of airports as network- and service-infrastructure have become more integral than ever to cities, business models and the location decisions of a broad spectrum of industries. For cities, especially those exposed to global competition, urban competitiveness is highly determined by connectivity and networks (Jones Lang Lasalle 2002: 1, Taylor et al. 2011).

Cities increasingly set out to treat their airports not only as a 'foyer or entrée' to their urban area, but also as a way to provide a competitive advantage within the global competition for future-oriented enterprises and highly skilled employees, especially of the knowledge economy. In order to increase the attractiveness of airports and their hinterland as office sites to future service companies, many cities, airport authorities and other actors have started strategic develop of the locations in and around airports. One of the most prominent examples is Amsterdam's Schiphol airport, which was one of the first to discover and tap into the wide economic potential of the airport.

Owing to the unique locational qualities and advantages of airports described above, many knowledge-intensive enterprises have started to favour airports and their vicinities as advantageous business sites. In the following chapter, the new office locational patterns around two selected international hub-airports, Amsterdam-Schiphol and Frankfurt Rhine-Main, will be analysed.

The Case of Amsterdam-Schiphol

Under the conditions of globalization, the spatial outlines of Amsterdam as a city have been reconfigured. The urban system of Amsterdam and its growth pattern were once perceived as 'prototypical expansion of the mono-centric city' (Salet and Majoor 2005: 19). Beginning in the early 1960s and continuing into the present day, the historical inner city, characterized by channels, listed buildings etc., has not been able to fulfil the increased demand of large-scale leasing on the part of the rising service and knowledge economy. As a consequence, and as a result of new accessibility requirements, companies started settling in the surroundings of the urban ring road or sometimes even further away. Through this trend, the spatial formation of Amsterdam has gradually been transformed into a polycentric urban landscape. New concentrations of urban activities appeared for example at the southern edge of Amsterdam reshaping the area into a dynamic growth zone (Bontje 2005). In this context, Schiphol has become 'the most prominent growth engine [...] and the largest employment concentration in the metropolitan area [...]' (Bontje 2009: 193).

Amsterdam-Schiphol, located 17.5 km southwest of Amsterdam, is the Netherlands' main airport, Europe's fourth biggest airport and one of the world's major hubs in international air traffic. Moreover, Schiphol is one of the two hubs of Air France-KLM. Although named and recognized as Amsterdam-Schiphol, the airport is actually located in the neighbouring municipality of Haarlemmermeer and not in the city proper of Amsterdam. Through the different airline networks, virtually every major city or economic market in the world is reachable for Amsterdam-Schiphol. This integration of the airport into international air traffic is supplemented by an ideal landside connection through all means of transportation. By road, Schiphol is linked via two major highways – A4 and A9 – to downtown Amsterdam and the broader metropolitan area. By rail, Schiphol is directly connected to Amsterdam and to important western European business centres such as Brussels, Paris, Frankfurt, Cologne or Dusseldorf. Through only an eight minute train ride, the airport is also in close spatial linkage to the Zuidas, Amsterdam's rapidly developing business district where a new high-speed train station will be opened in the next years.

A New 'Glocal' Nexus of Knowledge Exchange

At the end of the 1980s, the master plan for Schiphol proposed for the first time the idea of realizing office projects in the central area within the loop of the access roads that bring people in and out of the airport area (Kloos and de Maar 1996: 82). Today, this strip is known as Schiphol-Centre and since the beginning of the 1990s, new office sites have gradually been built up (Kloos and de Maar 1996, Schiphol Group 2010). Currently, the total stock of lettable office space comprises nearly 200,000 m² of office space (Jones Lang Lasalle 2010: 9). In the future, the office stock at Schiphol-Centre will grow by another 8–15 per cent due to a number of projects in the pipeline, such as the extension of the Outlook Building (Jones Lang Lasalle 2009a: 11).

The construction activities of the office complexes were simultaneously accompanied by the construction of an increasing number of high-quality facilities such as hotels of different categories, or meeting and conference centres. Similar to the office buildings, most of these premises are either directly linked to the terminal via walkways or promenades. All this helped to transform the location of Schiphol-Centre into a multifunctional and multimodal premium business site at the periphery of Amsterdam, which today is considered to be one of the top office locations in the whole of the Netherlands.

The high value of the airport sites is reflected in the office rents. In recent years, Schiphol-Centre has become the country's top office location, achieving the highest office rents countrywide. From 2004–2007, the recorded prime rents at Schiphol-Centre were at 350 €/m² per year (Jones Lang Lasalle 2009b 2010: 10). At the end of 2009, the annual top rent was around 365 €/m² (Jones Lang Lasalle 2010: 10). That was a decrease by 3 per cent compared with 2008 where a maximum of around 375 €/m² was reached (Jones Lang Lasalle 2010: 10). Since then, contractual agreements with maximum rents of 390 €/m² per year or even above have been registered (DTZ Zadelhoff 2009). In comparison to this, the South-Axis (Zuidas), the actual central business district of Amsterdam – halfway between city centre and Schiphol Airport – reached rents of approximately 335 €/m² per year in 2009. In the city centre itself, a prime rental value of around 255 €/m² was realized at the end of the fourth quarter of 2009 compared to 280 €/m² in 2008 (Jones Lang Lasalle 2009b 2010: 10).

Accordingly, two conclusions can be drawn: First, in the Amsterdam office market, contrary to what one might initially presume, it is not the city centre which is the most expensive office location, but Schiphol-Centre at the city's edge. This is a remarkable difference when compared to other selected European top office locations such as London, Paris or Frankfurt.

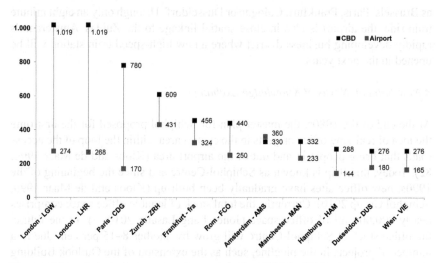

Figure 4.3   Selected annual prime rents for 2009 in €/m²

Source: own illustration, modified according to CB Richard Ellis (2009, 2010)

Second, despite the considerable turbulences, which have affected the real estate markets over recent years, the prime rents at Schiphol-Centre have remained relatively stable.

From the very beginning, the main strategy of the Schiphol Group was to attract companies that were either airport-related or had a strong affinity to the aviation business. However, scientific literature does not offer a standard definition for either of these terms. One approach defines airport-related companies as companies 'that have their business at the airport (such as airlines) or use the airport intensively (such as the head offices of international companies)' (Schaafsma 2008: 71). Indeed, Schiphol has been very successful in attracting internationally oriented companies offering superior business services, which have located their international or European headquarters at the airport. The demand for office space is generated from a broad spectrum of business sectors such as finance, consultancy, traffic and transportation, government or healthcare. Among the office space occupiers are prominent companies and institutions such as the American Chamber of Commerce, AXA Investment Managers, Citibank International, the Dutch Infrastructure Fund and Delta Hydrocarbons (WTC Schiphol 2010). Hence, the demand comes from enterprises that are not directly related to the aviation business. Today, this submarket has reached a certain level of maturity that is characterized by a manageable amount of high quality office properties with different locational qualities and price ranges. Basically, the closer the office is to the passenger terminal, the higher the office rent is. Future prospects expect a further densification of the strip and new office constructions, such as for example the Gateway building (Conventz 2008).

The Case of Frankfurt Rhine-Main

Frankfurt am Main is Germany's fifth-largest city and the centre of the Rhine-Main Metropolitan Region. Furthermore, it is continental Europe's leading financial centre harbouring more financial institutions than any other continental European city. With its two long-distance train stations – Central Station and Frankfurt airport – the city takes a key a position within the Trans-European railway network. Worldwide, Frankfurt is known for its international hub airport which, with its more than 53 million passengers a year, is ranked in the world's top ten busiest airports. According to the summer flight schedule of 2011, Frankfurt Rhine-Main airport serves 298 destinations in 110 countries, which is more than any other airport in the world. The airport serves as hub for Lufthansa and Condor Flugdienst. Within the Rhine-Main Metropolitan region, the airport is centrally located and only 12 km away from Frankfurt's city centre. From the landside accessibility standpoint, the airport is connected by road, rail and bus.

Frankfurt Airports as Prime Knowledge Hub

In recent years Frankfurt Rhine-Main Airport and the premises around the airport have become prime sites for knowledge-based activities. Despite its peripheral location, the airport largely resembles the inner cities' prime rents. Only 6 minutes southwest of the office city of Niederrad and 15 minutes south of Frankfurt's CBD by public transit, the airport location collects a top rent of approximately 360 €/m² (BNP Paribas Real Estate 2011). Occasionally, contractual agreements with maximum rents of over 420–480 €/m² have been registered (Immobilienzeitung 2011).

The dynamic real estate and infrastructure developments as well as the increase in letting success have contributed to the circumstance that the airport and its vicinity are considered as prime commercial locations for knowledge-based services as well as conference and exposition sites. Currently, 366,000m² of office stock is available on the airport grounds alone. Including the locations surrounding the airport, the office stock comprises more than 576,000 m² gross floor area. The demand for office space is mainly generated by knowledge economy industries such as human resources, traffic and transportation, IT and telecommunications, computer industries, accounting and consultancies or healthcare. Today, leading companies in these fields, such as Arthur D. Little, KPMG, Dell, Oracle, Nortel or MasterCard, have already settled in or around the airport. Other enterprises, such as the logistic companies DB Schenker or Imtec, have contractually assured their intention to move to the airport. Today's office locations are the Frankfurt Airport Centre (FAC) I and II, Cargo City South, Air Cargo Centre / Airbizz and Cargo City North, all being localized on the airport premises. In addition, there are office property sites that already exist, or are currently in the implementation phase, which are in close spatial linkage and sometimes within walking distance to the airport. Such locations are for example the Main Airport Centre (MAC), the

Square, formerly known as AirRail Centre, and Gateway Gardens. Furthermore, there is office space projected at the Mönchhof Area and at the Airport Office Centre (Fraport 2012).

New office real estate developments like The Winglet, The Cockpit or The Propeller will provide for a substantial contribution to the revenues of Fraport, the owner and operator of the airport, as well as to the locations' reputation as knowledge hub. According to Fraport, the need of airport office space due to the airport expansion is expected to increase from around 500,000 m² currently to approximately 650,000 m² in the year 2015. Office stock that is out of date or not in line with the market requirements will be taken out of the market (Hommerich 2006). Consequently, the current office stock will decrease by the year 2015. At the same time, modern office estates will gradually substitute this dated stock. These construction activities reflect the location's high dynamics as a new place for knowledge-based activities.

Discussion

Just as much as people were attracted to ports, railway stations and motorway intersections in centuries of the past, airports have rapidly become new urban growth generators, hubs of information and knowledge exchange, and centres of competence. The accessibility profile of international hub airports again induces a multitude of economic and regional catalytic effects such as settlement of companies, employment development, or stimulation of innovation, etcetera (ECAD 2007: 4). In recent years airports have become vital growth poles for urban and regional economies and centres of a new post-industrial spatial structure. As fundamental nodes of the networked post-Fordist knowledge society, airports take centre stage within the knowledge creation and the organization of chains of economic value added. Once planned as spatially seldom-integrated solitaires at the cities edge, airports have morphed into network and service infrastructures and places of highest centrality and accessibility. Like no other infrastructure facility, many European airport locations integrate two core, contemporary spatial qualities: worldwide connectivity by air and multimodal landside accessibility on local, regional and national scales.

As the examples of Schiphol and Frankfurt illustrate, airports are no longer mainly perceived as transportation nodes, but more generally as advantageous business sites. Multimodality of transportation infrastructure combined with an extensive business infrastructure is understood as a crucial competitive and developmental advantage within the international time-based competition. With the expanding floor space for office-based services in and around international airports, a new urban locational pattern is evolving. This kind of locational quality is exactly tailored to the locational requirements of knowledge-intensive companies. The willingness of those customer groups to pay top rents, i.e. far above the average, reflects the demand for such locations.

The recentralization of new functions formerly localized in the central city and the shifting perception of airports enable airports to appear as a modern kind of marketplace (Gottdiener 2001, Edwards 2005) where people can convene, exhibit, trade and change information. Thus, airports are in no way inferior to historic marketplaces of the medieval city such as Brussels' Grand Place. Hence, with the history of airports, the history of markets is repeated.

Although Airports have grown out of their niche as pure infrastructure facilities and morphed into attractive real estate sites, the complex dynamics that are taking place in and around international airports represent a crucially understudied element in the post-industrial restructuring of urban and regional systems. From our point of view, one of the most important keys in understanding these processes and dynamics are the locational requirements and changing internal and external value chains of knowledge-intensive companies. Thus, future research activities must deal with the following specific aspects. Firstly, in order to understand the spatial alteration around airports more thoroughly, we need a conceptual-analytical approach – an impact model – that combines the complex and multi-sided interplay between location strategies of knowledge enterprises, geographical proximity, airport-linked real estate developments and the way airports are used within the process of knowledge creation. Secondly, future research must place a special focus on intra-firm and extra-firm linkages of APS and High-Tech firms that are settled in the vicinity of airports. Thirdly, an additional qualitative investigation needs to be carried out, for example by means of qualitative network analysis. The combination of these approaches makes it possible to identify the role an airport plays and the potential it has within the site selection and the organization of value chains of knowledge-based companies.

Lastly growing inter-relatedness between hub airports, urban development and the knowledge economy certainly can have drawbacks. They may consist of an overly high degree of mutual dependency. Therefore a serious challenge for analysis, as well as for urban planning, is how to integrate urban functions more wisely in order to render the emerging structures more robust against the volatility of either natural disasters or external economic shocks. And, finally, new methods of analysing and visualizing airport-linked spatial developments need to be established in order to show and understand the changing role and potentiality of airports. Raising awareness of the spatial drivers is a prerequisite for sustainable and forward-looking planning at urban and regional level.

References

Airport Council International (ACI) 2004. *The Social an Economic Impact of Airports in Europe*. Available at: www.airports.org [accessed: April 8, 2007].

AT Kearney Consulting 2010. *Shoppen im Vorbeifliegen*. Available at: www. atkearney.de [accessed: March 2010].

AT Kearney Consulting 2007. *Verkehrsknotenpunkte – Handelsstandorte der Zukunft*. Available at: www.atkearney.de [accessed: 24 April 2009].

Beardsley, S.C., Johnson, B.C. and Manyika, J.M. 2006. Competitive advantage from better interactions. *McKinsey Quarterly*, 2.

BNP Paribas Real Estate 2011. *City Report Frankfurt 2011*. Frankfurt: BNP Paribas Real Estate.

Bontje, M. 2005. Der Amsterdamer Südraum – Eine dynamische Wachstumszone, in *Beiträge zur Regionalen Geographie: Europäische metropolitane Peripherien*, edited by J. Burdack, G. Herfert and R. Rudolph. Leipzig: Leibniz-Institut für Länderkunde, 193–205.

Bontje, M. 2009. The Amsterdam city region: A polycentric metropolis?, in *Metropolregionen – Restrukturierung und Governance. Deutsche und internationale Fallstudien: Volume 3 Metropolis und Region*, edited by L. Basten. Dortmund: Verlag Dorothea Rohn, 57–69.

Boston Consulting Group (BCG) 2004. *Airports – Dawn to a New Era*. Munich: The Boston Consulting Group (BCG).

Bowen, J. (2012) A spatial analysis of FedEx and UPS: Hubs, spokes and network structure. *Journal of Transport Geography*, 24, 419–31.

Castells, M. 1996. *The Information Age: Economy, Society and Culture. Volume 1 – The Rise of the Network Society*. Malden: Blackwell Publishers.

CB Richard Ellis 2009. *Zum Abheben gut. Investitionsnische Flughafen* [unpublished].

Childe, G. 1950. The urban revolution. *The Town Planning Review*, 21(1), 3–17.

Conventz, S. 2008. *Näher bei der Welt – Büroteilmärkte an internationalen Hub-Airports. Das Beispiel Frankfurt Rhein-Main im Vergleich zu Amsterdam-Schiphol* [unpublished]. The University of Bayreuth, Diploma Thesis.

Deimler, M., Love, R. and Stelter, D. 2004. *Airports - Dawn of a New Era. Preparing for One of the Industry's Biggest Shake-ups*. Munich: The Boston Consulting Group.

DTZ Zadelhoff 2009. *The Netherlands, a National Picture. Fact Sheets office and Industrial Property Market, mid 2009*. Available at: www.dtz.nl, accessed 24 April 2009.

Edwards, B. 2005. *The Modern Terminal. New Approaches to Airport Architecture*. London, New York: E & FN Spon.

European Center for Aviation Development (ECAD) 2007. Luftverkehr – ein zentraler Standortfaktor für die deutsche Volkswirtschaft. Ergebnisübersicht zur Studie "Katalytische volks- und regionalwirtschaftliche Effekte des Luftverkehrs in Deutschland" der European Center for Aviation Development – ECAD GmbH. Darmstadt. Berlin: Bundesverband der Deutschen Luftverkehrswirtschaft e.V.

Fraport AG 2012. Büroimmobilien. Available at: http://www.frankfurt-airport.de [accessed: 9 January 2012].

Garreau, J. 1991. *Edge City: Life on the New Frontier*. New York: Doubleday.

Gertler, M.S. 2003. Tacit knowledge and the economic geography of context, or the undefinable tacitness of being there. *Journal of Economic Geography*, 3 (1), 75–99.

Goebel, V., Thierstein, A. and Lüthi, S. 2007. *Functional Polycentricity in the Mega-City Region of Munich.* Annual Meeting of the Association of European Planning, (AESOP), Napoli, Italy, 11–14 July 2007.

Gottdiener, M. 2001. *Life in the Air. Surviving the New Culture of Air Travel.* Lanham: Rowman & Littlefield Publishers, Inc.

Güller, M. and Güller, M. 2003. *From Airport to Airport City.* Barcelona: Gustavo Gili.

Hall, P. and Pain, K. 2006. *The Polycentric Metropolis. Learning from Mega-City Regions in Europe.* London: Earthscan.

Hommerich, C. 2006. *Chancen für die Airport City. Fraport AG, Frankfurt am Main*, Seminar zum Immobilienstandort, Frankfurt, Germany, 6 December 2006.

Immobilien Zeitung 2011. Flughäfen: Vom Büro die Welt erreichen, *Immobilien Zeitung: Fachzeitung für die Immobilienwirtschaft*, 50, 1+14.

Jones Lang Lasalle 2002. *World Winning Cities – Paper 1.* Available at: http://www. joneslanglasalle.com/pages/worldwinningcities.aspx [accessed: 21 May 2009].

Jones Lang Lasalle 2009a. *Dutch office Market Outlook 2009 – Randstad Core Markets.* Amsterdam: Jones Lang Lasalle IP, Inc.

Jones Lang Lasalle 2009b. Selected office Market Key Numbers Amsterdam [unpublished].

Jones Lang Lasalle 2010. *Dutch office Market Outlook 2010 – Randstad Core Markets.* Amsterdam: Jones Lang Lasalle IP, Inc.

Kasarda, J 2001. From Airport City to Aerotropolis. *Airport World*, 6(4), 42–5.

Kloos, M. and de Maar, B. 1996. Schiphol Architecture. Amsterdam: Architectura & Natura.

Lang, R.E. 2000. *Edgeless Cities. Exploring the Exklusive Metropolis.* Washington, DC: Brookings Institute Press.

Läpple, D. 2001. Stadt und Region im Zeitalter der Globalisierung und Digitalisierung. *Deutsche Zeitschrift für Kommunalwissenschaften*, 40(2), 12–36.

Lüthi, S. 2011. *PhD Dissertation: Interlocking Firm Networks and Emerging Mega-City Regions. The Relational Geography of the Knowledge Economy in Germany.* Munich: Technical University of Munich.

Malecki, E. 2000. Creating and sustaining competitiveness. Local knowledge and economic geography, in *Knowledge, Space, Economy*, edited by J.Byrson, P. Daniels, N. Henry and J. Pollard. London, New York: Routledge, 103–19.

Polanyi , M. 1967. *The Tacit Dimension.* London: Loutledge & Kegan Paul.

Redondi, R., Malighetti, P. and Paleari, S. (2013) European connectivity: the role played by small airports. *Journal of Transport Geography*, 24, 86–94.

Ringbeck, J., Hauser, R., Franke, M. and Clayton, E. 2006. "Aero" – *Dynamik im Europäischen Flughafensektor. Neuausrichtung wegen veränderter Nachfrage und Kostendruck erforderlich.* Düsseldorf: Booz Allen Hamilton Consulting.

Salet, W. and Majoor, S. 2005. *Amsterdam Zuidas. European Space.* Rotterdam: 010 Publishers.

Schaafsma, M. 2008. Accessing global city regions: The airport as city, in *The Image and The Region: Making Mega-City Regions Visible!*, edited by A. Thierstein and A. Foerster. Baden: Lars Müller Publishers, 69–80.

Schamp, E.W. 2003. Knowledge, innovation and funding in spatial context: The case of Germany, in *Innovation, Finance and Space*, edited by A. Thierstein and E.W. Schamp. Frankfurt: Selbstverlag Institut für Wirtschaft und Sozialgeographie der Johann Wolfgang Goethe Universität, 179–93.

Schubert, J. and Conventz, S. 2011. Immobilienstandort Flughafen – Merkmale und Perspektiven der Airport Cities in Deutschland. *Informationen zur Raumentwicklung (IzR)*, 1, 13–26.

Simmie, J. 2003. Innovation and urban regions as national and international nodes for the transfer and sharing of knowledge. *Regional Studies*, 37(6), 607–20.

Soureli, K. and Youn, E. 2009. Urban restructuring and the crisis: A symposium with Neil Brenner, John Friedman, Margit Mayer, Allen J. Scott, and Edward W. Soja. *Critical Planning, A Journal of UCLA Department for Urban Planning*, 16, 35–9.

Taaffe, E.J. 1956. Air transportation and United States urban distribution. *Geographical Review*, 46(2), 219–38.

Taylor, P.J., Ni, P., Derudder, B. Hoyler, M., Huang, J. and Witlox, F. 2011. *Global Urban Analysis. A Survey of Cities in Globalization.* London, Washington, DC: Earthscan Publishing.

Thierstein, A., Kruse, C., Glanzmann, L., Gabi, S. and Grillon, N. 2006. *Raumentwicklung im Verborgenen. Untersuchungen und Handlungsfelder für die Entwicklung der Metropolregion Nordschweiz.* Zürich: NZZ Buchverlag.

Time Magazine 1960. *Airport Cities: Gateways to the Jet Age.* Available at: www.time.com/time/magazine/article/0,9171,939792-1,00.html [accessed: 22 June 2010].

van Wijk, M. 2007. Airprorts as cityports in the city region. Spatial-economic and institutional positions and institutional learning in Randstad-Schiphol (AMS), Frankfurt Rhein-Main (FRA), Tokyo Haneda (HND) and Narita (NRT). *Netherlands Geographical Studies*, 353.

WTC-Schiphol 2010. *WTC Schiphol Airport Tenants.* Available at: www.wtcschiphol.nl [accessed: 2 April 2010].

Chapter 5

European Port Cities: Embodiments of Interaction – Knowledge and Freight Flow as Catalysts of Spatial Development

Anne Wiese and Alain Thierstein

Introduction

Economic structural change and globalization exert a lasting impact on European port cities. The volume of goods, which are being shipped around the globe, has multiplied over the past decade. Consequently, the supply chains and markets have increased in complexity (Gereffi et al. 2005). Today, successful cities are nodes in a global network of knowledge creation and transformation (Sassen 1991, Castells 2000). As a result, the urban space itself is constituted via relations of networks – material and immaterial – at different interrelated scale levels from the global to the local (Dicken et al. 2001, Bunnell and Coe 2001, Allen 2009). In this framework, port cities can be places of encounter, as they facilitate the transportation of goods and knowledge. They thereby bear particular potential for the creation and exchange of knowledge (Hesse 2010, Jacobs 2008, Brown et al. 2010). The contemporary port – city relationship is shaped by spatial and functional interdependencies, which stretch beyond the individual port and city: The port in its functionality, formerly a contained industrial site, has extended its operations into other sectors. Notably the related advanced producer services of logistics, trade and supply are situated and embedded in the urban system (Jacobs et al. 2010). Individually, these are only to a limited extent spatially bound to the port operations (O'Connor 1989). Overall, the industrial value chain is functionally closely intertwined with the knowledge flows in the city system and gives rise to the modern maritime economy as a merged entity of industrial and service operations (Jacobs et al. 2010). At the same time, the urban milieu of port cities achieves new prominence in the light of location choice of producer service firms and property developers, seeking attractive urban locations with good infrastructure (Hein 2011, Warsewa 2004, Wilson 2002). On the one hand, the perpetual importance of ports in a global system of transport, the successful development of an advanced producer service sector and an advantageous geostrategic location and morphology might be considered a predictor for successful urban development trajectories in a port region. On the other hand, many port cities fail to succeed in their spatial ambitions and are faced with the functional realities of global competition and ongoing structural change. The regional scale has gained in importance for the development of port cities as it offers economies of scale and scope as well as space for the co-existence of overlapping network logics in a field of interaction (Notteboom and Rodrigue 2005, Hesse 2010).

This chapter looks at the spatial implications of the city's position in a network of national and international sites interlinked by knowledge flows and the port's position in a global system of physical production and transportation. Starting out from the recent planned redevelopment of many European port cities, we highlight the importance of physical space as a catalyst for exchange processes. We argue that functional differences between European port cities at the outset of regeneration attempts need to facilitate different approaches to planning and governance.

Applying a relational conception of space and taking the interrelatedness of different scale levels into consideration, our research results trace the dependencies of physical spatial configuration and functional development on a super-regional, regional and local scale, based on detailed data on the collaborative networks of the maritime economy of Northern Germany.

Planned Urban Redevelopment

Urban regeneration debates in European port cities have been going on for the last two decades. Port cities that have lost out in the fierce battle of port competition, mostly due their disadvantageous geographic location or dispositions, are trying to re-establish themselves as tourist destinations and/or service hubs. Those that remain geostrategic entry points for goods into the market economy have specialized and/or expanded. In most of these cases however, the relationship with the urban core seems to have vanished (Daamen 2007, Bird 1963, Hoyle 1989). The port is part of a network of logistic hubs, whereas the city is part of a network of knowledge hubs. Our argument is that those networks are closely intertwined, imprinting on the spatial configuration of those regions, which are benefiting from an enmeshed value chain of physical and non-physical flows.

In the attempt to compete with other locations to attract firms, talent and attention, urban development programs on the waterfront are strikingly similar: they contain a mix of private and corporate uses with offices and shops, water-related recreational uses, touristic, cultural and gastronomic offerings and a certain amount of entertainment and events (Warsewa 2004, Price Waterhouse Coopers 2010). Whether the port is still functional and just moved to far outside the city or the port has actually lost its role altogether seemingly makes no difference in how municipalities and property developers approach the redevelopment question. Projects generally dismiss the option of synergies between the modern port and the urban core, as it inflicts spatial conflict and consider the port rather to be an autonomous technical system of structures dedicated to its logistic use (Ducruet 2007, Wilson 2002).

As a result, the majority of waterfront redevelopments merely reference the heritage by presenting refurbished cranes as part of a mixed use gentrified, clean urban environment and fail to take on a more differentiated approach. The lack of coherence between existing economic structures and local specificities in the current practice are preventing successful regeneration (Hall and Soskice 2001, Warsewa 2010) for a number of reasons. Firstly, the geographic and economic challenges European port cities face from a maritime economy point of view vary greatly (Warsewa 2004). Secondly, the aforementioned structural changes in the economy have increased the strategic advantage of cities tied into the global network of knowledge and finance flows (Sassen 1991). Thirdly, the city's potential in both aspects increasingly depends on the retention it receives on a regional scale, strengthening its position as knowledge as well as a logistic hub (Lüthi et al. 2011, Notteboom and Rodrigue 2005).

Planning in this context requires a multi-scalar approach reaching beyond the built environment and encompassing an understanding of material, social and organizational space as major constituents of the living space (Boudon 1999). The potential of functional specialization and relational advantage for the development of cities mean that distinct non-physical capabilities should be capitalized for redevelopment in conjunction with the opportunities of the built and un-built environment. The abundance of docks and warehouse structures along the entire European coastline is the result of the embodiment of previous development phases and as such bears particular opportunities for urban redevelopment. However, the success of such efforts is likely to depend on other factors such as accessibility, presence of talent and above average amenities to attract the economic actors necessary (Thierstein and Wiese 2011).

Dealing with these – in any single case – limited opportunities requires an adaptation of current methods of planning, responding to the multi-layered challenges of a relational concept of place. Our framework suggests a stronger focus on the conceptualization and analysis of idiosyncratic resources, which are a result of and form the basis for the evolution of network relations. Therefore, the conception of the status-quo needs to precede any projection into a future trajectory in order to be sustainable. The aim is to strengthen the innovative capacity of future projects by the formulation of spatial strategies and promote the negotiation of unique solutions in this field of differing scale and activity levels adding to urban space diversity (Thierstein and Wiese 2012).

Space as an Ordering Principle

The diminished importance of traditional boundaries for the flow of goods, finance and money has stimulated the creation of a complex web of flows between places, which eludes itself from human perception. However, place still matters and the world is in no sense flat (Friedman 2005). Especially in an economic system, where knowledge is the key resource, space becomes the principal mode of social ordering and control (Harvey 1989, Soja 1989). Qualitatively different spaces are created through the unique constellation of superimposing network logics with the locally specific interrelations and conceptions. The immanent field of relations between nodes of a network manifests difference and is constituted via other nodes in the network, delineating new spatial entities. These are, rather than homogeneous planar levels, constituted by cross-relations between physical substance and non-physical flows as well as its position and meaning in the global network of interrelations (Lefebvre 1991). Rather than being a territorial unit, a city consequently consists of numerous sites in spatially stretched economic relations (Amin and Thrift 2002) or fields of interaction (Schumacher 2005). Space – as the three dimensional product – is hereby created and constantly recreated by processes of production and consumption, which imprint on the physical and non-physical environment.

Due to recent developments in the way we work and live in Europe, the importance of place has increased: Globalization has led to a fierce competition for talent and capital as a basis for prosperity (Thierstein and Wiese 2011). Local characteristics and conditions are attractors and anchors for firms and talent as they are seen to be conductive to the creation and exchange of certain types of knowledge (Boschma 2005) and lifestyle in a region, which is no longer differentiated by national specifics such as legislation and trade restrictions. Moreover, places are an integral part of the identity of humans within an increasingly individualized world, where splintering social groups seek cohesion in particular cities, neighbourhoods (Florida 2008) and imagery (Cresswell 2011). As a result, our habitat is not necessarily territorially continuous, but rather a discontinuous constellation of places interlinked by travel patterns (Amann and Mantia 1998) forming the dimension of human perceived space (Lefebvre 1991).

Physical Proximity as Catalyst

The argument of physical proximity as a catalyst for knowledge exchange closely relates to urban agglomeration economics. Localization economics, whereby a critical mass is created and urbanization economies, whereby a large variety of products and services are available create the urban milieu as a bustling marketplace for knowledge. The spatial differential is reinforced by positive externalities such as density and connectivity. As a socially, organizationally, culturally and physically embedded resource, knowledge is more easily transferred through face-to-face communication (Nohria and Eccles 1992, Storper and Venables 2004). Direct contact enables the participating parties to exchange imperfect knowledge or insight in a realm of mutual trust. Moreover, physical proximity opens up additional channels of non-verbal communication, where physical co-presence enables the transmission of knowledge embodied in processes and artefacts through observation and use (Pfeifer et al. 2007). Here again, the urban environment offers a rich and dense co-presence of functional and physical components stimulating the creation of new knowledge by mimicking and complementing.

The discussion of proximity in the context of innovation research has a long tradition. The successes of Silicon Valley and the Third Italy have been attributed to spatial proximity and local cohesion, which makes these clusters particularly vibrant economically (Saxenian 1991, Boschma and Lambooy 2002). The concept of regional innovation systems has stressed that the role of local ties between public and private organizations is creating a 'milieu' which bears positively on innovation activity (Cooke et al. 1997). However, very few studies have attempted to delineate the size or extent of such a system spatially (Crevoisier 2004). The research that has been undertaken into the structure, form and quality of milieus in the context of advanced producer service firms shows that polycentric Mega-City Regions (Hall and Pain 2006) will be better placed to constantly reinvent themselves and to sustain global competition. They are able to combine agglomeration economies and global network economies in a multi-scale innovation and production system, complemented by top-quality urban amenities. This results in overlapping and trans-scalar knowledge activities that manifest themselves in nodes of multiple knowledge connections of varying intensity and spatial distance, as a place in a web of trans-scalar and nonlinear connections, and as a relay point of circulating knowledge that cannot be territorially attributed with any measure of certainty or fixity (Amin and Cohendet 2004).

The role of physical proximity in the creation of regional clusters is strengthened by the co-presence of differing knowledge bases, dependencies within the value chain and industrial dynamics in regard to increased competition and globalized markets. In order to trace the resultant physical spatial configurations and qualities, multi-scalar sectoral studies could reveal the interrelatedness of different scales and the role of space for innovation activity within specific sectors.

The dynamic landscapes that these networks create are embodied in real spaces, which restrain and foster our physical movement and interaction by structural, functional and qualitative differentiation. By analysing the built and urban form in European port cities as the embodiments of the interaction and nodes in larger networks (Hein 2011), we intend to reveal potential future development paths.

Physical Space in a Relational World

Morphologically, the distinction between urban and rural areas has become blurred. The ancient city – well defined by means of its city walls – has been replaced by an urban landscape, which integrates farmland, settlement areas and industrial facilities into a hybrid spatial form (SAUL 2006, Batty 2001). Industrialization and prosperity have created new ecologies, representing the wishes and desires of the dominant actors (Shane 2011). Differentiation is generated by density, typology and relative attractiveness (Florida 2008). Recursivity is generated through agglomeration economies, where central spaces perpetually gain further in importance (Sassen 1991). As a result the functional hierarchy between places has steepened (Thierstein et al. 2011). Differentiation is generated by land price

(Alonso 1973), morphology and relative attractiveness (Myrdal 1957) and recursivity, generated through agglomeration economies (Hoover 1937). The surface area covered by urbanized structures has tremendously increased, spurred by mass transportation and car usage.

Today, the definition of a city as 'a relatively large, dense and permanent settlement of socially heterogeneous individuals' (Wirth 1938) can only serve as a minimal concept on the most general level. The qualities of the individual city and region need to be decoded from its co-existing and penetrating relational logics, which are exerting a strong impact on past, current and future development. Relational logics based on the physical flows of people and goods, as well as the non-physical flows of finance and knowledge creates fields of interaction (Amin 2004). The spatial extent of these fields and their intrinsic logic cannot be delineated a priori but has to be revealed empirically as part of the conception of the city (Boudon 1999). Only thereafter it can be stated which forces are exerting a lasting influence on the local distinctiveness and instruct the strategy of development (Bourdieu and Wacquand 1996, Berking and Low 2008). Successful places are a result of a multitude of inter-related network logics and fields of interaction imprinting on the local urban environment, perceived by the user (Montgomery 1998). Increasingly, the spheres of influence, perception and the network extend fail to coincide. The urban space has changed into a complex field of interrelated activities through changed boundary conditions and additional factors of influence, which evolve on other scale levels. Urban space diversity is the product of local and global factors, relational and positional qualities and material and immaterial components, which manifest themselves in a unique local configuration as a place, (Thierstein and Wiese 2012).

The context of the European port city, where space for development is scarce, poses particular challenges to the renewal and addition of 'urban space' into that mix. These cities are to a large extent built up and come with a history of development, which can hinder adaptation to changing demands locally and globally. The existing urban fabric can also restrain. Conditions of control, influence and objective can reach far beyond the city limits and inflict conflict locally. Interventions of larger scale are therefore increasingly complex endeavours (Thierstein et al. 2012). Immanent potentials and synergies have to be equally activated for the benefit of economic and spatial development.

Functional Realities

The globalization of production and consumption has changed the conditions for cities in global competition, shaping the evolution of spatial processes. Formerly prosperous cities have declined and other places – mostly outside Europe – have gained in strategic importance. Urban designers and planners are facing previously unknown functional realities: Most prominently, the cities in the Gulf region have rapidly gained geostrategic importance and established themselves in the first instance as logistics hubs located in-between Europe and Asia. Global shifts in the economic constellation have fuelled their development as hubs not only for trade and infrastructure, but later on also as leisure, entertainment, cultural and Islamic finance hubs on a global scale (Thierstein and Schein 2008). The functional specialization of places has become more pronounced. The global exchange of knowledge and goods has increased and made talent and capital sought after resources to secure prosperity. Many cities have gained in importance as sophisticated market places for services and goods locally as well as globally. The traditional urban environment catalyses knowledge-transfer through density, richness and diversity (Jacobs 1961, Montgomery 1998).

Simultaneously, knowledge with its various forms and focuses has become a more distinct feature of value creation in most sectors. Advanced Producer Services (APS), such as legal, banking, accountancy and advertising play an intermittent role in the value chains across various industries. They create an interlocking network through their global location strategies for situating offices and are as such generators of world city networks (Taylor et al. 2002, Taylor 2001). The supply of such complementary and competing knowledge via firms and employees is a key factor for agglomeration effects to evolve locally through innovation and subsequent growth. The risk of specialization and the division of labour is offset by a certain critical mass and a multitude of networking opportunities. In that sense, the urban reduces the transaction costs of knowledge at the benefit of the individual and the private firm (Thompson 2007). The urban density also serves as a device to reduce uncertainty for individuals and firms in terms of information gathering and interpretation. Knowledge exchange is also seen to be facilitated by other forms of proximity. Gertler (1995) has introduced the concept of relational proximity, determining how easily specialized knowledge can be jointly produced and shared through distributed innovation processes. It refers to 'the degree to which individuals, firms, and communities are bound by relations of common interest, purpose, or passion, and held together by routines and varying degrees of mutuality' (Amin and Cohendet 2004: 74). Within the regional context of a successful city global pipelines and local networks of material and immaterial flows coincide and bear particular potential for development (Jacobs et al. 2010, Bathelt et al. 2004).

Against this background only selected port cities have the opportunity to re-invent themselves as primary platforms in the knowledge economy based on pre-existing resources and achieve a sustainable balance which fosters development. The urban core is only one component in a regional economic system, which – as a whole- stands in competition with other regions (Thierstein et al. 2011, Jacobs 2008).

Figure 5.1 illustrates the spread of APS firms in accordance to their importance within the firm network applying the extended Globalization and World City rational of interlocking intra- and inter-firm networks (Taylor 2001, Lüthi et al. 2010). The darker the colour, the higher is the ranking of this location in the overall firm network. Among the port cities of Kiel, Bremerhaven, Bremen and Hamburg, only the greater Hamburg region shows a relative concentration of APS firms.

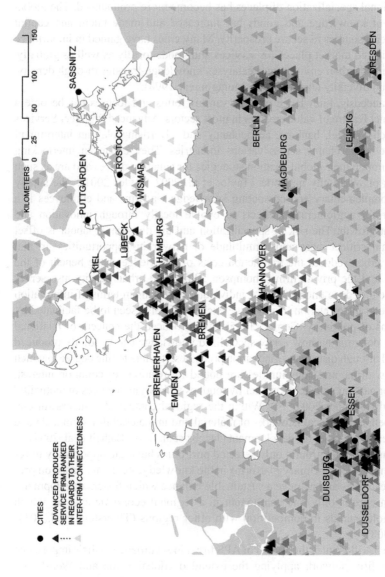

Figure 5.1 Advanced Producer Service firms in the North of Germany with port cities marked in black

Although the agglomeration of Hamburg is less compact than the Rhine-Ruhr region or Berlin, the map illustrates the importance of a regional conception in all cases as higher ranked locations (darker colour) extend far beyond the city limits.

The relatively dense population and high levels of income make Europe a major consumer market in the world. Structural change exerts however a lasting impact on the functional interdependencies. The high demand for land and high labour costs make labour intensive mass production economically not viable in the long run. As a result, firms with labour and space intensive operations have a propensity to relocate to places where labour and land are cheaper. Moreover, the differentiation of tastes and cultures has spurred the demand for customized solutions in products and services. Advances in technology have enabled a large part of the working population to shift from manual work to more complex coordination tasks. With rising educational levels the workforce possesses more universal capabilities and becomes more flexible (Hansen and Winther 2010). In the European context, the relocation of labour and space intensive operations to other parts of the world has reinforced the importance of highly specialized and knowledge intensive tasks in the value creation (Dicken 1998). Location has gained in importance and defines differentiated markets for customers, talent and infrastructure (Florida 2002, Van Geenhuizen and Nijkamp 2009).

Port City Development

For centuries port development was closely related to urban development in Europe. The primary historic interdependence of city and port is obvious: goods are imported via the port and traded in the city. The urban population is provided with consumer goods and local industry with raw products. Trade means that locally available finance and/or products can be exchanged for locally unavailable goods. Vice versa local products are exported via the port in exchange for finance, available for re-investment. Access to global markets strengthens the local economy and enables economic development based on extra-local demand. Since the 1990s however, the economic development paths of port and city show no correlation anymore (Ducruet and Lee 2006), but have been simultaneously subjected to fragmented debates across the disciplines of urban planning, port and transport economics and economic geography. Ports have developed spatial structures beyond the city boundaries increasing the efficiency of their operations, leading to sophisticated new spatial constellations of hub and feeder ports (Lee et al. 2008, Notteboom and Rodrigue 2005) and integrated corporate supply chains (Olivier and Slack 2006, Robinson 2002). As a result, the port is tied into a network of transport from the seaside and landside. Equally the port is tied to a number of other activities beyond its territory and agency, inserting it into different relational networks (Bichou and Gray 2005). This reflects the interplay between logistics demand and the supply and trade channels fuelled by production and consumption. The contemporary port and city are therefore linked by more complex exchange processes, which evolve on various interrelated scale levels locally, regionally and globally, which are only partially visible (Bunnell and Coe 2001, Jacobs et al. 2010).

In several ways the regional scale gains importance over the individual port. Logistically, inland distribution becomes of foremost importance in port competition, favouring the emergence of transport corridors and logistics poles. As a consequence of decisions and subsequent actions of shippers and third party logistics providers (Robinson 2002) aiming at an optimization of costs and access, competition emerges between port regions rather than the individual port (Notteboom 2010). Logistically, a regional cluster of ports offers the opportunity of functional specialization and/ or the establishment of feeder systems, increasing the efficiency of shipping lines (Notteboom and Rodrigue 2005). Sites for cargo handling and distribution are connected by high capacity infrastructure and stretched out on a regional level. Third and fourth party logistics suppliers are orchestrating global supply chains with regional subsidiaries and provide knowledge intensive services beyond the physical handling of goods. Suppliers, shipping companies, shipbuilders, service providers and research institutions form a regional system of knowledge exchange, which is embedded in the urban as well as the port system. From a knowledge economy perspective regionalization results from the functional specialization and differentiation of locations across a region, critically affected by the availability of skilled labour and connectivity in order to capture the advantages of complementarity and competition in the advanced producer service sector on a regional level (Hall and Pain 2006). The relative physical proximity within a region fosters knowledge exchange. The distinction between places that are central places in a network of knowledge flow and those that are transport places, which are specialized in offering transport and wholesale services, thanks to their strategic location on transport channels (Hesse 2010), needs to be complemented by a more differentiated relational conception capturing the relationship between the two subsystems on a regional level. The urban market remains the raison d'être of production and consumption activities as ports and transport players are bound to the markets they serve and their location patterns (Ducruet 2007).

The result is a region consisting of qualitatively different locations characterized by physical and non-physical parameters such as structural composition, functional definition and spatial quality. On a European scale the coexistence of hubs of the transportation network and hubs of the knowledge network on a regional level can be confirmed empirically.

Figure 5.2 superimposes the Alpha, Beta and Gamma cities (Classification of cities 2010[1]), which are characterized by a relative concentration of advanced producer services (APS) with the most frequented ports and multi-port gateway regions as defined by Notteboom (2010a). This division of cities into three different classes has been carried out based on their importance in the four segments advertising, banking, legal and accountancy (Beaverstock et al. 1999).

---

1   Available through: http://www.lboro.ac.uk/gawc/world2010t.html; accessed 9th January 2012

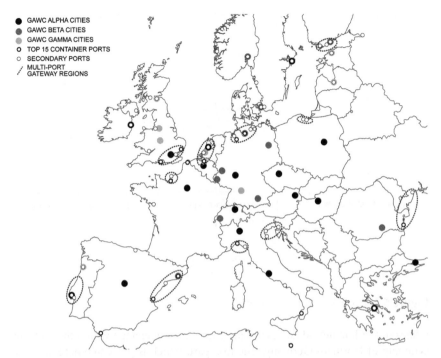

GAWC ALPHA CITIES
GAWC BETA CITIES
GAWC GAMMA CITIES
TOP 15 CONTAINER PORTS
SECONDARY PORTS
MULTI-PORT
GATEWAY REGIONS

Figure 5.2   Superposition of multi-port gateway regions and APS hubs

Strikingly, they coincide in the majority of cases supporting our argument that despite their spatial separation on the city scale they form functional regional clusters. In some cases the physical relationship is more distant but might still be of relevance from a functional perspective. Based on the above insight and the theoretical background laid out above, our research focuses on the spatial configuration of port city regions under the impact of material and immaterial flows.

Research Framework

Based on a relational conception of space and the increasing importance of advanced producer services for the development of urban regions, our analysis of the northern German region traces inter-related spatial development at different scale levels. Existing research on the supra-regional scale of European port cities (Figure 5.2) is informing the selection of the super-regional context of Northern Germany (Figures 5.1, 5.5 and 5.7). The regional context is preliminarily defined as an intermittent scale of functional urban areas (Figure 5.1) or metropolitan areas (BBSR 2011) and the local level as variable inner-city scale.

Based on the previously outlined argument, the aim of this ongoing research project is to evaluate the specific use value of the built environment, which

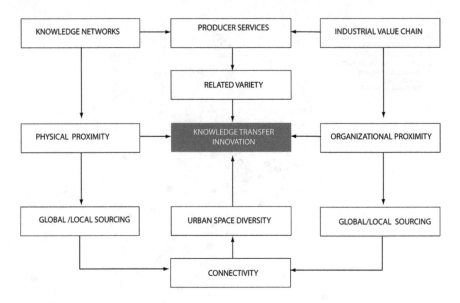

Figure 5.3   Research framework

relates to the immaterial and material processes of exchange within the maritime economy of Northern Germany. The first part, which is presented here, analyses the networks of interrelations at different scale levels in order to define extent and reach of potential spaces of encounter between the two systems, which in turn will guide the morphological analysis. The research framework (Figure 5.3) brings together the functional perspectives of knowledge networks and industrial value chains with the spatial perspective of proximity and connectivity as mutually reinforcing processes for increased knowledge transfer and innovation propensity. The capability to innovate is considered a prerequisite for competitiveness. The interrelatedness of scale levels results in physical and organizational proximity equally catalysing exchange processes.

The potential arises from the proximity of firms and technologies, which are complementary as well as in competition with each other. Formal and informal ties provide different opportunities for the exchange of knowledge. The regional scale bears a particular potential in that it enables physical proximity with sufficiently differentiated spaces for functional specialization to arise, thereby accommodating material and knowledge based activities simultaneously. This co-existence is hypothesized to increase the competitiveness of port cities as it fosters advances in technology and functional specialization based on the mutual functional dependency of industrial value chains and knowledge networks. In the following section we present a number of empirical results in this framework.

Own Research

We have based our analysis on survey data of 4495 firms in the maritime sector, which was gathered between 2008 and 2010 by the Norddeutsche Landesbank, one of Germany's major state owned regional banks. The dataset comprises locations and typologies of firms in the five northern Bundeslaender of Germany, the second tier level in decentralized Germany. These are: Hamburg, Bremen, Schleswig Holstein, Niedersachsen and Mecklenburg-Vorpommern, which we consider the super-regional scale in the context of this research. The multi-port gateway region of Northern Germany as indicated in Figure 5.2 forms part of this extent. The relational data represents collaborations between firms for the purpose of innovation. Functionally, these firms are part of the maritime economy consisting of seven distinct fields of competence: shipbuilding, suppliers, shipping companies, service providers, port logistics and research institutions.

Organizational Proximity

The globalization of production and consumption, the increasing specialization of firms and the acceleration of trade have increased the amount of interfaces within value chain systems (Brown et al. 2004, Gereffi et al. 2005, Storper 2009). Producer services play a crucial role in setting up and sustaining global production networks (Daniels and Bryson 2002), as a number of these interfaces require constant co-ordination and very close co-operation in order to realize the benefits of spatial des-integration, others are more standardized and easily codifiable.

Within the maritime economy of Northern Germany data on the collaboration among firms for innovation shows strong links on either side of the traditional divide between knowledge intensive and more manufacturing based competence fields. Figure 5.4 illustrates the cumulated interrelationships between fields of competence within the Maritime Industry of Northern Germany. The strong ties between shipping companies and shipbuilding as well as suppliers to the shipbuilding industry stand out as relations across traditional manufacturing boundaries. These can be considered as traditional value chain relationships, with the shipping company providing the finance and scope to the builder and the supplier providing specialist parts to the latter. A large number of ties between Research and Maritime Technology indicate a high degree of knowledge exchange and compatibility reflecting the research-intensive nature of this activity. Within the competence field of Maritime Technology strong internal ties are present. This high degree of collaboration can be attributed to complementary knowledge bases between firms. The ties between Port Logistics and Service Providers support our assumption that the industry-service interface is fundamentally important for a successful maritime network (Jacobs 2008, Brown et al. 2004).

The relative lack of ties between shipping companies and port logistics hints at the absence of relational proximity between these firms and their activities. The value chains of vessel construction and commissioning and the logistic value

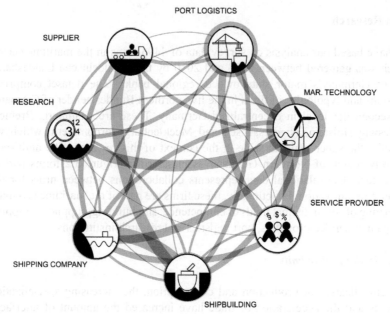

Figure 5.4   Maritime network of cooperation for innovation

Source: own illustration, NordLB data base (2010), Brandt et al. 2010

chain, which is involved in the formation of multi-modal networks (Robinson 2002), cannot be regarded as intertwined according to this.

In summary, the super-regional level exhibits functional ties, which reflect both organizational and technological proximity. The spatial consequences thereof require further analysis. The debate on knowledge spillovers centres on the local context as a milieu, which makes it easy to establish contacts with potential cooperation partners and to exchange knowledge without the pre-existence of formalized value chain relationships. Thereby certain localities foster informal exchange and provide a raised potential for innovation by providing knowledge spill overs (Marshall 1930, Bathelt et al. 2004, Storper and Venables 2004) and 'untraded interdependencies' (Storper 1997) due to physical proximity. The following analysis attempts a delineation of those localities on the regional level.

Functional Connectivity

The hypothesis that APS and maritime industry are building collaborative ties on a regional level generating a particular type of spatial configuration informs the spatial analysis of the functional connectivity of the sampled firms.

Based on the survey data in the maritime sector we have mapped their aggregated interconnectedness of spatial units (Kreise) for innovation and training within the northern German region (Figure 5.5a). On the regional scale, Hamburg clearly dominates with the majority of firms locating there, generating a high

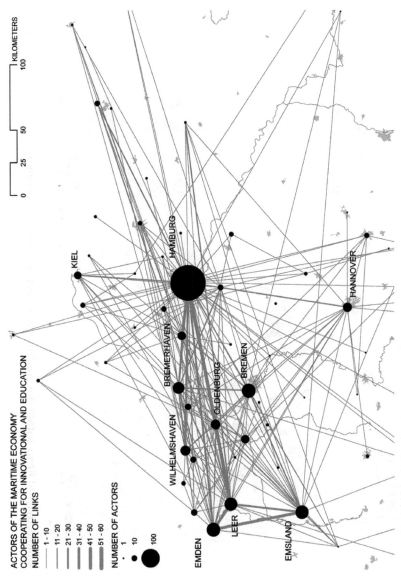

ACTORS OF THE MARITIME ECONOMY
COOPERATING FOR INNOVATION AND EDUCATION

NUMBER OF LINKS

1 - 10
11 - 20
21 - 30
31 - 40
41 - 50
51 - 60

NUMBER OF ACTORS

· 1
• 10
● 100

KILOMETERS

0   25   50   100

KIEL

HAMBURG

BREMERHAVEN

WILHELMSHAVEN

OLDENBURG

BREMEN

HANNOVER

EMDEN

LEER

EMSLAND

Figure 5.5a   Aggregated network of firms on a super-regional level

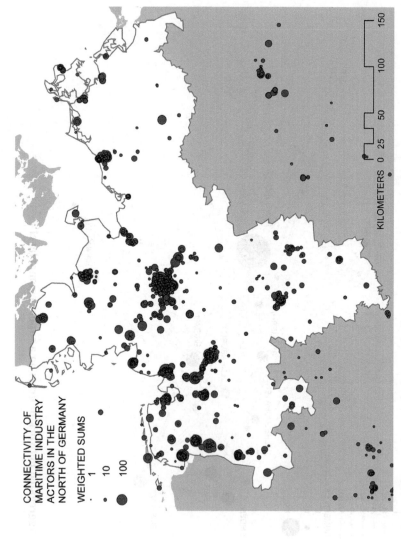

Figure 5.5b Connectivity of firms within the maritime economy of Northern Germany

degree of centrality in the overall network. The secondary port cities Bremerhaven, Cuxhaven and Wilhelmshaven exhibit strong links with Hamburg. A secondary axis of collaboration is evident along the river Ems to the west, also strongly linking into Hamburg. The network gravitates along the coast of the North Sea, where the main seaports are located.

Focusing on the connectivity of firms, derived from the total of connections per firm weighted according to their intensity (Figure 5.5b), a more distinct spatial pattern becomes evident on the super-regional scale. Those locations in vicinity to the larger, established agglomerations of Hamburg, Bremen and Hannover stand out as particularly clustered and connected. We also observe high degrees of connectivity in more remote locations, namely along the river Ems and the area north of Hamburg. The majority of firms are located in relative proximity to the ports, which are respectively in the main urban agglomerations in the case of Bremen and Hamburg. In these two areas, we therefore seek to establish more insight into the local spatial configuration from a functional and qualitative angle.

Physical Proximity

By applying a spectral algorithm, we have computed non-overlapping communities, delineated by fewer than expected interconnections between them. These communities are treated as functionally related modules in regard to innovation activity. The analysis has computed 21 modules of more than ten firms, which are more strongly connected internally than externally within the overall network (Newman 2006). These modules are considered as clusters and analysed in accordance with their spatial configuration on the local level. Interestingly, we can identify complementary as well as competitive clusters of firms are related by input-output relationships (Figure 5.6a), but also compete with each other Figure 5.6b).

Also, there is a clear spatial demarcation of operational alliances versus strategic alliances. In the case of Hamburg, operational alliances stretch along the south of the river Elbe towards more de-central locations (Figure 5.5a) whereas strategic alliances cluster more centrally (Figure 5.5b).

The module analysis shows however, that very few real co-operations for the purpose of innovation and education evolve at the local level. Despite the technology park of Bremen (Figure 5.6c) no single area accommodates a critical number of actors within a five kilometre radius, which could be considered walking distance and therefore accounted as local. The relevance of other scale levels needs to be followed up in more detail as part of a further study. As we hypothesize that knowledge flows and freight flows are interrelated on the regional level, the analysis of physical connectivity bears potential to further delineate spatial units, which are of particular relevance.

**Figures 5.6a, b and c   Local clusters of firms within three separate
                            modules in Hamburg**

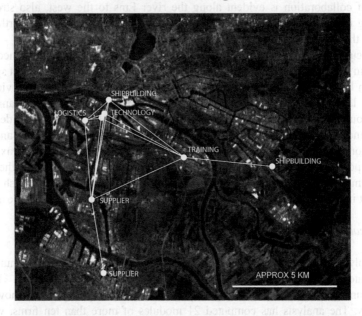

5.6a

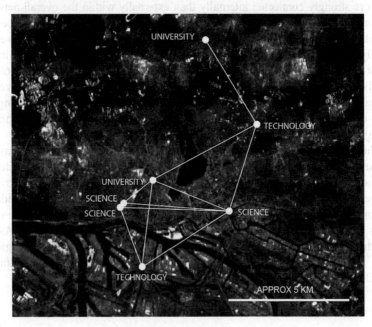

5.6b

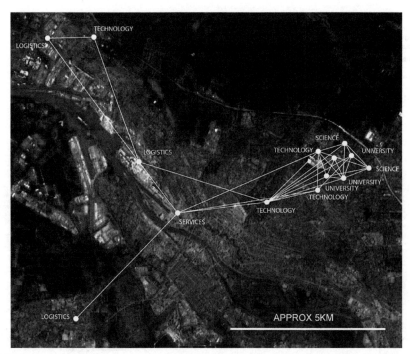

5.6c

Physical Connectivity

Based on maritime transport (Eurostat 2005a) and railway freight data (Eurostat 2005b), this analysis maps the physical connectivity by freight flow (Figure 5.7). The port of Hamburg is dominating in terms of seaside connectivity with Bremen and the ports of the Weser-Ems Region representing secondary hubs. Hamburg stands out as a centre of landside distribution, but Bremen and Weser-Ems also clearly show their relevance on the regional level. Logistically, Braunschweig and Hannover appear as major destinations of goods within the region. Set into relation with the functional connectivities of the former analysis, the strong link between Bremen and Hamburg persists. The relevance of Hannover in the logistic flow however is absent in the analysis of the data on collaboration. This could suggest that there are relevant organizational ties, which reach beyond those captured in the maritime economy or that the two systems are to be regarded independent of each other.

The lack of relational data on other modes of transport limits the validity of these findings. However, the need for further studies on the spatial consequences of the interrelationship of logistics and maritime industry becomes apparent.

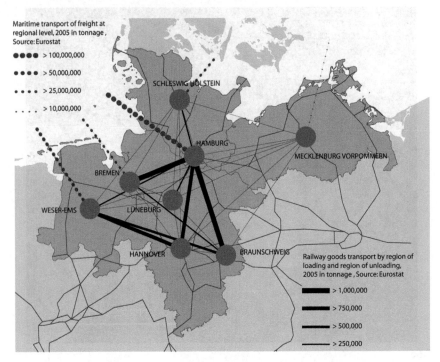

Figure 5.7   Freight traffic within the northern German region via rail

Conclusion

We intended to explore the spatial consequences of knowledge and freight flows on different scale levels in the multi-port gateway region in the north of Germany. The empirical results reveal the dominance of the metropolitan area of Hamburg as a centre for advanced producer service firms as well as for the maritime economy and cargo handling. The role of the metropolitan area of Hannover within the maritime economy remains limited, although it clearly features in the survey of APS firm locations (Figure 5.1), as well as in the material flow analysis (Figure 5.8). The Weser-Ems region appears logistically independent from Hamburg, whereas its network of collaboration shows strong functional ties in the more established urban cores of Hamburg and Bremen.

On the local inner city level, we have identified clusters of complementary and competitive activities, albeit at a scale which is regarded too large for unintended knowledge spillovers to occur. With the exemption of the Bremen Technology Park, where such spillovers could occur due to the scale and structure, the local level appears to have limited importance. The module analysis reveals a potentially more relevant intermediate scale, indicating spatially differentiated specialized milieus, focusing on research, strategic management and operative tasks. These coincide in the centre of the super-region of Northern Germany between the metropolitan areas of Hamburg, Bremen, Hannover and Braunschweig.

The interrelatedness of spatial scales and interconnectedness of different spheres of activity through knowledge exchange points towards spatial integration rather than fragmentation on a regional and sub-regional (intermediate) scale. The empirical delineation of relevant scale levels has to be further explored. Hamburg serves as the dual dominating core of the region, with other regional clusters being functionally more specialized such as the Weser-Ems Region.

Collaboration within the maritime economy can be observed in different areas with distinct spatial reach and centres of gravity. We have identified spaces of encounter on a sub-regional level as well as spatial differentiation at that scale. The majority of results are preliminary in that they require confirmation through triangulation by complementary methods. Further research is required to identify distinct patterns of spatial organization informing planning and governance in port city regions. This research is crucial as further insight into the interrelationship of urban design, planning and economic geography at the regional scale could inform location strategies and inform the governance of European port cities, facing ongoing structural change and intensified competition in the future.

References

Allen, S. 2009. From object to field: Field conditions in architecture and urbanism, in *Space Reader. Heterogeneous Space in Architecture*, edited by Michael Hensel, Christopher Hight and Achim Menges. Padstow: Wiley, 119–43.

Amann, K. and Mantia, G. 1998. No where. Vorschläge zur Analyse der urbanen Realität. *Daidalos*, 69/70, 82–91.

Amin, A. 2004. Regions unbound: Towards new politics of place. *Geografiska annaler: series B, Human Geography*, 86(1), 33–44.

Amin, A. and Cohendet, P. 2004. *Architectures of Knowledge. Firms, Capabilities, and Communities*. Oxford, New York: Oxford University Press.

Amin, A. and Thrift, N. 2002. *Cities Reimagining the Urban*. Cambridge: Blackwell.

Bathelt, H., Malmberg, A. and Maskell, P. 2004. Clusters and knowledge local buzz, global pipelines and the process of knowledge creation. *Progress in Human Geography*, 28(31), 31–56.

Batty, M. 2001. Polynucleated urban landscapes. *Urban Studies*, 38(4), 635–56.

BBSR. 2011. *Metropolitan areas in Europe*. BBSR-Online-Publikation 01/2011. Eds.: Federal Institute for Research on Building, Urban Affairs and Spatial Development (BBSR) within the Federal Office for Building and Regional Planning (BBR), Bonn.

Beaverstock, J., Smith, R.G. and Taylor, P.J. 1999. A roster of world cities. *Cities*, 16(6), 445–58.

Berking, H. and Löw, M. 2008. *Die Eigenlogik der Städte*. Frankfurt: campus.

Bichou, K. and Gray, R. 2005. A critical review of conventional terminology for classifying seaports. *Transportation Research*, Part A, 39, 75–92.

Bird, J. (1963) *The Major Seaports of the United Kingdom*. London: Hutchinson of London.

Boschma, R.A. 2005. Proximity and innovation: A critical assessment. *Regional Studies*, 39(1), 61–74.

Boschma, R.A. and Lambooy, J.G. 2002. Knowledge, market structure, and economic coordination: Dynamics of industrial districts. *Growth and Change*, 33(3), 291–311.

Boudon, P. 1999. The point of view of measurement in architectural conception: From questions of scale to scale as question. *Nordic Journal of Architectural Research*, 12(1), 7–18.

Bourdieu, P. and Wacquand, L.1996. *Reflexive Anthropologie*. Frankfurt: Suhrkamp.

Brandt, A., Dickow, M.C. and Drangmeister C. 2010. Entwicklungspotenziale und Netzwerkbeziehungen maritimer Cluster in Deutschland. *Zeitschrift für Wirtschaftsgeographie*. 54 (3–4), 238–53.

Brown, E., Derudder, B., Parnreiter, C., Pelupessy, W., Taylor, P.J. and Witlox, F. 2010. World city networks and global commodity chains: Towards a world-system's integration. *Global Networks – A Journal of Transnational Affairs*, 10 (1), 12–34.

Bunnell, T.G., and Coe, N.M. 2001. Spaces and scales of innovation. *Progress in Human Geography*, 24(4), 569–89.

Castells, M. 2000. *The Rise of the Network Society. The Information Age: Economy, Society and Culture*. Malden: Blackwell Publishers.

Cooke, P, Uranga, M.G. and Etxebarria, G. 1997. Regional innovation systems: Institutional and organisational dimensions. *Research Policy*, 26, 475–91.

Cresswell, T. 2011. *Geographies of Mobilities: Practices, Spaces, Subjects*. Farnham: Ashgate.

Crevoisier, O. 2004. The innovative milieus approach: Toward a territorialized understanding of the economy? *Economic Geography*, 80(4), 367–79.

Daamen, T. 2007. *Sustainable Development of the European Port-City Interface*. Paper to European Network for Housing Research international conference: Sustainable urban areas, Rotterdam 25–28.6.2007.

Daniels, P.W. and Bryson, J.R. 2002. Manufacturing services and servicing manufacturing: Knowledge-based cities and changing forms of production. *Urban Studies*, 39(5–6), 977–91.

Dicken, P. 1998. *Global Shift. Transforming the World Economy*. London: Paul Chapman.

Dicken, P., Kelly, P., Olds, C. and Yeung, H. 2001. Chains and networks, territories and scales: Towards a relational framework for analysing the global economy. *Global Networks*, 1(2), 89–112.

Ducruet, C. 2007. The metageography of port-city relationships, in *Ports, Cities, and Global Supply Chains*, edited by J.J Wang et al. Aldershot: Ashgate, 157–73.

Ducruet, C., and Lee, S.W. 2006. Frontline soldiers of globalisation: Port–city evolution and regional competition. *Geojournal*, 9, 67(2), 107–22.

Eurostat. 2005a. *Maritime transport of freight by NUTS 2 regions* [online]. Available at: http://appsso.eurostat.ec.europa.eu/nui/show.do?dataset=tran_r_mago_nm&lang=en [accessed 15.01.12]

Eurostat. 2005b. *Annual national and international railway goods transport by region of loading and region of unloading* [online]. Available at: http://appsso.eurostat.ec.europa.eu/nui/show.do?dataset=tran_r_rago&lang=en [accessed 15.01.12]

Florida, R. 2002. *The Rise of the Creative Class*. New York: Basic Books.

Florida, R. 2008. *Who's your City? How the Creative Economy is Making Where to Live The Most Important Decision of your Life*. New York: Basic Books.

Friedman, T.L. 2005. *The World is Flat. A Brief History of the Twenty-first Century*. New York: Farrar, Strauss and Giroux.

Gereffi, G., Humphrey, J. and Sturgeon, T. 2005. The governance of global value chains. *Review of International Political Economy*, 12(1), 78–104.

Gertler, M.S. 1995. 'Being there': Proximity, organization, and culture in the development of advanced manufacturing technologies. *Economic Geography*, 71(1), 1–26.

Hall, P.A. and Soskice, D. 2001. An introduction to varieties of capitalism, in *Varieties of Capitalism: The Institutional Foundations of Comparative Advantage*, edited by P. Hall et al. New York: Oxford University Press, 1–68.

Hall, P. and Pain, K. 2006. *The Polycentric Metropolis. Learning from Mega-City Regions in Europe*. London: Earthscan.

Hansen, H.K. and Winther, L. 2010. The spatial division of talent in city regions: Location dynamics of business services in Copenhagen. *Tijdschrift voor Economische en Sociale Geografie*. 101(1), 55–72.

Harvey, D. 1989. *The Condition of Postmodernity*. Oxford: Blackwell.

Hein, C. 2011. *Port Cities: Dynamic Landscapes and Global Networks*. London: Routledge.

Hesse, M. 2010. Cities, material flows and the geography of spatial interaction: Urban places in the system of chains. *Global Networks*, 10(1), 75–91.

Hoyle, B. 1989. The port-city interface: trends, problems, and examples. *Geoforum* 20(4), 429–35.

Jacobs, J. 1961. *The Death and Life of Great American Cities*. New York: Random House.

Jacobs, W. 2008. Global value chains, port clusters and advanced producer services. A framework for analysis. Annual Meeting of the Association of American Geographers, 15–19 April, Boston, MA.

Jacobs, W., Koster, H. and Hall, P. 2010 The location and global network structure of maritime advanced producer Services. *Urban Studies*, 48(13), 2749–69.

Jacobs, W., Ducruet, C. and De Langen, P. 2010b. Integrating world cities into production networks: The case of port cities. *Global Networks*, 10(1), 92–113

Lee, S., Song, D. and Ducruet C. 2008. A tale of Asia's world ports: The spatial evolution in global hub port cities. Geoforum, 39, 372–85.

Lefebvre, H. 1991. *The Production of Space*. Oxford and Cambridge: Blackwell.

Lüthi, S., Thierstein, A. and Goebel V. 2010. Intra-firm and extra-firm linkages in the knowledge economy: The case of the emerging mega-city region of Munich. *Global Networks*, 10(1), 114–37.

Lüthi, S., Thierstein, A. and Bentlage, M. 2011. Interlocking firm networks in the German knowledge economy. On local networks and global connectivity. *Raumforschung und Raumordnung*, 69(3), 161–74.

Marshall, A. 1930. *Principles of Economics*. London: Macmillan.

Montgomery, J. 1998. Making a city: Urbanity, vitality and urban design. *Journal of Urban Design*, 3(1), 93–116.

Newman, M.E. 2006. Modularity and community structure in networks. *PNAS.* 103(23), 8577–82.

Nohria, N., and Eccles, R. 1992. Face-to-Face: Making network organizations work, in *Networks and Organizations: Structure, Form, and Action*, edited by N. Nohria et al. Boston, MA: Harvard Business School Press.

Notteboom, T. 2010. Concentration and the formation of multi-port gateway regions in the European container port system: An update. *Journal of Transport Geography*, 18(4), 567–83.

Notteboom, T. and Rodrigue, J.-P. 2005. Port regionalization: Towards a new phase in port development. *Maritime Policy and Management*, 32(3), 297–313.

O'Connor, K. 1989. Australian ports, metropolitan areas and trade-related services. *Australian Geographer*, 20(2), 167–72

Olivier, D. and Slack, B. 2006. Rethinking the port. *Environment and Planning A*, 38(8), 1409–27.

Pfeifer, R., Bongard, J. and Grand, S. 2007. *How the Body Shapes the Way we Think: A New View of Intelligence*. Boston: MIT Press.

PriceWaterhouse Coopers, PWC Wertewandel an der Wasserkante – von der Terra Incognita zur Urban Waterfront. http://www.pwc.de/portal/pub, 13.10.2010.

Robinson, J. 2002. Global and world cities: a view from off the map. *International Journal of Urban and Regional Research*, 26(3), 531–54.

Sassen, S. 1991. *The Global City: New York, London, Tokyo*. Princeton, NJ: Princeton University Press.

SAUL, Sustainable & Accessible Urban Landscapes 2006. *Vital Urban Landscapes*. The Vital role of sustainable and accessible urban landscapes in Europe's city regions. SAUL, Sustainable & Accessible Urban Landscapes, London.

Saxenian, A.L.1991. The origins and dynamics of production networks in Silicon Valley. *Research Policy*, 20(5), 423–37.

Schumacher, P. 2005. Spatializing the complexities of contemporary business organization, in *Corporate Fields- New Office Environments*, edited by B. Steele. London: AA Publications.

Shane, D.G. 2011. *Urban Design since 1945 – a global perspective.* Chichester: Wiley.

Soja, E. 1989. *Postmodern Geographies: The Reassertion of Space in Critical Social Theory.* London: Verso Press.

Storper, M. 1997. *The Regional World. Territorial Development in a Global Economy.* New York, London: The Guilford Press.

Storper, M. 2009. Roepke lecture in economic geography regional context and global trade. *Economic Geography*, 85(1), 1–21.

Storper, M. and Venables, A.J. 2004. Buzz: Face-to-face contact and the urban economy. *Journal of Economic Geography*, 4(4), 351–3=70.

Taylor, P.J. 2001. Specification on the world city network. *Geographical Analysis*, 33, 181–1=94.

Taylor, P.J., Catalano, G. and Walker, D.R.F. 2002. Measurement of the world city network. *Urban Studies*, 39(13), 2367–76.

Thierstein, A. and Schein, E. 2008. Emerging cities on the Arabian peninsula: Urban space in the knowledge economy context. *International Journal of Architectural Research*, 2(2), 178–95.

Thierstein, A., Lüthi, S. and Hoyler, M. 2011. Introduction: German cities in the world city network. *Raumforschung und Raumordnung*, 69(3), 141–6.

Thierstein, A. and Wiese A. 2011. Attracting talents. Metropolregionen im Wettbewerb um Humankapital. *RegioPol, Zeitschrift für Regionalwissenschaft*, Heft 1+2, 127–37.

Thierstein, A. and Wiese, A. 2012. Diversity as a unique constellation of superimposing network logics. Open House International Special Issue. *Urban Space Diversity: paradoxes and realities*, 37(2).

Thierstein, A., Wiese, A. and Förster, A. 2012. Creative, competitive, attractive. The city lost in transition, in *urbanRESET How to Activate Immanent Potentials of Urban Spaces*, edited by A. Eisinger et al. Basel: Birkhäuser.

Thompson, W. 2007. The city as distorted price system, in *The City Reader*, edited by F. Stout. London: Routledge Chapman & Hall.

Van Geenhuizen, M. and Nijkamp, P. 2009. Place-bound versus footloose firms: Wiring metropolitan areas in a policy context. *The Annals of Regional Science*, 43, 879–96.

Warsewa, G. 2004. *Strukturwandel und Identität - Die europäischen Hafenstädte erfinden sich neu.* Bremen.

Warsewa, G. 2010. Lokale Kultur und die Neuerfindung der Hafenstadt. *Raumforschung und Raumordnung*, 68, 373–87.

Wilson, A. 2002. Alte und neue Identitäten. Zur Typologie der Hafenstädte und der Gefahr ihrer Selbstauflösung. *Werk, Bauen + Wohnen*, 89/56(5), 10–17.

Wirth, L. 1938. Urbanism as a way of life. *The American Journal of Sociology*, 44(1), 1–42.

PART II

PART II

Chapter 6

Hub Cities in the Evolving Internet

Edward J. Malecki

Introduction

The global economy is overseen and controlled from a network of urban centres, a network of world cities. The standard literature thus far on world cities or global cities has given precedence to advanced producer services (APS), including banking and other financial services (Sassen 2001, 2006). Taylor and his collaborators in the Globalization and World Cities (GaWC) project have painstakingly gathered data on the locations of firms in several producer service sectors: accountancy, advertising, banking/finance, insurance, law, and management consultancy (Taylor 2004, Taylor et al. 2011).

World cities are among the 'sticky' places of the global economy – that is, they are able to attract and retain both investment and talented people (Markusen 1996). To function as a world city requires that infrastructures for travel (airports, railway stations, subways) and communications (Internet) be in place and constantly updated. These infrastructures are maintained at the highest levels in large cities with agglomeration economies, and these cities attract offices and facilities of transnational corporations (TNCs) and of APS firms that serve the TNCs. The Internet facilitates flows of data and codified knowledge but also to some degree of tacit knowledge via e-mail, messaging and teleconferencing. It has not completely replaced travel: the Internet is seen as a complement to travel rather than a substitute (Salt 2010). Much of the Internet's infrastructure is invisible to the eye, however, buried underground or in tiny devices (Dodge and Kitchin 2004, Graham 2010). Other parts of its infrastructure – and the focus of this chapter – are massive buildings where data are stored and where networks interconnect.

This chapter examines the phenomenon of Internet interconnection, or peering, of the networks that form the Internet. The chapter utilizes a global data base and focuses on four Internet content giants – Apple, Amazon.com, Facebook, and Google – firms whose decisions matter for millions of users worldwide. All four firms have large data centres and deliver content to users by interconnecting through peering hubs. The locational choice for both data centres and peering hubs are among the important location decisions in the Internet-based digital economy (Malecki and Moriset 2008). As a result of these decisions, some established cities continue to function as Internet hubs, and other cities have emerged as new ones. We look first at world cities as control points, and APS as urban functions. Then, the chapter examines the recent evolution of the Internet toward video and user-generated content and their impact. Empirical data on Internet interconnection, systemwide and of the four giant firms, identify several different corporate geographies.

World Cities and Hub Cities

Managerial control in business services is not confined to London, New York and Tokyo. In investment banking and management consultancy, control is diffused throughout a transnational network of management-level employees and strategic power resides with a relatively large and dispersed group of actors (Jones 2002). Geographically, the actors themselves are located in a large and dispersed set of urban areas. Lists and rankings can be made at any point in time (e.g. Taylor et al. 2011), but they ultimately depend on the mediating élites and the financial and business professionals who collectively form and maintain the networks. Even if cities appear to compete for investment, they do not compete in a zero-sum manner, but must cooperate within global networks. 'It is more about the power to 'run' the networks, to exercise power with rather than over others, than it is about domination and control' (Allen 2010: 2896–97).

Internet services such as Internet exchange points (IXPs) function as a new APS found in (some) world cities to support global firms. Just as some cities have attracted maritime or port-related APS activities (Jacobs et al. 2008; Wiese and Thierstein, this volume)), Internet interconnection has agglomerated in some cities more than in others. Although Internet access is nearly ubiquitous, now spreading even in Africa, it is not present in all cities at a standard attractive to global firms. In addition, finance and Internet infrastructure are co-evolving, with some international financial centres (IFCs) and stock exchanges, such as London, New York and Frankfurt, now attracting the bandwidth and facilities to support low-latency trading. Hibernia Atlantic (2012), for example, operates an 'ultra-low latency' Global Financial Network (GFN) that focuses on 'key financial cities' and 'the financial community, including global broker dealers, hedge funds, and capital markets across the U.S., Canada, Europe, the Pacific Rim and beyond'. Meyer (1998) suggests that the high fixed cost of telecommunications networks and the concentration of their infrastructure at a small number of high-capacity switching nodes seem to require that financial firms locate at – or very near – those nodes. The primary data centres of NYSE Euronext, for example, are located in Basildon, just east of London, and in Mahwah, New Jersey, across from New York City (Rath 2010).

In general, the process of internationalization of the Internet is continuing (Kim 2005). As a result, the formerly US-centric network has become a global network. The Internet, in terms of the number of access/hosting, transit and content providers, is nearly as large in Europe as in North America (Dhamdhere and Dovrolis 2011). Infrastructure also is moving to emerging sources of demand, such as Asia (Malecki and Wei 2009). Two Indian firms, for example, have become global players. The FLAG (Fiberoptic Link Around the Globe) cable system, originally a project of AT&T and KDD (Warf 1998), is now part of Reliance Globalcom, itself part of Reliance Communications. Tata Communications absorbed VSNL as well as both Tyco Global Network and Teleglobe, forming a second Indian powerhouse in global telecom.

Despite the Internet's global reach, there are relatively few *global* studies of the Internet as a differentiated infrastructure. Townsend (2001) identified IXPs through traceroutes, and found a small set of global cities to be Internet hubs. Choi et al. (2006) have compared air transport and Internet networks at a global scale, and Devriendt et al. (2008, 2010) and Tranos (2011) have done the same for cities within Europe. Finally, D'Ignazio and Giovannetti (2007) have examined interconnection at IXPs in Europe, and conclude that interconnection is predominantly random rather than distance-dependent.

The Internet: Old and New

The emergence of the Internet coincided with a number of other disruptions in the telecommunications industry. Digital convergence broke down the distinction between sectors, deregulation changed the ground rules for long-protected monopolies, and waves of mergers and acquisitions transformed the corporate landscape. The result has been a *new ICT ecosystem* (Fransman 2010). The standard model of Internet interconnection has also changed from that of the 1990s, based in universities and research institutes, to one that works within the new ecosystem and the demands of consumers for mobile computing and video content.

The growth of content – and especially video – is altering the geography of the Internet. A key feature of the 'new' Internet is the presence of *content networks* – particularly the 'hyper giants' such as Google – in widespread locations (Labovitz et al. 2010). Web content now frequently embeds video and dynamic advertising, unlike the static web pages of the past, and content delivery networks (CDNs), such as Akamai and Limelight, deliver a great deal of content to users for their corporate customers (Buyya et al. 2008). A CDN delivers content, particularly large files such as video, through a network of servers located close to users, who may have Internet access through any of a number of Internet service providers (ISPs). CDNs are intermediaries, then, contracted by content providers to bring content to users no matter which local ISP they use (Pathan et al. 2008). Mobile Internet, including video, has become the greatest area of growth (West and Mace 2010).

The user-generated content of Web 2.0 and the bandwidth and storage demands of digital video, music, and photos have combined to make three technologies and infrastructures become more important to the functioning of the Internet: first, data centres, where content is stored; second, CDNs to deliver that content reliably, and, third, Internet exchange points (IXPs) to connect the various networks. Therefore, Internet infrastructure now means much more than simply the 'fibre tracks' of networks and cables that link Internet users.

A Brief Overview of Internet Interconnection

The Internet has always been a 'network of networks', with long-haul backbones, national networks, and regional and local networks interconnected to form a global system. Interconnection between networks takes place at IXPs, which have replaced the original network access points (NAPs) of the early US Internet. IXPs also link directly the content networks with the local and regional networks that serve 'eyeballs' of consumers (Faratin et al. 2008, Norton 2011).

Interconnection between two networks can be accomplished by *transit* (a paid customer-supplier relationship) or by *peering* (free exchange of Internet traffic between two equal or peer networks). The traditional understanding of peering has focused on the network service providers (NSPs), or backbone networks (Huston 1999, Crémer et al. 2000). The growing heterogeneity and sheer size of the Internet, as well as the emergence of large content networks, have led to a variety of contract types, including 'paid peering', instead of a simple binary choice between peering and transit (Faratin et al. 2008, Norton, 2011, Valancius et al. 2011). There is now a 'bewildering web of real-world peering relationships' (Rasti et al. 2010: 197). In practice, all interconnection often is referred to as peering, regardless of whether a payment is required (Savageau 2010). Gilmore (2011) points out that peering involves many choices, and it is not free, requiring both operating expense and capital expenditure for equipment and fibre connections.

Private peering emerged as firms chose to avoid the (typically congested) public peering 'fabric' in IXPs. By interconnecting directly in private peering facilities, rather than through the IXP, they were able to guarantee faster, lower latency flows to their customers. Low latency is particularly critical for video (including telemedicine and teleconferencing) and for financial transactions. Public and private peering facilities are frequently located within the same building; a firm can readily decide just how it might choose to interconnect with others – through the 'public fabric' at an IXP, through direct connection with a peer, or both (Titley 2010, Norton 2011). Some firms, such as Equinix, InterXion, TelecityGroup, and Telehouse, were created explicitly to capitalize on providing these choices: public peering, colocation space for private peering, and in many cases data centre space from which content can be distributed throughout the Internet.

The rise of content networks – and their interconnection at strategic locations – is redefining the Internet. This redefinition is changing the traditional hierarchical model to a new structure that is complex, the result of many individual decisions about where to interconnect and with which other networks. This growing complexity means that we cannot always know about all types of connections. One trend is evident: the largest and most global (Tier-1) networks have the most restrictive peering polices, preferring to sell transit and to peer privately outside IXPs (Norton 2011).

Content networks, such as Google, Microsoft, and Yahoo, are now more important than the traditional 'backbone' networks (Labovitz et al. 2010). Google now accounts for 6.4 per cent of all Internet traffic, and has direct peering (i.e. not transit) with more than 70 per cent of all providers around the world. As a result, friction arises between content networks and NSPs: France Telecom believes that Google and other content providers should be billed according to how much traffic they generate on French networks rather than to get free transmission via peering (Rooney 2011).

In the next section, the structure of Internet interconnection is described, along with its growth and change from 2009 to 2011. These trends are elaborated and illustrated with the examples of several prominent networks.

PeeringDB as a Data Source

This chapter utilizes peering data from PeeringDB [www.peeringdb.com], a database of networks, public Internet exchange points, and private peering facilities. PeeringDB is recommended to networks by many involved in peering (Ho 2010, Titley 2010, Levy 2011) and by those who want to peer with Google (Guzman 2008). PeeringDB began in 2004 as a hobby project of Richard Steenbergen, the chief technology officer (CTO) of nLayer, and 'has grown into the largest depository of information regarding interconnection (peering, colocation, contact, etc.) on the Internet' (Gilmore 2010). The number of networks in PeeringDB increased 32.3 per cent – from 1,558 in 2009 to 2,061 in 2010.[1] It is a cooperative venture, 'created by and for peering coordinators'. PeeringDB is maintained by its users; both its administrators and developers are from the peering community (Gilmore 2011). The server hosting the database is located in West Lebanon, New Hampshire, USA (Themecraft.net 2012).

The database distinguishes among several types of networks (Table 6.1). The three largest types are: (1) NSPs, which tend to be global or national backbone networks, (2) networks of cable, digital subscriber line (DSL) and Internet service providers (ISPs), which tend not to peer beyond their market regions, and (3) content networks, which range from small to large and include both content 'hyper giants' such as Google and CDNs.[2] A small number of networks are categorized as corporate, education/research, and non-profit, but the three largest types account for 89.7 per cent of all networks in the PeeringDB data. Also noted in Table 6.1 is the extent of private peering by firms in the database. Private peering represents just over one-half of all interconnections.

Table 6.2 summarizes some key indicators about peering of Internet networks, as recorded in PeeringDB in October 2010. The public IXPs are fewer and larger

---

1   Augustin et al. (2009) attempt to identify all IXPs, and find that PeeringDB is incomplete compared with Packet Clearing House (PCH), but that PCH also contains many inactive or defunct exchanges. Steady additions to PeeringDB over the past two years, however, as well as data on peers, make it preferable as a sole data source.

2   CDNs, delivering content for customers, account for nearly 10 per cent of all Internet traffic (Labovitz et al. 2010).

Table 6.1   Types of networks and the prevalence of private peering, 2010

Network type	Number of networks 2010	Number of peering locations	Private peering (%)
Network service provider	658	5,259	54.9
Cable/DSL/ISP	661	2,804	45.8
Content	530	2,758	51.9
Enterprise	53	194	55.2
Education/research	82	382	33.8
Non-profit	63	378	31.7
Not disclosed	14	11	36.4
All networks	2,061	11,786	50.6

Source: Calculated from data in PeeringDB

Table 6.2   Public peering at IXPs and private peering in the PeeringDB data base, October 2010

	Public (IXPs)	Private facilities
Total number of exchanges/facilities	312	764
Total number of participants	9075	6025
Number of exchanges/facilities with 10 or more participants	122 (39.1%)	141 (18.5%)
Number of exchanges/facilities with 100 or more participants	28 (9.0%)	8 (1.05%)
Participants in exchanges/facilities with 10 or more participants	8,532 (94.0%)	4,674 (77.6%)
Participants in exchanges/facilities with 100 or more participants	5,451 (60.1%)	1,024 (17.0%)

Source: Calculated from data in PeeringDB

than facilities for private peering: the 312 IXPs include 28 IXPs that have 100 or more participants; ten years earlier, in 2000, only one IXP was so large (MAE-East) (Malecki 2002). These 28 IXPs account for 60.1 per cent of all participants in all public Internet exchanges in the PeeringDB data base. A second tier of interconnection hubs includes 122 IXPs that had 10 or more participants and account for 94.0 per cent of all participants in public peering.

Private peering is typically ignored in research on peering for lack of data. Private peering points are 'a type of IXP [but] they are generally not counted in the number of IXPs' (Paltridge 2006: 21). PeeringDB, however, lists the firms present

Table 6.3   Largest Internet exchange points (IXPs) for public peering

Exchange	Exchange full name	City	Participants
AMS-IX	Amsterdam Internet Exchange	Amsterdam	576
NL-IX	Netherlands Internet Exchange	Amsterdam	569
Equinix Ashburn	Equinix Ashburn Exchange	Ashburn, VA (Washington)	520
Equinix Chicago	Equinix Chicago Exchange	Chicago	254
ECIX Düsseldorf	European Commercial Exchange Düsseldorf	Düsseldorf	234
DE-CIX	Deutscher Commercial Internet Exchange	Frankfurt	220
KleyReX	KleyReX	Frankfurt	201
HKIX	Hong Kong Internet Exchange	Hong Kong	196
LINX Brocade LAN	London Internet Exchange Ltd.	London	194
LINX Extreme LAN	London Internet Exchange Ltd.	London	180
LONAP	London Network Access Point	London	178
Equinix Los Angeles	Equinix Los Angeles Exchange	Los Angeles	178
CoreSite - Any2 California	CoreSite - Any2 California	Los Angeles and Bay Area	176
NOTA	NAP Of The Americas	Miami	153
MSK-IX	Moscow Internet Exchange	Moscow	135
NYIIX	New York International Internet eXchange	New York	134
Equinix New York (was: PAIX)	Equinix Internet Exchange New York	New York	126
Equinix Palo Alto (PAIX)	Equinix Internet Exchange Palo Alto	Palo Alto	123
PaNAP	Paris Network Access Point	Paris	122
SFINX	Service for French INternet eXchange	Paris	121

Equinix Paris	Equinix Paris Exchange	Paris	117
Equinix San Jose	Equinix San Jose / Bay Area Exchange	San Jose	113
SIX	Seattle Internet Exchange	Seattle	111
Equinix Singapore	Equinix Singapore Exchange	Singapore	110
NetNod Stockholm	NetNod Internet Exchange i Sverige AB	Stockholm	106
TorIX	Toronto Internet eXchange	Toronto	102
VIX	Vienna Internet Exchange	Vienna	101
SwissIX	Swiss Internet Exchange	Zurich	101

Source: Compiled from PeeringDB, October 2010

in each of 764 private peering facilities (although it does *not* provide peering matrices of who peers with whom). Of 764 private peering facilities in October 2010, only 8 have 100 or more participants or peering networks. The 141 facilities with 10 or more participants (18.5 per cent of the 764 facilities) account for 77.6 per cent of all participants in all private peering facilities. This pattern suggests that private peering is more competitive, provided by a larger number of facilities, and that it is less dominated a small group of facilities.

PeeringDB makes the distinction between public Internet exchanges (IXPs) and private peering facilities. The data for 2010 show that private peering accounts for 50.6 per cent of all peering records. The information on IXPs (which PeeringDB calls public peering exchange points) is relatively limited, reporting only which networks peer there, its autonomous system number (ASN), Internet Protocol (IP) address, and its peering policy (open, selective, or restrictive). More detailed information is offered in the peering listing for each company, which reports the peering point name, IP address, and the speed (Mbit/sec) of its connection there. The information is more limited for private peering facilities, which only lists the facility name and its city but not the bandwidth of the interconnection.

We turn now to the locations of peering, including both public exchanges (IXPs) and private peering facilities. Of the 312 public exchange points listed on PeeringDB in October, 2010, 28 have more than 100 networks that are members or participants, the typical metric for measuring an IXP. In general, cities that have major IXPs also have private peering facilities. In 2000, by this measure, the largest IXPs were still in the United States, followed closely by LINX in London

Table 6.4   Leading private peering facilities, 2010

Facility	Location	Number of participants
Telehouse London (Docklands North)	London	168
Equinix Ashburn (DC1-DC5)	Ashburn, VA (Washington)	153
Telehouse London (Docklands East)	London	131
Ancotel Frankfurt	Frankfurt	126
TelecityGroup Amsterdam 2 (South East)	Amsterdam	116
CoreSite Los Angeles (One Wilshire)	Los Angeles	115
Telehouse Paris 2 (Voltaire)	Paris	112
Equinix Chicago (CH1/CH2)	Chicago	103

Source: Compiled from PeeringDB, October 2010

and AMS-IX in Amsterdam (Malecki 2002). The landscape has shifted: 15 of the 28 largest IXPs are in Europe, 11 in North America, and two in Asia (Table 6.3).

During the past decade, Internet interconnection has shifted away from the early NAPs and toward the facilities of private firms that tend to offer both public and private interconnection (Norton 2011). This shift is particularly marked in the US, where the participants in commercial exchanges are 'customers', not 'members' as in Europe. The cost structure also determines the amount of participation in an IXP. Norton (2011) suggests that US IXPs charge what the market will bear, whereas European IXPs tend to charge nearer to the cost of operations. The very different models of Internet exchanges in Europe and in America at least partly explain why European IXPs have larger numbers of members and much more peering bandwidth.[3]

The 122 private peering facilities with 10 or more networks as participants are located in 43 cities, suggesting an average of three facilities in each city. However, they are agglomerated in a much more restricted set of cities: 69 facilities (56.6 per cent) are located in eight cities, each of which has four or more private peering facilities. Just five cities have 56 (45.9 per cent) of all private peering facilities with 10 or more participants: London (16), Frankfurt (13), and Amsterdam, New York, and Paris (9 each). The general pattern is that cities that have one or more large IXPs also have one or several private peering facilities. The eight cities in Table 6.4 are also sites of large IXPs (as seen in Table 6.3). This suggests that private peering is a complement, rather than a substitute, for public peering. Although

---

3   Three of the original NAPs in the US (MAE Central, East, and West) still appear in PeeringDB, but none with more than three networks peering, one of which is Verizon Business, which now owns them.

Norton (2011) suggests that private peering is much more common in the US, it appears to be prevalent wherever large IXPs are found.

Geographically, the 28 IXPs with 100 or more participants in Table 6.3 are found in 19 urban areas. Only London and Paris have three IXPs; five urban areas have two: Amsterdam, Frankfurt, Los Angeles, New York, and the San Francisco Bay Area.[4] Two large exchanges are in Asia (in Hong Kong and Singapore), while all 26 others are in Europe or North America. Several urban areas have more than the two IXPs preferred or recommended by the peering community (Norton 2009). Indeed, only seven urban areas have five or more: New York (7), London, San Francisco Bay, Paris, Los Angeles, and Tokyo (6), and Washington (5). Chicago, Dallas, and Seattle have 4 each. The cities on this 'short list' of major hubs are the world cities of the Internet (Malecki 2011).

Growth and Change in Peering: A Look at Four Networks

In this section we look more closely at four companies that manage content networks and at changes in the geography of their peering. The networks are: Amazon.com, Apple, Facebook, and Google. Apple was primarily a hardware company until its iTunes store began to sell music for Apple's popular iPod in 2003. The iTunes store also sells applications (apps) for the iPhone and the iPad. Through its products, then, Apple has become a content provider for millions of Internet users. The other three companies have always been content-based, but are moving to provide full 'ecosystems'. Google also now sells mobile phones that use its Android operating system, competing with Apple. Amazon sells not only books but also Kindle e-book readers and tablets, and sells music and rents movies online. Jin et al. (2010) cite Google and Amazon as exemplars of cloud computing. All four firms have built huge data centers to house their content, and these connect to the rest of the Internet through peering connections.

Apple

To store its music, apps, and other content, Apple operates two data centres in California (in Newark and Cupertino), and recently completed a massive data centre in Maiden, North Carolina. It is reported to be planning to build a second massive data centre (adjacent to a new Facebook facility in Oregon) (Miller 2011). Thus, all of Apple's infrastructure is located in the US. Apple also makes significant use of major commercial content delivery networks, particularly Akamai, to deliver software and digital files (Miller 2010b, 2010c). PeeringdB

---

4   The San Francisco Bay urban area here includes San Francisco-Oakland-Fremont metropolitan statistical area (MSA) as well as the San Jose-Sunnyvale-Santa Clara (Silicon Valley) MSA.

data on Apple in November, 2011 show only private peering and only in three locations: in Ashburn, Palo Alto, and San Jose – all major US hubs.

Google

Google is the preeminent 'hyper giant' of the new content-rich Internet, as identified by Labovitz et al. (2010). Google is active beyond its ubiquitous search engine. The firm purchased video site YouTube in 2008, and has consolidated all YouTube activities within Google. Google Earth, Google Maps, Google Apps, and Gmail are major examples of cloud computing (Helft and Hempel 2011). As its services have expanded, Google continues to add not only data centres – currently 39 (Table 6.5) – but also peering locations and, at those peering locations, higher-bandwidth connections.

Table 6.5   Google data centers

USA (20)	Europe (12)	Other Locations (7)
Mountain View, CA	Berlin, Germany	Toronto
Pleasanton, CA	Frankfurt, Germany	Sao Paulo
San Jose, CA	Munich, Germany	Beijing
Los Angeles, CA	Zurich, Switzerland	Hong Kong
Palo Alto, CA	Groningen, Netherlands	Tokyo
Seattle, WA The Dalles, OR	Eemshaven, Netherlands	Singapore (planned) Taiwan (planned)
Portland, OR	Mons, Belgium	
Atlanta, GA (2)	Paris	
Chicago	London	
Miami, FL	Dublin, Ireland	
Reston, VA	Milan, Italy	
Ashburn, VA	Moscow, Russia	
Virginia Beach, VA	Hamina, Finland	
Houston, TX		
Lenoir, NC		
Goose Creek, SC		
Pryor, OK		
Council Bluffs, IA		

Source: Miller 2008a, 2008b, 2008c, with updates to 2011

Google presents a sharp contrast with Apple because it has more peering entries than any other network in the PeeringDB data. Indeed, from September 2009 to October 2011, Google increased its number of peering locations from 98 to 128 (45 public and 53 private to 66 public and 62 private). More importantly, perhaps, is the more than doubling of bandwidth connections at IXPs, from a total of 676,000 Mbps to 1,490,000 Mbps in 2011. The geography of Google's peering locations expanded from sites in 27 urban areas in 2009 to encompass ten new ones in 2010 (Berlin, Düsseldorf, Madrid, Milan, Turin, Warsaw, Moscow, Stockholm, Cape Town, and Kuala Lumpur) and four additional in 2011 (Budapest, Zagreb, Lagos, and Manchester) (Table 6.6). In its corporate geography, Google is a pioneer – or an imperialist – in being the only major firm to locate in India, Malaysia, Nigeria, and South Africa, and in Russia and cities in eastern Europe. Indeed, Google's presence in these cities signals their suitability for foreign investment and encourages local Internet firms (Rose 2011).

Table 6.6   Google: public and private peering locations, 2009–2011

Google	2009	2010	2011
Public peering			
	28 cities *Asia (5):* Hong Kong, Perth, Singapore, Sydney, Tokyo *Europe (12):* Amsterdam, Dublin, Frankfurt, Groningen, Hamburg, London, Moscow, Munich, Paris, Prague, St. Petersburg, Zurich *North America (10):* Atlanta, Chicago, Los Angeles, Miami, New York, Portland, San Francisco Bay, Seattle, Toronto, Washington *South America (1):* São Paulo	37 cities *Africa (1):* Cape Town *Asia (6):* Hong Kong, Kuala Lumpur, Perth, Singapore, Sydney, Tokyo *Europe (18):* Amsterdam, Berlin, Dublin, Düsseldorf, Frankfurt, Groningen, Hamburg, London, Madrid, Milan, Moscow, Munich, Paris, Prague, St. Petersburg, Stockholm, Warsaw, Zurich *North America (10):* Atlanta, Chicago, Los Angeles, Miami, New York, Portland, San Francisco Bay, Seattle, Toronto, Washington *South America (1):* São Paulo	41 cities *Africa (2):* Cape Town, Lagos *Asia (5):* Hong Kong, Kuala Lumpur, Singapore, Sydney, Tokyo *Europe (21):* Amsterdam, Berlin, Budapest, Dublin, Düsseldorf, Frankfurt, Groningen, Hamburg, London, Madrid, Manchester, Milan, Moscow, Munich, Paris, Prague, St. Petersburg, Stockholm, Warsaw, Zagreb, Zurich *North America (10):* Atlanta, Chicago, Los Angeles, Miami, New York, Portland, San Francisco Bay, Seattle, Toronto, Washington *South America (1):* São Paulo

Private peering			
	34 cities *Asia (8)*: Chennai, Hong Kong, Kuala Lumpur, Mumbai, Singapore, Sydney, Taipei, Tokyo *Europe (14)*: Amsterdam, Berlin, Budapest, Dublin, Frankfurt, Kiev, London, Milan, Moscow, Munich, Paris, Prague, Stockholm, Zurich *North America (11)*: Atlanta, Chicago, Dallas, Los Angeles, Miami, New York, Portland, San Francisco Bay, Seattle, Toronto, Washington *South America (1)*: Sao Paolo	37 cities Africa (1): Cape Town *Asia (8)*: Chennai, Hong Kong, Kuala Lumpur, Mumbai, Singapore, Sydney, Taipei, Tokyo *Europe (16)*: Amsterdam, Berlin, Budapest, Dublin, Frankfurt, Kiev, London, Madrid, Marseille, Milan, Moscow, Munich, Paris, Prague, Stockholm, Zurich *North America (11)*: Atlanta, Chicago, Dallas, Los Angeles, Miami, New York, Portland, San Francisco Bay, Seattle, Toronto, Washington *South America (1)*: Sao Paolo	38 cities *Africa (2)*: Cape Town, Lagos *Asia (8)*: Chennai, Hong Kong, Kuala Lumpur, Mumbai, Singapore, Sydney, Taipei, Tokyo *Europe (16)*: Amsterdam, Berlin, Budapest, Dublin, Frankfurt, Kiev, London, Madrid, Marseille, Milan, Moscow, Munich, Paris, Prague, Stockholm, Zurich *North America (10)*: Atlanta, Chicago, Dallas, Los Angeles, Miami, New York, San Francisco Bay, Seattle, Toronto, Washington *South America (1)*: Sao Paolo

Amazon.com

Amazon began as an online bookseller but has evolved into a pioneer in cloud computing services. Amazon Web Services (AWS) allows anyone to use its storage and computing power. Amazon's Elastic Compute Cloud (EC2) services and Simple Storage Service (S3) were among the first to permit not only storage but also access to computer time, which is increasingly used for an array of scientific purposes (Fox 2011).

Amazon's data centres are located in Asia, Europe, and North America but, like those of Google, the majority of them are in the US (Table 6.7). The firm's evolving global geography is seen in its peering locations: Amazon in 2009 peered publicly in just seven IXPs located in five urban areas, only one of which was located outside the USA (Dublin, Ireland). By 2011, Amazon had expanded its public and private peering to 23 IXPs in 17 cities – adding peering in several US cities and Amsterdam, Frankfurt, London, and Paris in Europe and Singapore and

Table 6.7   Amazon data centres

USA (8)	Europe (4)	Asia (3)
Ashburn, VA	Amsterdam	Hong Kong
Dallas	Dublin	Singapore
Los Angeles	Frankfurt	Tokyo
Miami	London	
Newark, NJ		
Palo Alto, CA		
Seattle		
St. Louis		

Source: Miller (2008d, with updates)

Tokyo in Asia. In 2011, Osaka and São Paulo were added as private peering sites (Table 6.8). Like Google, the bandwidth of Amazon's peering connections has also grown, more than quadrupling from 61,000 Mbps in 2009 to 273,000 Mbps in 2011. Alone among the four firms, Amazon does private peering in two mid-size US cities which are not hubs: Jacksonville, Florida and St. Louis, Missouri.

Facebook

Facebook is the youngest of the four companies. Founded only in 2004, it has experienced explosive growth (Stone 2009, Kirkpatrick 2010). Facebook currently accounts for about 9.5 per cent of all Internet traffic, slightly more than Google (Miller 2010a). As Facebook grew, it leased data centres in several key hubs, mainly in the San Francisco Bay area (Miller 2010a). Like its content competitors, however, Facebook has begun to build its own data centres, the first in rural Prineville, Oregon (to be joined by another at the same site), a second in Forest City, North Carolina, and a third in Lulea, Sweden.

Facebook currently leases space in about six different data centres in Silicon Valley. The company has also leased space in three wholesale data centre facilities in Ashburn, Virginia (Miller 2010d).

In 2009, Facebook peered publicly at 12 locations in 10 cities, three of them outside the US (Amsterdam, Frankfurt, and London). A year later, October 2010, public peering had expanded to 13 cities (now including Hong Kong, Singapore, and London as well as Amsterdam and Frankfurt) (Table 6.9). Private peering in 2009 was available at 11 sites in 9 cities (including only Amsterdam and London outside the US), expanding to 16 facilities in 14 cities (five outside the US) in 2011. This could be considered a 'narrow' globalization, focusing on only a small set of global cities. Facebook increased its peering bandwidth nearly sevenfold from 120,000 Mbps in October 2009 to 830,000 Mbps in October 2011.

Table 6.8   Amazon: public and private peering locations, 2009–2011

Amazon.com	2009	2010	2011
Public peering			
5 cities *Europe (1)*: Dublin *North America (4)*: Miami, San Francisco Bay, Seattle, Washington	12 cities *Asia (2)*: Singapore, Tokyo *Europe (1)*: Dublin *North America (9)*: Atlanta, Chicago, Dallas, Los Angeles, Miami, New York, San Francisco Bay, Seattle, Washington	18 cities *Asia (3)*: Hong Kong, Singapore, Tokyo *Europe (5)*: Amsterdam, Dublin, Frankfurt, London, Paris *North America (9)*: Atlanta, Chicago, Dallas, Los Angeles, Miami, New York, San Francisco Bay, Seattle, Washington *South America (1)*: Sao Paulo	
Private peering			
10 cities *Asia (2)*: Hong Kong, Tokyo *North America (8)*: Dallas, Los Angeles, Miami, New York, San Francisco Bay, Seattle, St. Louis, Washington	17 cities *Asia (3)*: Hong Kong, Singapore, Tokyo *Europe (5)*: Amsterdam, Dublin, Frankfurt, London, Paris *North America (9)*: Dallas, Jacksonville, Los Angeles, Miami, New York, San Francisco Bay, Seattle, St. Louis, Washington	19 cities *Asia (4)*: Hong Kong, Osaka, Singapore, Tokyo *Europe (5)*: Amsterdam, Dublin, Frankfurt, London, Paris *North America (9)*: Dallas, Jacksonville, Los Angeles, Miami, New York, San Francisco Bay, Seattle, St. Louis, Washington *South America (1)*: Sao Paulo	

Source: compiled from PeeringDB

Table 6.10 summarizes the four firms and their connections with the Internet. The four firms – all major Internet content networks – represent three distinct Internet geographies: Apple maintains close control over a very small number of data centres and private peering sites – all in the US. Google, at the opposite extreme, is the most global Internet firm, continually adding new infrastructure and connections in new locations. Already global in 2009, Google is the only firm of the four to peer in Africa, and the only one to peer in Asia outside the 'safe' locations (Hong Kong, Singapore, and Japan). Google's footprint in Europe also continues to expand, adding to the Internet ecosystem in Europe that is now larger and more dynamic than in North America (Dhamdhere and Dovrolis 2011).

Table 6.9   Facebook: public and private peering locations, 2009-2011

Facebook	2009	2010	2011
Public peering			
	10 cities *Europe (3)*: Amsterdam, Frankfurt, London *North America (7)*: Chicago, Dallas, Los Angeles, Miami, New York, San Francisco Bay, Washington	13 cities *Asia (2)*: Hong Kong, Singapore *Europe (3)*: Amsterdam, Frankfurt, London *North America (8)*: Chicago, Dallas, Los Angeles, Miami, New York, San Francisco Bay, Seattle, Washington	14 cities *Asia (2)*: Hong Kong, Singapore *Europe (3)*: Amsterdam, Frankfurt, London *North America (9)*: Atlanta, Chicago, Dallas, Los Angeles, Miami, New York, San Francisco Bay, Seattle, Washington
Private peering			
	9 cities *Europe (2)*: Amsterdam, London *North America (7)*: Chicago, Dallas, Los Angeles, Miami, New York, San Francisco Bay, Washington	13 cities *Asia (2)*: Hong Kong, Singapore *Europe (3)*: Amsterdam, Frankfurt, London *North America (8)*: Chicago, Dallas, Los Angeles, Miami, New York, San Francisco Bay, Seattle, Washington	14 cities *Asia (2)*: Hong Kong, Singapore *Europe (3)*: Amsterdam, Frankfurt, London *North America (9)*: Atlanta, Chicago, Dallas, Los Angeles, Miami, New York, San Francisco Bay, Seattle, Washington

Source: compiled from PeeringDB

Between the extremes represented by Apple and Google, Amazon and Facebook, their growth more recent, have been more cautious in their global expansions. Both have kept much of their infrastructure in the US and their peering at established hubs in Asia and Europe. As the older of the two firms, Amazon is creating a more global footprint: it recently added São Paulo as a peering location and has added a data centre there as well. Facebook remains restricted to only three European and two Asian peering hubs.

Conclusions

The global spread of Internet interconnection facilities – public and private – has encompassed a large number of cities, including cities not in the footprints of

Table 6.10   Comparison of the four large content networks

	Amazon.com	Apple	Facebook	Google
Total IXPs 2009	7	0	11	98
Total IXPs 2010	17	0	17	121
Total IXPs 2011	24	0	18	128
Bandwidth at IXPs 2009	61,000	0	120,000	746,000
Bandwidth at IXPs 2010	191,000	0	250,000	1,352,000
Bandwidth at IXPs 2011	273,000	0	830,000	1,489,000
Number of cities where peering at IXPs 2009	5	0	10	36
Number of cities where peering at IXPs 2010	12	0	13	46
Number of cities where peering at IXPs 2011	20	0	14	50
Number of cities where peering privately 2009	10	2	9	34
Number of cities where peering privately 2010	18	2	13	37
Number of cities where peering privately 2011	20	2	14	38

Source: Calculated from data in PeeringDB

the four firms. Such is the agglomeration of facilities and firms, however, that a relatively small number of places act as key hubs in the global network, where public and private peering facilities have agglomerated (Malecki 2011). The established hubs in advanced countries have multiple interconnection sites for public and private peering as well as redundancy of fibre providers. These hubs provide a resilient infrastructure for Internet connectivity. While individual interconnection facilities in such places – such as London, New York, and Tokyo – are certainly vulnerable, these urban regions have enough aggregate redundancy that they could be called resilient hubs. A growing number of other cities, particularly those with a substantial corporate and financial sector presence, have attracted investment in Internet peering infrastructure.

Amazon, Facebook, and Google, although US-based, have added new locations in hubs near major markets elsewhere. Google is more aggressive, adding new locations in potential hubs for the future – and emerging world cities – such as Lagos, Kuala Lumpur, Chennai, and Mumbai. Apple, with few data centres and little peering, appears to be cautious and less-than-global in outlook. However, because Apple has so far chosen to be served by Akamai (perhaps the largest CDN), this means its content is actually provided through dozens of IXPs and private peering facilities.

As Tranos and Gillespie (2009: 433) describe it, 'the Internet has a distinctive geography […] it is not thinly spread and ubiquitous, but rather highly aggregated and geographically differentiated'. This aggregation is seen in the agglomeration of peering facilities and of major networks that connect in them, in major hubs. Thus, we see in the PeeringDB data the pattern of concentration of peering hubs in established places and hints of new places being added by Google, a pioneer in its Internet geography.

References

Allen, J. 2010. Powerful city networks: more than connections, less than domination and control. *Urban Studies*, 47(13), 2895–911.

Augustin, B., Krishnamurthy, B. and Willinger, W. 2009. IXPs: mapped? In *Proceedings of the 9th ACM SIGCOMM Internet measurement conference 2009*, Chicago, Illinois, USA, 4–6 November 2009 [*IMC'09*]. New York: ACM, 336–49.

Buyya, R., Pathan, M. and Vakali, A. 2008. *Content Delivery Networks*. Berlin: Springer.

Choi, J.H., Barnett, G.A. and Chon, B.S. 2006. Comparing world city networks: A network analysis of Internet backbone and air transport intercity linkages. *Global Networks*, 6(1), 81–99.

Crémer, J., Rey, P., and Tirole, J. 2000. Connectivity in the commercial Internet. *Journal of Industrial Economics*, 48(4), 433–72.

Devriendt, L., Derudder, B. and Witlox, F. 2008. Cyberplace and cyberspace: Two approaches to analyzing digital intercity linkages. *Journal of Urban Technology*, 15(2), 5–32.

Devriendt, L., Derudder, B. and Witlox, F. 2010. Conceptualizing digital and physical connectivity: The position of European cities in Internet backbone and air traffic flows. *Telecommunications Policy*, 34(8), 417–29.

Dhamdhere, A. and Dovrolis, C. 2011. Twelve years in the evolution of the Internet ecosystem. *IEEE/ACM Transactions on Networking* 19(5), 1420–1433.

D'Ignazio, A. and Giovannetti E. 2007. Spatial dispersion of interconnection clusters in the European internet. *Spatial Economic Analysis*, 2(3), 219–36.

Dodge, M. and Kitchin, R. 2004. Charting movement: Mapping Internet infrastructures, in *Moving People, Goods, and Information in the 21st Century: The Cutting-Edge Infrastructures of Networked Cities*, edited by R. Hanley. London: Routledge, 159–85.

Faratin, P., Clark, D., Bauer, S., Lehr, W., Gilmore, P. and Berger, A. 2008. The growing complexity of Internet interconnection. *Communications and Strategies*, 72, 51–71.

Fox, A. 2011. Cloud computing – What's in it for me as a scientist? *Science*, 331, 406–7.

Fransman, M. 2010. *The New ICT Ecosystem: Implications for Policy and Regulation*. Cambridge: Cambridge University Press.

Gilmore, P.W. 2010. Inaugural post, *PeeringDB Blog*. [Online]. Available at: http://blog.peeringdb.com/2010_02_01_archive.html [accessed: 29 March 2012].

Gilmore, P.W. 2011. *Peering Strategies: How do Networks Decide?*, presentation at The 2nd Workshop on Internet Economics [WIE'11], San Diego, US, December. Available at: http://www.caida.org/workshops/wie/1112/slides/wie1112_pgilmore.pdf [accessed: 5 March 2012].

Graham, S. 2010. *Disrupted Cities: When Infrastructure Fails*. London: Routledge.

Guzman, J.M. 2008. *Google Peering Policy: Latin America – 2008*, presentation at LACNIC 2008, Curacao, July. [Online]. Available at: http://www.lacnic.net/documentos/lacnicxi/presentaciones/Google-LACNIC-final-short.pdf [accessed: 14 December 2011].

Helft, M. and Hempel, J. 2011. Facebook vs. Google: the battle for the future of the Web. *Fortune*, 164(8) (November 21), 114–24.

Hibernia Atlantic 2012. *The Global Financial Network* (GFN). [Online]. Available at: http://www.hiberniagfn.com/documents/GFN_statsheet_3-2.22.12.pdf [accessed: 29 March 2012].

Ho, R. 2010. *How to build an Internet Exchange in Asia*, presentation at APNIC 29, Kuala Lumpur, March. [Online]. Available at: http://meetings.apnic.net/__data/assets/pdf_file/0011/18893/Peering-Forum_Raphael-Ho.pdf [accessed: 14 December 2011].

Huston, G. 1999. Interconnection, peering, and settlements. *INET'99 Proceedings*. [Online]. Available at: http://www.isoc.org/inet99/proceedings/1e/1e_1.htm [accessed: 14 December 2011].

Jacobs, W., Ducruet, C. and De Langen, P. 2008. Integrating world cities into production networks: the case of port cities. *Global Networks*, 10(1), 92–113.

Jin, H., Ibrahim, S., Bell, T., Qi, L., Cao, H., Wu, S. and Shi, X. 2010. Tools and technologies for building clouds, in *Cloud Computing: Principles, Systems and Applications*, edited by N. Antonopoulos and L. Gillam. Berlin: Springer, 3–20.

Jones, A. 2002. The 'global city' misconceived: The myth of 'global management' in transnational service firms. *Geoforum* 33(3), 335–50.

Kim, B.-K. 2005. *Internationalizing the Internet: The Co-evolution of Influence and Technology*. Cheltenham: Edward Elgar.

Kirkpatrick, D. 2010. *The Facebook Effect: The Inside Story of the Company That Is Connecting the World*. New York: Simon & Schuster.

Labovitz, C., Iekel-Johnson, S., McPherson, D., Oberheide, J. and Jahanian, F. 2010. Internet inter-domain traffic. *SIGCOMM'10*, New Delhi, India, 30 August–3 September 2010, 75–86.

Levy, M.J. 2011. *PeeringDB and why everyone should use it*, presentation at AfPIF-2, Accra, Ghana, August. [Online]. Available at: http://www.isoc.org/isoc/conferences/afpif/2011/docs/martin_levy_hurricane-electric-peeringdb.pdf [accessed: 29 March 2012].

Malecki, E.J. 2002. The economic geography of the Internet's infrastructure. *Economic Geography*, 78(4), 399–424.

Malecki, E.J. 2011. Internet networks of world cities: Agglomeration and dispersion, in *International Handbook of Globalization and World Cities*, edited by B. Derudder, M. Hoyler, P.J. Taylor and F. Witlox. Cheltenham: Edward Elgar, 117–25.

Malecki, E.J. and Moriset, B. 2008. *The Digital Economy: Business Organization, Production Processes and Regional Developments*. London: Routledge.

Malecki, E.J. and Wei, H. 2009. A wired world: The evolving geography of submarine cables and the shift to Asia. *Annals of the Association of American Geographers*, 99(2), 360–82.

Markusen, A.R. 1996. Sticky places in slippery space: A typology of industrial districts. *Economic Geography*, 72(3), 293–313.

Meyer, D.R. 1998. World cities as financial centres, in *Globalization and World Cities*, edited by F. Lo and Y. Yeung. Tokyo: United Nations University Press, 410–32.

Miller, R. 2008a. Google data center FAQ. *Data Center Knowledge* March 27. [Online]. Available at: http://www.datacenterknowledge.com/archives/2008/03/27/google-data-center-faq/ [accessed: 14 December 2011].

Miller, R. 2008b. Google data center FAQ, part 2. *Data Center Knowledge* August 26. [Online]. Available at: http://www.datacenterknowledge.com/google-data-center-faq-part-2/ [accessed: 14 December 2011].

Miller, R. 2008c. Google data center FAQ, part 3. *Data Center Knowledge* August 26. [Online]. Available at: http://www.datacenterknowledge.com/google-data-center-faq-part-3/ [accessed: 14 December 2011].

Miller, R. 2008d. Where Amazon's data centers are located. *Data Center Knowledge* November 18. [Online]. [Available at: http://www.datacenterknowledge.com/archives/2008/11/18/where-amazons-data-centers-are-located/ [accessed: 14 December 2011].

Miller, R. 2010a. The Facebook data center FAQ. *Data Center Knowledge* September 27. [Online]. Available at: http://www.datacenterknowledge.com/the-facebook-data-center-faq/ [accessed: 14 December 2011].

Miller, R. 2010b. The Apple data center FAQ. *Data Center Knowledge* November 22. [Online]. Available at: http://www.datacenterknowledge.com/the-apple-data-center-faq/ [accessed: 14 December 2011].

Miller, R. 2010c. The Apple data center FAQ, part 2. *Data Center Knowledge* November 22. [Online]. Available at: http://www.datacenterknowledge.com/the-apple-data-center-faq-part-2/ [accessed: 14 December 2011].

Miller, R. 2010d. Facebook plans North Carolina data center. *Data Center Knowledge* November 11. [Online]. Available at: http://www.datacenterknowledge.com/archives/2010/11/11/facebook-plans-north-carolina-data-center/ [accessed: 14 December 2011].

Miller, R. 2011. Report: Apple may build near Facebook in Oregon. *Data Center Knowledge*, December 3. [Online]. Available at: http://www.

datacenterknowledge.com/archives/2011/12/03/report-apple-may-build-near-facebook-in-oregon/ [accessed: 14 December 2011].

Norton, W.B. 2009. How many IXes per metro? *Ask DrPeering*, August 27. [Online]. Available at: http://drpeering.net/AskDrPeering/blog/articles/Ask_DrPeering/Entries/2009/8/27_How_many_IXes_per_metro.html [accessed: 14 December 2011].

Norton, W.B. 2011. *The Internet Peering Playbook*. Palo Alto, CA: DrPeeringPress.

Paltridge, S. 2006. *Internet Traffic Exchange: Market Developments and Measurement of Growth*. Paris: Organisation for Economic Co-operation and Development.

Pathan, M., Buyya, R. and Vakili, A. 2008. Content delivery networks: State of the art, insights, and imperatives, in *Content Delivery Networks*, edited by R. Buyya, M. Pathan and A. Vakali. Berlin: Springer, 3–32.

Rasti, A.H., Magharei, N., Willinger, W. and Rejaie, R. 2010. Eyeball ASes: From geography to connectivity. *Proceedings of the 10th Annual Conference on Internet Measurement, Melbourne*. New York: ACM, 192–98.

Rath, J. 2010. NYSE Euronext plans global trading hubs. *Data Center Knowledge* November 30. [Online]. Available at: http://www.datacenterknowledge.com/archives/2010/11/30/nyse-euronext-plans-global-trading-hubs/ [accessed: 30 March 2012].

Rooney, B. 2011. Content providers must pay, says France Telecom. *The Wall Street Journal Tech Europe*, 4 February. [Online.] Available at: http://blogs.wsj.com/tech-europe/2011/02/04/content-providers-must-pay-says-france-telecom/ [accessed: 14 December 2011].

Rose, K. 2011 AfPIF: growing Africa's Internet infrastructure. *IEEE Internet Computing*, 15(6), 94–96.

Salt, J. 2010. Business travel and portfolios of mobility within global companies, in *International Business Travel in the Global Economy*, edited by J.V. Beaverstock, B. Derudder, J. Faulconbridge and F. Witlox. Farnham: Ashgate, 107–24.

Sassen, S. 2006. *Cities in a World Economy*. 3rd Edition. Thousand Oaks, CA: Sage.

Sassen, S. 2001. *The Global City: London, New York, Tokyo*. Princeton: Princeton University Press.

Savageau, J. 2010. The utility and pain of Internet peering, *John Savageau's Technology Topics*, August 9. [Online]. Available at: http://john-savageau.com/2010/08/09/the-utility-and-pain-of-internet-peering/ [accessed: 14 December 2011]

Stone, B. 2009. Is Facebook growing up too fast? *The New York Times* March 29, BU1.

Taylor, P.J. 2004. *World City Network*. London: Routledge.

Taylor, P.J., Ni, P., Derudder, B., Hoyler, M., Huang, J. and Witlox, F. 2011. *Global Urban Analysis: A Survey of Cities in Globalization*. London: Earthscan.

Themecraft.net. 2012. Peeringdb.com. [Online]. Available at: http://themecraft.
net/www/peeringdb.com [accessed: 29 March 2012]
Titley, N. 2010. Peering and network deployment at 10G, presentation at SANOG
12, Kathmandu, Nepal. [Online]. Available at: http://www.sanog.org/resources/
sanog12/sanog12-nigel-peering-at-10gig.pdf [accessed: 14 December 2011].
Townsend, A.R. 2001. Network cities and the global structure of the Internet.
American Behavioral Scientist, 44(10), 1697–716.
Tranos, E. 2011. The topology and the emerging urban geographies of the Internet
backbone and aviation networks in Europe: A comparative study. *Environment
and Planning A*, 43(2) 378–92.
Tranos, E. and Gillespie, A. 2009. The spatial distribution of Internet backbone
networks in Europe: A metropolitan knowledge economy perspective.
European Urban and Regional Studies, 16(4), 423–37.
Valancius, V., Lumezanu, C., Feamster, N., Johari, R. and Vazirani, V.V. 2011.
How many tiers? Pricing in the Internet transit market. *SIGCOMM'11*, August
15–19, 2011, Toronto. [Online]. Available at: http://conferences.sigcomm.org/
sigcomm/2011/papers/sigcomm/p194.pdf [accessed: 14 December 2011].
Warf, B. 1998. Reach out and touch someone: AT&T's global operations in the
1990s. *The Professional Geographer*, 50(2), 252–67.
West, J. and Mace, M. 2010. Browsing as the killer app: Explaining the rapid
success of Apple's iPhone. *Telecommunications Policy*, 34(5–6), 270–86.

Chapter 7

Urban and Regional Analysis and the Digital Revolution: Challenges and Opportunities

Emmanouil Tranos and Peter Nijkamp

Introduction

The current discussion on the importance of Information and Communication Technologies (ICTs) for cities and regions is not something new in the literature. At the beginning of the twentieth century, Britain's hegemony in the world economy was reflected in London's dominance in the global telegraph network and in its role (inter)connecting London with North America and the outskirts of the British Empire (Hugill 1999). Some thirty years ago, Toffler was talking about the emergence of tele-cottages (1980), Hepworth in the late 1980s was analysing the Geography of the Information Economy, and later on, heated debates around the 'death of cities' (Gilder 1995, Drucker 1998 Kolko 1999), the Internet's anti-spatial nature (Mitchell 1995) and the 'death of distance' (Cairncross 2001) occurred more frequently in the relevant literature. A common denominator in this stream of studies was the lack of empirical analysis in support of the policy-related discussion about the pervasive character of ICTs, at least from a spatial perspective.

Indeed, the empirical geographic analysis of ICTs attracted limited interest from geographers, planners and spatial scientists in general. The intangible and technical nature of ICTs is the main reason why this subject stayed out of mainstream research. Economic and urban geographers as well as spatial scientists usually deal with tangible objects, contrary to the elusive nature of ICTs (Bakis 1981, Hepworth 1989, Kellerman 1993). Additionally, the digital infrastructure, just like any other network infrastructure, is fairly invisible when it works accurately and only becomes visible when it stops working (Star 1999). Moreover, the complex technical structure of the digital infrastructure deteriorates the spatial scientists' ability to fully comprehend the topology, structure and design principles of such networks (Kellerman 1993).

On top of the above constraints, the lack of empirical analysis – which prevented researchers from mapping and fully understanding the digital layer which supports the function of cities and regions – may be attributed to the lack of relevant data about the digital infrastructure (supply side) and the use of this infrastructure (demand side). Firstly, because of the private and fragmented nature of digital infrastructure and the derived services, there is no central agency with responsibility for collecting and retrieving data, such as digital connectivity and capacity of cities or telecommunication and Internet Protocol (IP) traffic flows (Kende 2000). Despite the fact that companies which own and manage digital infrastructures, such as Internet Service Providers (ISPs), collect both demand and supply side data for calibrating their networks, such data is not published for competition reasons, a trend which intensified by the private nature of these companies (Graham and Marvin 1996). However, this is not new. Batty in the early 1990s argued that there is no interest in the impact of information flows on cities (Batty 1990), Moss in the late 1980s characterized telecommunications infrastructural networks as a mystery to most cities (1987), and Graham and Marvin (1996) admitted that many city planners were not aware of the telecommunications infrastructure supply in their cities.

Nonetheless, we are currently entering a new era which is characterized by the abundance of digitally collected bottom-up data. Examples of such sources include mobile phone and landline providers for telecommunication patterns and *real time* urban analysis, ISPs for IP communications and Internet infrastructure, transport operators for commuting patterns based on e-ticketing facilities, Web 2.0, participatory Geographic Information Systems (GIS), and virtual social networks etc. The availability of such exciting data sources provides new opportunities and challenges for urban and regional analysis. On the one hand, we are able not only to map the underpinning layers of the digital economy, but also to better understand the way cities and regions function. On the other hand, the analytical tools that spatial sciences traditionally use need to be enriched with methods and concepts developed in other disciplines such as *complexity* and *network science*. The use of toolboxes from such disciplines in combination with new, bottom up, digitally collected data for entire populations will enable spatial scientists to better understand and model the dynamics of the digital economy and its underpinning layers and also to evaluate the efficiency of urban and regional policies.

In total, spatial scientists cannot afford to ignore the digital revolution and the intensification of the digital economy for two reasons. Firstly, new digital phenomena, such as the Internet, have spatial reflections that need to be approached from a geographic perspective. Secondly, the profusion of new bottom-up data derived from digital sources enables the research community to study and quantify traditional geographic questions from a new perspective achieving greater spatio-temporal resolution. In addition, it needs to be noted here that despite the still evident *digital divide* in various aspects of the digital economy between the developed and developing world, the wide penetration of mobile technologies such as (smart) mobile phones, smoothens such divides and at the same time can potentially provide bottom-up data for places that even traditional secondary sources are in scarcity or not trust-worthy. From a policy perspective, such analytical efforts will enable researchers to inform policy makers and to include digital themes in the local policy agenda.

The above two elements are the main focus of this chapter. After providing a background of the digital revolution, this chapter will continue with empirical examples of digital phenomena with spatial reference and traditional geographic phenomena which can be approached with digital data. This chapter ends with some concluding remarks summarizing the 'digital' challenges and opportunities for urban and regional scientists.

The Digital Revolution in Social Science Literature

This section provides the necessary background on the discussion around the digital revolution from a social science perspective. Apart from critically presenting the notion of the digital economy, this section will briefly discuss Castells' seminal work on the space of flows. The latter will enable us to better understand how the digital revolution affects cities and urban networks.

The Digital Economy

The most recent attempt to conceptualize the current economic system is summarized under the term *digital economy*. The latter is usually related with economic transactions taking place in the Internet (Atkinson and McKay 2007). However this is only part of what the digital economy really is. Atkinson and McKay (2007: 7) define it as follows:

> The digital economy represents the pervasive use of IT (hardware, software, applications and telecommunications) in all aspects of the economy, including internal operations of organizations (business, government and non-profit); transactions between organizations; and transactions between individuals, acting both as consumers and citizens, and organizations. Just as 100 years ago the development of cheap, hardened steel enabled a host of tools to be made that drove economic growth, today information technology enables the creation of a host of tools to create, manipulate, organize, transmit, store and act on information in digital form in new ways and through new organizational forms. (Cohen et al. 2001)

The main characteristic of the digital economy is the pervasive character of ICTs in all sectors of the economy. This is the distinctive element in comparison to other conceptual vehicles used to understand the post-industrial economy such as the *information* economy and the *knowledge economy*. The former is linked with specific sectors of the economy. For instance, Porrat (1977) identified the *informational worker* and he developed an inventory with 422 informational occupations based on the US Census of Population workforce classification. Additionally, concepts such as *quaternary employment*, which refers to services 'closely related to the production, processing and distribution of information' (Gottmann 1983: 66) and the *informational sector* were introduced to support the concept of the information economy (Hepworth 1989).

The *knowledge economy*, which is a fairly recent concept, is more widely framed: no explicit knowledge sector was identified and the definition of knowledge-based occupations was also extended out of the service sector (Neef 1998). Knowledge is directly linked to information because 'knowledge is more than information as information is more than simply data' (Malecki and Moriset 2008: 29). The relation between these notions is hierarchical: one place higher in the hierarchy is related with a higher level of sophistication, codification and therefore value. In the same way, Nijkamp and Jonkhoff (2001: 2) identified knowledge as the 'accumulated stock of information based on synergies' contrary to these 'structured flows of data', which form information. Because of the above, knowledge, as a commercialized entity, has become one of the factors of production, in advance of capital and labour (Drucker 1998). According to OECD's (1996: 7) definition, knowledge based economies are economies 'which are directly based on the production, distribution and use of knowledge and information'.

However, such a sectoral definition does not exist for the digital economy. Indeed, the latter refers to the impacts that economy in total can enjoy – mostly through productivity gains – because of the extensive use of ICTs in all aspects of the economy (Atkinson and McKay 2007). In simple words, computers, telecommunications and their combined function known as *infocommunications*, support downstream industries in all sectors of the economy (Malecki and Moriset 2008). This process results in productivity effects, which can be distinguished in *capital deepening* and *total factor productivity* gains (Atkinson and McKay 2007). While the former refers to the fact that increased capital results in increased labour productivity, the latter refers to productivity increases when the same amount of capital is used more efficiently. Additionally, OECD (2003) suggests a third path for expanding productivity gains: the productivity acceleration in the ICTs-producing sector and the expansion of the ICTs-producing sector in the economy. In a nutshell, such productivity gains can significantly affect economic growth.

To sum up, a common characteristic of the above analysed concepts is that they span across the different sectors of the economy and are not limited to the Internet-based new economy (Malecki and Moriset 2008). As explained above, the challenges and changes the post-industrial economic system underwent and is still experiencing are wider than this. Additionally, despite the different starting points, there are overlaps between the three different concepts discussed above, since they approach the same phenomenon from different perspectives: the new techno-economic paradigm of the post-industrial economy. While the first two approaches mostly focus on the soft factors of this paradigm (i.e. information, knowledge and the learning process), the digital economy framework mostly emphasizes the hard factors (i.e. ICTs). However, all the three theoretical concepts agree on the central role of ICTs in this new paradigm. This led Antonelli (2003: 197) to characterize advanced telecommunications services as the backbone of the new economy.

The Space of Flows

From an urban perspective, both the digital revolution and the underlying new techno-economic paradigm are associated with creating drastic social changes. The starting point for understanding these changes is the seminal work of Castells on the *space of flows*. In his work about the *network society* (Castells 1996), he illustrated the emergence of a new spatial form due to the structural transformation that our society is undergoing because of the extensive use of ICTs. He identified this new spatial form as the space of flows and he defined it as the 'managerial organization of time-sharing social practices that work through flows' (Castells 1996: 442). Such flows are the outcome of the digitally enhanced interaction between remote social actors. To better describe this new spatial form, Castells decomposed the space of flows to a three layer system. The first layer can be parallelled with what Batty (1997) identified as the *cyberplace* (Malecki 2002) and consists of the technical network infrastructure, upon which the flows of Castells' network society are transported. This infrastructural layer of communications 'defines the new space, very much like railways defined *economic regions* and *national markets* in the industrial economy' (Castells 1996: 433).

The second layer refers to the nodes and the hubs of the space of flows. These are the real places with 'well-defined social, cultural, physical, and functional characteristics' (Castells 1996: 443). These places – cities in reality – are interlinked through the first – infrastructural – layer of the space of flows. An example of this layer is the global financial network, which consists of specific places around the world where the global financial markets are located. Lastly, the third layer of the space of flows refers to 'the dominant managerial elites' and analyses the spatial organization of these privileged social groups, which are increasingly located in isolated communities, but at the same time in highly connected places (Castells 1996: 433).

While Castells highlighted the importance of the first layer as an underpinning layer of the space of flows, not surprising his analysis was mostly focused on the upper layers due to the data constraints discussed above.

Digital revolution and cities

This new spatial configuration has affected cities dramatically. The development of digital technology has prompted many questions on its space-time trajectories and its socio-economic and spatial implications. It is often argued that the digital world is not a result of technological determinism, but to a large extent a technological response to social and economic needs and challenges. This holds true not only at macro levels (e.g. nations), but also at local and regional levels.

The physical world of urban (infra)structure and transport, and the virtual world of urban communications and interactions, are often regarded as two disjointed domains. Structuralist explanations for the spatial constellations of cities – such as Von Thünen's concentric model or Burgess' ecological lay-out of cities – did not take into account the close interwovenness between the real and the cognitive dimensions of city life. In the past years, the emergence of ICTs has prompted an overwhelming interest in the cyber constituents of modern cities (see e.g. Graham and Marvin 1996, Cohen et al. 2002, Cohen-Blankshtain and Nijkamp 2004, Cohen-Blankshtain et al. 2004, Melody 1996). It turns out that ICTs do not only generate benefits of all kinds for the urban economy, but also act as a driver that shapes novel urban structures and influences its metabolism.

In addition, it is safe nowadays to (re)confirm that geography still matters! Cities are strategic nodal centres in a complex spatial network. The linkage structure in such networks may be both physical and virtual. Despite the 'death of cities' hypothesis, cities have turned out to strengthen their position in a digital world. In most cases, ICT technology has not led to a flat landscape (Friedman 2005), but even more to a 'spiky' landscape (Florida 2005, Rodríguez-Pose and Crescenzi 2008). Geography still matters apparently, while ICTs add only another complicating factor for the locational analysis of people and firms.

Rising agglomeration benefits prompt firms to seek a central location, but the high land rents in cities may stimulate firms to choose more peripheral and low-cost areas, while still having a high – local and global – connectivity through ICT use.

Clearly, distance may lose part of its importance as a major impediment, but agglomeration benefits may grow even faster. Under such circumstances, ICTs may help to reduce the cost of physical movement and hence stimulate more real transport flows.

At a different scale, it is noteworthy that the virtual world has opened up a complex ramification of global linkages between cities, with a surprising variety in intensity and complexity, which calls for novel quantitative geographic network analysis. Before moving to such empirical examples, these global inter-urban links can be approached through the lens of the space of flows. According to Castells (1996: 417): 'the global city is not a place but a process. A process by which centres of production and consumption of advanced services, and their ancillary local societies, are connected in a global network, while simultaneously downplaying the linkages with their hinterlands, on the basis of informational flows.'

ICTs, just like transportation, support this process. ICTs are friction-reducing technologies, because they reduce the cost of distance (Cohen et al. 2002, Cohen-Blankshtain and Nijkamp 2004), enable global interactions by facilitating global economic activity (Malecki and Wei 2009) and finally support the emergence of a world cities network. As Derudder (2006: 2029) emphasizes, 'in a networked context, important cities derive their status from what flows between them rather than from what remains fixed within them' (Allen 1999, Amin and Graham 1999, Castells 2001). Moreover, Smith and Timberlake (2002: 139) identify world cities as the 'spatial articulations of the global flows that constitute the world economy' and Rimmer (1998 p. 439) 'as junctions in flows of goods, information and people rather than as fixed locations for the production of goods and services' (Tranos 2011b). Although geography still matters and cities retained, if not increased, their importance in the frame of the digital economy, what has changed is the importance of global urban interdependencies, the existence of which is, to a great extent, owing to ICTs and the derived socio-economic paradigm.

Examples of 'Digital' Urban Research

Given the importance of the above, the emerging question is how urban and regional analysis and spatial sciences in general can respond to the digital economy and the derived socio-economic changes. As briefly discussed in the introduction section, two paths can be identified. Firstly, digital phenomena have geographic representations. For instance, despite what an average Internet user experiences as a *placeless cyberspace*, the latter depends on *real world's fixities*, which are found on cyberplace (Kitchin 1998a, 1998b, for a discussion about the spatiality of cyberplace and cyberspace see also Devriendt et al. 2008). Secondly, traditional spatial phenomena can be better analysed with the use of digital data. Owing to the extensive penetration of ICTs, a great part of human actions and interactions is channelled through digital infrastructure. For instance, commuting is heavily based nowadays in electronic ticketing and communications are handled by various digital providers such as mobile phone carriers and ISPs. This section provides some examples of research along these lines. Although the list is not exhaustive, it reflects the urban analysis' responses to the digital economy.

Digital Phenomena with Spatial Reflections

Firstly, using the analysis conducted by Tranos and Gillespie, the Internet physical infrastructure is analysed from a relational urban geography perspective (Tranos and Gillespie 2011). Using the highest tier of the Internet infrastructure, identified as the Internet backbone network, the cited paper analyses how European cities are (inter)connected via this infrastructural network. Using methods derived from the network analysis domain, such as different centrality measures, which are then summarized with cluster analysis, this paper discusses the different urban connectivities. The outcome of this analysis is not just another urban hierarchy, but rather an understanding of the new roles cities perform in the digital economy. While cities such as London, Paris, Amsterdam and Frankfurt form the *golden diamond* of the European Internet – with London being always the dominant node, cities such as Vienna, Milan, Budapest, Athens, Lisbon and Palermo have distinctive roles either as hub cities or as gateways to other continents.

The emerging question is if and how cities can take advantage of such infrastructure. From a geographic perspective, we know that the capacity of the digital infrastructure can affect local economic activity (Greenstein 2004). From an economic perspective, it is known that at the macro (state) and micro (firm) level, the Internet improves productivity due to its General Purpose Technology nature. It is a generic technology, which was gradually developed, but once it reached a specific threshold – privatization in this case – was radically expanded across the economy with a huge variety of different applications, creating spillovers which enable the emergence of the digital economy (Tranos 2011b, Lipsey et al. 2005). Such spillovers represent productivity increases in downstream sectors (Helpman 1998, Malecki 2002) which can result in economic growth and development. However, for the above to be materialized, physical digital infrastructure is necessary such as the physical infrastructural layer of the Internet.

Nonetheless, the research community knows little yet about the impact that such infrastructure generates on the meso (urban and regional) level. After performing econometric analysis based on Granger causality tests and panel data, the positive and significant impact of digital infrastructure on regional economic development can be verified (Tranos 2012). However, the latter mostly applies to northern European regions, which are characterized by the necessary *absorptive* capacity to take advantage of such infrastructure. This capacity is related with the sophistication of national and local economies. Just like other traditional types of infrastructure, digital infrastructure is a necessary, but not sufficient factor for economic development in the framework of the digital economy (Gillespie and Robins 1989, Graham 1999, Gibbs and Tanner 1997, Hackler 2003).

Finally, questions emerge of how well we can understand the structure and the topology of digital infrastructure. The complex structure of this infrastructure requires methodological input from other disciplines such as complexity theory and network analysis. After applying complex network analysis methods, the structural characteristics of the Internet backbone network in Europe were revealed (see Tranos 2011b). The analysis depicted the physical constraints affecting the structure of this complex system. Although the Internet and its physical infrastructure appear to be a-spatial, its structure and topology are characterized in reality by significant spatiality. While the golden diamond performs as the core of the European Internet, the connectivity of these cities is not high enough to support the formation of scale-free networks, which are linked in the literature with super-connected hubs. Such quantitative exercises and hard evidence improve our understanding of the nature of this infrastructure, the derived urban roles and the resilience of such systems (Tranos 2011a).

Real World Phenomena Approached with Digital Data[1]

The second stream of empirical examples refers to the use of data from phone communications in geography, which is undergoing a second golden age: while landline phone call data was traditionally used in spatial analysis and fed spatial interaction models to understand intercity relations, nowadays the interest has moved towards data derived from mobile phone communications. Geographers and other spatial scientists have started recently utilizing this new data source to gain new insights on spatial structures, population geography human patterns and interactions at different levels of aggregation in high space-time resolution.

---

1   This work is in collaboration with John Steenbruggen and Henk Scholten

For example, MIT's SENSEable City Lab has examined concentrations of people in a city (Reades et al. 2009), population distribution due to non-recurrent mass events such as pop festivals (Reades et al. 2007), the use of private or public spaces by individuals (Calabrese et al. 2010) and the use of location-based services as a form of insight into complex and rapidly changing spatial phenomena (Ratti et al. 2006, Ratti et al. 2007). Human geographers such as Ahas et al. (2006) studied commuting, but also tourist patterns (Ahas et al. 2007, Ahas et al. 2008). Such data has been also used in mobility studies (Lambiotte et al. 2008, Licoppe et al. 2008) to shed light on the displacement and mobility paradigm (Sheller and Urry 2006). In complexity and network science fields, researchers such as Barabási and his colleagues explored the statistical mechanisms governing the formation of complex networks of human communication in cellular networks. For example, the work of Song et al. (2010a, 2010b) links mobility discussions with statistic physics, while Candia et al. (2008) illustrate individual human dynamics using mobile phone records as the main instrument. Other examples in relevant research fields include Eagle et al. (2009) who analysed spatial friendship network structures and Steenbruggen et al. (2011) in the transport and incidents management field.

The reason behind the recent flourishing of these studies is twofold. Mobile phone penetration has increased dramatically over the last decade: at the end of 2011 there were 6 billion mobile phone subscriptions and global penetration reached 87 per cent (ITU 2011). Due to the nature of such devices and their underpinning technology, data from mobile phone usage can provide insights on various geographic questions, which otherwise would be impossible to quantitatively understand and model. In addition, it seems that we are reaching the point that such data has become available to researchers, not because privacy issues have been largely solved, but mostly because telephone carriers are interested in exploiting the huge pool of data generated by their services for reasons other than network optimization.

To facilitate the discussion on utilizing digital data to capture traditional urban phenomena, a simple example is presented here. This is an explanatory econometric model explaining the relation between urban land use types and mobile phone intensity. The value added by this approach is the fine temporal resolution of mobile phone data. Indeed, the basic input for this model is aggregated data for mobile phone usage at the level of the GSM (Global System for Mobile Communications) cell for the city of Amsterdam, Netherlands. In total the city of Amsterdam is covered by circa 800 GSM cells and the data is available for the period of one month in hourly intervals. This results to a very large dataset, which can provide valuable empirical insights on the temporal variation of the usage of different land use types during the course of a week (i.e. working versus non-working days) and during the course of a day (i.e. different hours of the day). The underlying assumption is that population concentration is highly correlated with mobile phone usage due to the almost universal mobile phone penetration.

In order to capture these temporal effects, three way interaction terms are introduced in model (1):

$$mob_{it} = B_1 X_i * T_t * H_t + B_2 X_i + a_1\ control_i + a_0 + \varepsilon_{it} \quad (1)$$

According to this model, mobile phone activity (mob_{it}) in area i and time t, as depicted by the total volume of mobile usage known as *erlang*, is affected by a vector X_i of land use types interacting with a vector T_t, which distinguishes between working and non-working days, and a vector H_t, which introduces hour-to-hour variability. In addition, the model includes a vector of control variables *control_i* such as the total area of the cell (*area*) and the volume of the build space (*volume*). Such a model exploits the panel data nature of the mobile phone data. Simply put, we consider the dual dimension of the dataset: space and time. In regards to the model estimation, panel data regressions have been used. In more detail, a GLS estimator is employed to estimate (1) as a random effect panel model. Most importantly, first order serial autocorrelation which can be a source of bias in our data, is addressed here with the use of the xtregar module of Stata software. Serial autocorrelation in our case reflects the dependence of the mobile phone intensity in cell i in time t on time $t-1$.

The estimation of this model is presented in Table 7.1. On the vertical axis we can identify the different land use types on working and non-working days and on the horizontal axis the different times of the day are presented. In overall, this regression represents the *heart-beat* of Amsterdam. For instance, we can see that the impact of traffic land use type becomes positive earlier on working days than on non-working days. Similarly, there is a 2-3 hours difference before the impact of residential, business, recreation and nature land use types becomes positive. In addition, we can see that the magnitude of the impact is higher on working days for traffic land use and its variation during these days is also higher. The difference between working and non-working days is marginal for residential areas, but this is not the case for business areas, where the impact is more than double on working days. As these are only preliminary results, more analysis needs to be done for the recreation and nature land use types, as the magnitude of impact is higher than expected. Attention needs also to be paid to potential spatial autocorrelation issues. Nonetheless, the estimations come as no surprise as they reflect the heart-beat of Amsterdam.

Conclusions

The digital revolution has clearly created a type of less visible digital – or cyber – infrastructure that is difficult to understand and imagine in terms of its impacts on spatial development. But in addition, it has prompted a wealth of less visible information and data flows that have a great variety of interaction impacts on human behaviour and on social as well as economic systems. Such interwoven space-time connectivity patterns embody all elements of a complex system, with dynamic changes – sometimes unforeseen - and with a myriad of actors involved. The final outcomes of these complex feed-back and feed-forward systems call for

Table 7.1   Amsterdam's heart-beat using mobile phone data

Hours		00:00	01:00	02:00	03:00	04:00	05:00	06:00	07:00	08:00	09:00	10:00	11:00	12:00
lu. traffic	w.d.	BASE	-0.012 (0.000)***	-0.02 (0.001)***	-0.023 (0.001)***	-0.022 (0.001)***	-0.003 (0.001)***	0.016 (0.001)***	0.03 (0.001)***	0.045 (0.001)***	0.048 (0.001)***	0.045 (0.001)***	0.045 (0.001)***	0.045 (0.001)***
	non-w.d.		-0.012 (0.001)***	-0.022 (0.001)***	-0.024 (0.001)***	-0.021 (0.001)***	-0.014 (0.001)***	-0.004 (0.001)***	0.004 (0.001)***	0.011 (0.001)***	0.017 (0.001)***	0.021 (0.001)***	0.023 (0.001)***	0.024 (0.001)***
lu. residential	w.d.		-0.01 (0.000)***	-0.019 (0.000)***	-0.026 (0.000)***	-0.031 (0.000)***	-0.034 (0.000)***	-0.026 (0.000)***	-0.01 (0.000)***	0.002 (0.000)***	0.008 (0.000)***	0.011 (0.000)***	0.012 (0.000)***	0.012 (0.000)***
	non-w.d.		-0.006 (0.000)***	-0.012 (0.000)***	-0.016 (0.000)***	-0.02 (0.000)***	-0.025 (0.000)***	-0.029 (0.000)***	-0.024 (0.000)***	-0.013 (0.000)***	-0.002 (0.000)***	0.005 (0.000)***	0.008 (0.000)***	0.01 (0.000)***
lu. business	w.d.		-0.008 (0.000)***	-0.015 (0.000)***	-0.019 (0.000)***	-0.023 (0.000)***	-0.022 (0.000)***	-0.009 (0.000)***	0.011 (0.000)***	0.025 (0.000)***	0.032 (0.000)***	0.036 (0.000)***	0.037 (0.000)***	0.038 (0.000)***
	non-w.d.		-0.006 (0.000)***	-0.011 (0.000)***	-0.014 (0.000)***	-0.017 (0.000)***	-0.02 (0.000)***	-0.021 (0.000)***	-0.017 (0.000)***	-0.008 (0.000)***	0.001 (0.000)***	0.007 (0.001)***	0.012 (0.001)***	0.014 (0.001)***
lu. recreation	w.d.		-0.011 (0.000)***	-0.021 (0.000)***	-0.028 (0.000)***	-0.031 (0.000)***	-0.025 (0.000)***	-0.009 (0.000)***	0.008 (0.000)***	0.021 (0.000)***	0.026 (0.001)***	0.026 (0.001)***	0.027 (0.001)***	0.027 (0.001)***
	non-w.d.		-0.007 (0.000)***	-0.015 (0.001)***	-0.021 (0.001)***	-0.027 (0.001)***	-0.027 (0.001)***	-0.024 (0.001)***	-0.015 (0.001)***	-0.004 (0.001)***	0.006 (0.001)***	0.012 (0.001)***	0.016 (0.001)***	0.017 (0.001)***
lu. nature	w.d.		-0.035 (0.002)***	-0.067 (0.003)***	-0.084 (0.003)***	-0.088 (0.004)***	-0.063 (0.004)***	-0.007 (0.004)*	0.045 (0.004)***	0.077 (0.004)***	0.086 (0.004)***	0.088 (0.004)***	0.089 (0.004)***	0.088 (0.004)***
	non-w.d.		-0.021 (0.003)***	-0.04 (0.004)***	-0.059 (0.005)***	-0.07 (0.005)***	-0.085 (0.005)***	-0.077 (0.005)***	-0.038 (0.005)***	-0.005 (0.005)***	0.025 (0.005)***	0.047 (0.006)***	0.054 (0.006)***	0.054 (0.006)***

Table (BASE model)

Hours	13:00	13:00	14:00	15:00	16:00	17:00	18:00	19:00	20:00	21:00	22:00	23:00
Lu. traffic w.d.	0.045	0.045	0.046	0.048	0.048	0.044	0.036	0.03	0.026	0.02	0.012	-0.011
	(0.001)***	(0.001)***	(0.001)***	(0.001)***	(0.001)***	(0.001)***	(0.001)***	(0.001)***	(0.001)***	(0.001)***	(0.001)***	(0.003)***
Lu. traffic w.d.-non	0.023	0.022	0.021	0.02	0.02	0.02	0.02	0.02	0.016	0.012	0.005	-0.009
	(0.001)***	(0.001)***	(0.001)***	(0.001)***	(0.001)***	(0.001)***	(0.001)***	(0.001)***	(0.001)***	(0.001)***	(0.001)***	(0.003)***
Lu. residential w.d.	0.012	0.012	0.012	0.013	0.014	0.014	0.013	0.014	0.015	0.013	0.008	0.009
	(0.000)***	(0.000)***	(0.000)***	(0.000)***	(0.000)***	(0.000)***	(0.000)***	(0.000)***	(0.000)***	(0.000)***	(0.000)***	(0.002)***
Lu. residential w.d.-non	0.009	0.009	0.008	0.008	0.008	0.008	0.008	0.009	0.009	0.007	0.003	0.01
	(0.000)***	(0.000)***	(0.000)***	(0.000)***	(0.000)***	(0.000)***	(0.000)***	(0.000)***	(0.000)***	(0.000)***	(0.000)***	(0.002)***
Lu. business w.d.	0.038	0.039	0.038	0.037	0.035	0.03	0.024	0.021	0.019	0.015	0.01	-0.02
	(0.000)***	(0.000)***	(0.000)***	(0.000)***	(0.000)***	(0.000)***	(0.000)***	(0.000)***	(0.000)***	(0.000)***	(0.000)***	(0.002)***
Lu. business w.d.-non	0.015	0.015	0.015	0.015	0.014	0.011	0.01	0.009	0.009	0.006	0.003	-0.016
	(0.001)***	(0.001)***	(0.001)***	(0.001)***	(0.001)***	(0.001)***	(0.001)***	(0.001)***	(0.001)***	(0.001)***	(0.001)***	(0.002)***
Lu. recreation w.d.	0.027	0.028	0.029	0.031	0.032	0.03	0.024	0.022	0.021	0.018	0.011	-0.008
	(0.001)***	(0.001)***	(0.001)***	(0.001)***	(0.001)***	(0.001)***	(0.001)***	(0.001)***	(0.001)***	(0.001)***	(0.001)***	(0.002)***
Lu. recreation w.d.-non	0.017	0.017	0.016	0.016	0.016	0.014	0.012	0.013	0.013	0.01	0.006	-0.005
	(0.001)***	(0.001)***	(0.001)***	(0.001)***	(0.001)***	(0.001)***	(0.001)***	(0.001)***	(0.001)***	(0.001)***	(0.001)***	(0.002)**
Lu. nature w.d.	0.088	0.088	0.089	0.091	0.092	0.084	0.071	0.07	0.068	0.056	0.035	-0.003
	(0.004)***	(0.004)***	(0.004)***	(0.004)***	(0.004)***	(0.004)***	(0.004)***	(0.004)***	(0.004)***	(0.004)***	(0.004)***	(0.004)***
Lu. nature w.d.-non	0.057	0.055	0.052	0.05	0.051	0.047	0.045	0.051	0.049	0.038	0.02	-0.013
	(0.006)***	(0.006)***	(0.006)***	(0.006)***	(0.006)***	(0.006)***	(0.006)***	(0.006)***	(0.006)***	(0.006)***	(0.006)***	(0.006)***

area	0	(0.000)***
volume	0	(0.000)***
Constant	-0.477	(0.153)***
Observations	371981	
Number of cells	520	

Note to Table 7.1: Standard errors in parentheses; ** significant at 5%; *** significant at 1%; l.u. = land use; w.d. = working days

quantitative, data-instigated data analysis, using the fruit from modern complexity science. Such an analytical approach can provide the necessary tools to empirically support research focusing on the digital revolution from a spatial perspective.

To conclude, this chapter demonstrated the need for spatial sciences to focus more on the digital revolution. The plethora of new digital data – which is a direct impact of the digital revolution - calls towards an *e-regional science* (Tranos 2011a), which will address digital phenomena from a spatial perspective and utilize digital data to approach traditional geographical questions. Such a research direction can provide useful feedback to policy makers and enable them to include 'digital' elements in the local policy agenda. Although ICTs appear to be a black box for urban and regional planners, hard evidences summarized here suggest that digital infrastructure and the digital revolution in general have a place in a regional development policy framework.

References

Ahas, R., Saluveer, E., Tiru, M. and Silm, S. 2008. Mobile positioning based tourism monitoring system: Positium barometer, in *Information and Communication Technologies in Tourism*, edited by P. O'Connor, W. Höpken and U. Gretzel. Vienna: Springer, 475–85.

Ahas, R., Aasa, A., Silm, S., and Tiru, M. 2007. Mobile positioning data in tourism studies and monitoring: Case study in Tartu, Estonia, in *Information and Communication Technologies in Tourism*, edited by P. O'Connor, W. Höpken and U. Gretzel. Vienna: Springer, 119–28.

Allen, J. 1999. Cities of power and influence: Settled formations, in *Unsettling cities*, edited by J. Allen, D. Massey and M. Pryke. London: Routledge, 186–237.

Amin, A. and Graham, S. 1999. Cities of connections and disconnection, in *Unsettling cities*, edited by J. Allen, D. Massey and M. Pryke. London: Routledge, 7–48.

Antonelli, C. 2003. The digital divide: Understanding the economics of new information and communication technology in the global economy. *Information Economics and Policy*, 15(2), 173–99.

Atkinson, R.D. and McKay, A. 2007. *Digital Prosperity*. Washington, DC: ITIF.

Bakis, H. 1981. Elements for a geography of telecommunication. *Geographic Research Forum*, 4, 31–45.

Batty, M. 1990. Invisible cities. *Environment and Planning B*, 17(2), 127–30.

Batty, M. 1997. Virtual Geography. *Futures*, 29(4–5), 337–52.

Cairncross, F. 2001. *The Death of Distance 2.0*. London: Texere Publishing Limited.

Calabrese, F., Reades, J. and Ratti, C. 2010. Eigenplaces: Segmenting Space through Digital Signatures. *IEEE Pervasive Computing*, 9, 936–9.

Candia, J., Gonzalez, M.C., Wang, P., Schoenharl, T., Madey, G. and Barabási, A.-L. 2008. Uncovering individual and collective human dynamics from mobile phone records. *Journal of Physics A: Mathematical and Theoretical*, 41, 1–11.

Castells, M. 1996. *The Rise of the Network Society*. Oxford: Blackwell.

Castells, M. 2001. *The Internet Galaxy*. Oxford: Oxford University Press.

Cohen-Blankshtain, G. and Nijkamp, P. 2004. The appreciative system of urban ICT policies: An analysis of perceptions of urban policy makers. *Growth and Change*, 35(2), 166–97.

Cohen-Blankshtain, G., Nijkamp, P. and van Montfort, K. 2004. Modelling ICT perceptions and views of urban front-liners. *Urban Studies*, 41(13), 2647–67.

Cohen, S.S., DeLong, J.B., Weber, S. and Zysman, J. 2001. *Tracking a Transformation: E-Commerce and the Terms of Competition in Industries. BRIE-IGCC E-conomy Project Task Force*. Washington, DC: Brookings Press.

Cohen, G., Salomon, I. and Nijkamp, P. 2002. Information-communications technologies ICT and transport: Does knowledge underpin policy? *Telecommunication Policy*, 26(1), 31–52.

Derudder, B. 2006. On conceptual confusion in empirical analyses of a transnational urban network. *Urban Studies*, 43(11), 2027–46.

Devriendt, L., Derudder, B. and Witlox, F. 2008. Cyberplace and cyberspace: Two approaches to analyzing digital intercity linkages. *Journal of Urban Technology*, 15(2), 5–32.

Drucker, P.F. 1998. From capitalism to knowledge society, in *The Knowledge Economy*, edited by D. Neef. Woburn, MA: Butterworth-Heinemann, 15–34.

Eagle, N., Pentland, A. and Lazer, D. 2009. Inferring friendship network structure by using mobile phone data. *PNAS*, 9, 15274–8.

Florida, R. 2005. The world is spiky. *Atlantic Monthly*, 296, 48–51.

Friedman, T.L. 2005. *The World Is Flat: A Brief History of the Twenty-First Century*. New York: Farrar, Straus and Giroux.

Gibbs, D. and Tanner, K. 1997. Information and communication technologies and local economic development policies: The British case. *Regional Studies*, 31(8), 765–74.

Gilder, G. 1995 *Forbes ASAP*, pp. 56.

Gilder, G. and Peters, T. 1995. City vs. Country: The impact of technology on location. *Forbes ASAP*, 155(5), 56–61

Gillespie, A. and Robins, K. 1989. Geographical Inequalities: the spatial bias of the new communications technology. *Journal of Communication*, 39(3), 7–18.

Gottmann, J. 1983. *The Coming of the Transactional City*. College Park: University of Maryland, Institute for Urban Studies.

Graham, S. 1999. Global grids of glass: On global cities, telecommunications and planetary urban networks. *Urban Studies*, 36(5–6), 929–49.

Graham, S. and Marvin, S. 1996. *Telecommunications and the city*. London and New York: Routledge.

Greenstein, S.M. 2004. The economic geography of Internet infrastructure in the United States, in *Handbook of Telecommunications Economics*, Volume II, edited by M. Cave, S. Majumdar and I. Vogelsang. Amsterdam: Elsevier, 289–372.

Hackler, D. 2003. Invisible infrastructure and the city: The role of telecommunications in economic development. *American Behavioral Scientist*, 46(8), 1034–55.

Helpman, E. 1998. General purpose technologies and economic growth: Introduction, in *General Purpose Technologies and Economic Growth*, edited by E. Helpman. Cambridge, MA: MIT Press, 1–13.

Hepworth, M. 1989. *Geography of the Information Economy*. London: Belhaven Press.

Hugill, P.J. 1999. *Global Communications since 1844: Geopolitics and Technology*. Baltimore: Johns Hopkins University Press.

ITU. 2011. *The World in 2011: ICT Facts and Figures*. Geneva: ITU.

Kellerman, A. 1993. *Telecommunications Geography*. London: Belhaven Press.

Kende, M. 2000. *The Digital Handshake: Connecting Internet Backbones. OPP Working Paper No. 32*. Washington, DC: Federal Communications Commission, Office of Plans and Policy.

Kitchin, R. 1998a. *Cyberspace*. New York: Wiley.

Kitchin, R. 1998b. Towards geographies of cyberspace. *Progress in Human Geography*, 22(3), 385–406.

Kolko, J. 1999. The death of cities? The death of distance? Evidence from the geography of commercial Internet usage, in *Selected Papers from the Telecommunications Policy Research Conference 1999*. Newcastle.

Lambiotte, R., Blondel, V.D., de Kerchove, C, Huens, E., Prieur, C., Smoreda, Z. and Van Dooren, P. 2008. Geographical dispersal of mobile communication networks. *Physica A*, 387, 5317–532.

Licoppe, C., Diminescu, D., Smoreda, Z. and Ziemlicki, C. 2008. Using mobile phone geolocalisation for 'socio-geographical' analysis of co-ordination, urban mobilities, and social integration patterns. *Tijdschrift voor Economische en Sociale Geografie*, 99(5), 584–601.

Lipsey, R.G., Carlaw, K.I. and Bekar, C. 2005. *Economic Transformations: General Purpose Technologies, and Long Term Economic Growth*. Oxford: Oxford University Press.

Malecki, E.J. 2002. The economic geography of the Internet's infrastructure. *Economic Geography*, 78(4), 399–424.

Malecki, E.J. and Moriset, B. 2008. *The Digital Economy*. New York: Routledge.

Malecki, E.J. and Wei, H. 2009. A wired world: the evolving geography of submarine cables and the shift to Asia. *AAA Geograghers*, 99(2), 360–82.

Melody, W.H. 1996. Towards a framework for resigning information society policies. *Telecommunication Policy*, 24, 243–59.

Mitchell, W.J. 1995. *City of Bits: Space, Place and the Infobahn*. Cambridge, MA: MIT Press.

Moss, M.L. 1987. Telecommunications. World cities and urban policy. *Urban Studies*, 24(6), 534–46.

Neef, D. 1998. The knowledge economy: An introduction, in *The Knowledge Economy*, edited by D. Neef. Woburn, MA: Butterworth-Heinemann.

Nijkamp, P. and Jonkhoff, W. 2001. The city in the information and communication technology age: A comparative study on path dependency. *International Journal of Technology, Policy and Management*, 1(1), 78–99.

OECD. 1996. *The Knowledge-Based Economy*. Paris: OECD.

OECD. 2003. *The Sources of Economic Growth in OECD Countries*. Paris: OECD.

Porat, M. 1977. *The Information Economy: Definition and Management*. Washington, DC: Special Publication 77–12, Office of Telecommunications, US Department of Commerce.

Ratti, C., Pulselli, R.M., Williams, S. and Frenchman, D. 2006. Mobile Landscapes: using location data from cell phones for urban analysis. *Environment and Planning B*, 33(5), 727–48.

Ratti, C., Sevtsuk, A., Huang, S. and Pailer, R. 2007. Mobile landscapes: Graz in real time, in *Location Based Services and Telecartography*, edited by G. Gartner, W. Cartwright and M.P. Peterson. Heidelberg: Springer, 433–44.

Reades, J., Calabrese, F., Sevtsuk, A. and Ratti, C. 2007. Cellular census: Explorations in urban data collection. *IEEE Pervasive Computing*, 6, 30–38.

Reades, J., Calabrese, F. and Ratti, C. 2009. Eigenplaces: Analyzing cities using the space-time structure of the mobile phone network. *Environment and Planning B*, 36(5), 824–36.

Rimmer, P.J. 1998. Transport and telecommunications among world cities, in *Globalization and the world of large cities*, edited by F.-C. Lo and Y.-M. Yeung. Tokyo: United Nations University Press, 433–70.

Rodríguez-Pose, A. and Crescenzi, R. 2008. Mountains in a flat world: why proximity still matters for the location of economic activity. *Cambridge Journal of Regions, Economy and Society*, 1(3), 371–88.

Sheller, M. and Urry, J. 2006. The new mobilities paradigm. *Environment and Planning A*, 38(2), 207–26.

Smith, D. and Timberlake, M. 2002. Hierarchies of dominance among world cities: A network approach, in *Global Networks; Linked Cities*, edited by S. Sassen. New York, London: Routledge, 117–41.

Song, C., Koren, T., Wang, P. and Barabási, A.-L. 2010a. Modelling the scaling properties of human mobility. *Nature Physics*, 6(10), 818–23.

Song, C., Qu, Z., Blumm, N. and Barabási, A.-L. 2010b. Limits of Predictability in Human Mobility. *Science*, 327(5968), 1018–21.

Star, S.L. 1999. The ethnography of infrastructure. *American Behavioral Scientists*, 43(3), 377–91.

Steenbruggen, J., Borzacchiello, M.T., Nijkamp, P. and Scholten, H. 2013. Mobile phone data from GSM networks for traffic parameter and urban spatial pattern assessment: A review of applications and opportunities. *GeoJournal*, 78, 223–243.

Toffler, A. 1980. *Third Way*. New York: William Morrow.

Tranos, E. 2011a. e-Regional Science: why should regional science focus on the digital revolution? *Regional Insights*, 2, 5.

Tranos, E. 2011b. The topology and the emerging urban geographies of the Internet backbone and aviation networks in Europe: A comparative study. *Environment and Planning A*, 43(2), 378–92.

Tranos, E. 2012. The causal effect of the Internet infrastructure on the economic development of the European city-regions. *Spatial Economic Analysis*, 7(3), 319–37.

Tranos, E. and Gillespie, A. 2011. The urban geography of Internet backbone networks in Europe: roles and relations. *Journal of Urban Technology*, 18(1), 35–49.

Chapter 8

Mediating the City: The Role of Planned Media Cities in the Geographies of Creative Industry Activity

Oli Mould

Introduction

The start of this century saw the acceleration in the global recognition of the creative industries as a viable industrial sector and one that has huge potential for economic growth (Flew 2011). Perhaps fuelled by the rapid increase in technological development and the ease at which creative content can be created, modified, delivered and consumed, the creative industries are now seen at 'the apex of the knowledge economy' (Knell and Oakley 2007). Moreover, urban governments have realized the importance of the creative sector in revitalizing urban areas in need of regeneration. The popularity of Richard Florida's (2002) creative class thesis along with the 'creative city' eulogies of Landry (2008) and other self-styled urban 'gurus' has catalysed the uptake of policies that have put creative industry activity and the attraction of creative workers firmly at the centre of regenerative urban policies. Urban governance (notably more so in cities of the Global North however) is now focused on trying to create urban environments that help to foster creativity and innovation by making them attractive places to live, work and play.

One such policy initiative that is gaining in popularity is the construction of so-called 'media cities'. While the term 'media city' is relatively new (and perhaps slightly popularist), they can be defined as large, planned, highly developed urban areas designated specifically to media and creative industry production (in its broadest sense) – although this definition has been subject to evolution. Krätke (2003: 605, added emphasis) in attempting to define 'media cities' suggests that: "'media city' is a term *currently* used to describe cultural and media centres operating at very different geographical levels. They range from small-scale local urban clusters in the media industry to the cultural metropolises of the global urban and regional system'.

In the short period since this was written, the popularity of the media city as a physical urban policy development has mushroomed. Hence, the term 'media cities', has been used to indicate cities in a global network of media industry activity (Krätke 2003, Krätke and Taylor 2004, Watson and Hoyler 2010). However, the usage of media cities in this chapter, while relating to this ideology of global media cities (in that they do indeed contribute to a city's capacity to operate in the media industry internationally), it will refer to the media city as the physical, meta-planned, purpose-built area of media and creative industry production in any given urban locale. A number of examples across the world can be cited, the most recognized being Media City Dubai, DR Byen in Copenhagen, Digital Media City in Seoul and MediaCityUK in Salford. They will often have large office, studio and exhibition spaces (usually at high rental costs), and house auxiliary leisure and cultural services. Other examples of similar developments include TechCity in London and the digital mile in Zaragoza, which focus on digital technological companies rather than media, but have similar planning principles. Also, many cities have large film studios that have been constructed to attract 'runaway film production' from Hollywood (Mould 2008). These areas, including Fox Studios in Sydney and Vancouver Film Studios, but they also share many of the characteristics of the more recently constructed media cities. In all cases however, there is a large area of the city that is given over the multiple buildings and landscaped outdoor areas, designed to cater for and attract national and international creative and media industry companies. They are also often part of a wider urban renewal program which includes other leisure and consumption activities – such as the Salford Quays development surrounding MediaCityUK and the Moore Park area of Sydney which includes Fox Studios as well as two sports stadia.

These media cities, while a relatively new development are already beginning to change to geography of creative industry production globally, for example the British Broadcasting Corporation (BBC) recently moved (i.e. in the back end of 2010 and first half of 2011) approximately 50 per cent of its production capabilities from their base in London's White City to the brand new facility in MediaCityUK located in Salford, Greater Manchester. Other examples from across the world are seeing large, internationally recognized companies re-locate to these media cities to take advantage of the industry specific, often highly technologically capable, facilities on offer. As such, we are witnessing a shift in the global geographies of creative industry activity. This chapter then will explore the characteristics of these media cities and how they are changing the spatialities of national and international creative industry activity, as well as how they are affecting locally, incumbent activity that existed beforehand. Using examples from around the world, but focusing primarily on MediaCityUK in Salford, this chapter will first outline the descriptive characteristics of media cities. Second, the chapter will focus on how they have affected local creative industry activity through engagement with, but also dislocation of pre-existing creative industry companies and freelancers. Finally, the chapter will highlight how media cities have started to shift the geographies of world city connectivity and how this may affect the world city network of media and creative industry activity.

Media Cities – A Foundation

The importance of culture and creativity to urban regeneration is a policy development that has gained popularity in recent years (Peck 2005, Evans 2009). Based largely on the desire to attract the mobile creative class that are often seen as the critical ingredient in regeneration, many urban governments have invested heavily in cultural heritage and/or the creative industries. Many cities have chosen to adopt a sophisticated marketing campaign in order promote themselves internationally. The prefix 'creative' has been used seemingly at will (again, in predominantly Global North cities), with Creative London, Creative New York, Creative Sheffield, Creative Toronto just some of the cities to have used it to an garner international reputation as somewhere that is amenable to creative professionals (Evans 2009). In these instances, it is a city-wide campaign that is the focus of policy and 'on the ground' development, often leading to beautifying specific areas, investing in heritage and in local and regional transport infrastructure (Pratt 2008). However, more recently some local councils and urban officials have been providing an altogether more focused and pragmatic creative industry policy that entails the manifestation of a purpose built cluster of creative industry activity. Media Cities then, as they have become known, are being constructed around the world as councils, often led by private real estate and investment interests, are offering large swaths of their city as potential sites of massive redevelopment. Many cities already had recognizable clusters of creative industry activity mainly due to incumbent businesses recognizing the value of agglomeration and assimilating a cluster over time (Scott 2006). However, these media cities are large-scale, meta-planned, hi-tech media and creative industry facilities designed to attract companies internationally. Goldsmith and O'Regan (2003: 33) noted that the media city has been 'recast as a form of commercial property/industrial park development' which has a primary goal of attracting international business.

While each one is different in style, content and provisions, there are common characteristics that are shared, among the world's media cities, which can be distilled into three areas: technological capacity, diversity of real estate provision and private ownership. Each of these will now be discussed in turn.

Technological Capacity

Part of the mantra of all media cities is to provide the latest 'cutting edge' technological facilities. In terms of both hardware and software, the buildings that constitute these areas will have superfast broadband connectivity in order to transfer the large (often high-definition quality) content. MediaCityUK in Salford boasts broadband speeds of 10 gigabytes, which is needed by many of its tenants, including the BBC who have to transfer high-definition film between Salford and its base in White City in London. The ability to store large amounts of data on-site which can be accessed anywhere across the world is also often a pre-requisite. Cloud computing, file storage and remote digital access are modern data-handling methods used by creative industry professionals. Hence media cities need to cater for this by having large server capacity which often takes up large amounts of square footage (often underground with sophisticated cooling techniques). One such example is where BBC producers based in London will need to virtually 'touch up' animated children's programs made in Salford's studios. Much of the animation is created digitally and requires large software packages to manipulate them (such as Adobe Premier or Final Cut Pro). Previously, many of the changes or enhancements (changing colours, erasing errors etc.) had to be done on-site as the software was too large to be hosted via existing broadband connectivity. But the vast broadband capabilities of MediaCityUK allows for these changes to be made in real time by producers or creative professionals off-site (in London or elsewhere).

As well as the on-site and off-site broadband capabilities, the hardware to make the creative content in media cities needs to be of very high quality. The TV studios, editing suites and radio studios of contemporary usage all require high definition (and in some cases) 3D capabilities, which brings with it very different spatial and equipment needs. For example television studio space needs to be larger with more rigging on the ceiling and room for larger high definition and 3D cameras to move around. The spaces at many of these media cities have been designed specifically with these needs in mind and so, are more accessible for the modern methods of television, radio and film production. Also, many of the outside spaces in media cities have hi-tech provisioning with video walls, interactive screen and smart phone accessibility.

Real Estate Provisions

In order to attract the creative professionals to live as well as work in these media cities, often there will be high specification living accommodation built alongside the creative industry facilities. In most cases, these are high-rise condominium style constructions, often situated on or by a waterfront development. Earlier descriptions of media cities included the presence of these extra-curricular attractions: 'In addition many media cities also include extensive public areas comprising cinemas, concert halls, restaurants, function and conference centres, retail areas, theme parks, studio tours and, in the case of Fox in Sydney, a farmer's market' (Goldsmith and O'Regan 2003: 33).

Also, Copenhagen's media city for example has a purpose built large water feature with multi-story living quarters situated on either side. Salford's MediaCityUK was purposely located in the Salford Quays area as this was the location targeted for regeneration. Waterfront regeneration has been an intrinsic part of urban regeneration policies for some time (Norcliffe et al. 1996) and the attraction of Salford Quays as a site for MediaCityUK includes its waterfront location. As such, high-rise, waterfront facing apartments surround the main MediaCityUK buildings in Salford, with luxury fittings and services on offer. Most buildings will offer concierge services, high-speed broadband, fully fitted luxury apartments, and other services that creative professionals (an identified sub-set of the creative class (Florida 2002)) are thought to require. The proximity to their working environment (no more than a short walk or cycle away) is also viewed as a requirement for this group of workers. The provision of luxury accommodation nearby is a deliberate attempt by the planners of these media city sites to create a 'lived' atmosphere; an area that is not solely for work, but a place where people can see out their leisure time. As mentioned in the introduction, the creative industries are characterized by the high levels of social networking and the fact that much of the industrial learning and knowledge acquisition is done 'outside' of the work environment, in the after-work locations. As such, not only do the planners of these media cities offer luxury living quarters, but also there are hotels, bars, shops and other auxiliary leisure facilities. In Salford's MediaCityUK, the planners have offered building space for a high-end Holiday Inn, and the space for a number of cafés, food outlets and bars to be opened. The provision for this diversity of real estate is then crucial for the planners of media cities as it offers the workers the opportunity to interact socially as well as in the work environment, which is seen as critical to the success of a creative industry community.

Private Ownership

The media cities of the world are clearly seen as key strategic policies by local and national governments. By providing state-of-the-art facilities, they attract large international media companies, but of course, these provisions are extremely expensive. Many of these media cities around the world are owned by wealthy real estate companies, who have been invited by the local authority and governance structures to construct the facilities. However, this results in these areas being privatized, with strict enforcement of exclusion and spatial laws. The company that owns MediaCityUK for example, the Peel Group have strict vendor laws for the 'public square' area of MediaCityUK which prohibits street vendors beyond a certain point. For example, mobile food and beverage sellers are forced to move temporary stalls from one side of the road (which was owned by Peel) to the other (council land). Private security personnel often patrol the outside areas and the restriction of public activities (i.e. busking, begging, street vending etc.) is much higher than in other local council operated land. Often, the outside 'public' areas are highly landscaped with art installations and local transport hubs designed to give the impression of a public environment, which is an attempt to create a more 'relaxed' environment, which in turn is an attempt to stimulate the attractiveness and 'buzz' of the area.

Given these three characteristics of media cities, it is possible to see how they are beginning to represent attractive places for the world's prominent media and creative companies. MediaCityUK in Salford already has the BBC, but ITV (the UK's largest commercial TV channel) is relocating there, as well as many of the country's leading independent TV production companies. In Dubai, Reuters and CNN are already located there, with Disney and HBO looking into the potential of setting up regional bases. Other media cities such as in Copenhagen and Seoul house the national broadcasting corporations as well as a host of other small and medium sized enterprises. As such, these media cities are becoming important spaces of creative industry activity.

Mediating Local Talent?

Literature on the creative industries often extols the virtues of vibrant locally orientated communities of talent or 'creative clusters' (see O'Connor 2004, Cooke and Lazaeretti 2008). The tacit knowledge and shared learning that is embedded in local networks of creative industry practitioners is key to learning the latest trends, obtaining employment opportunities (as many freelancers and project-based workers operate in this manner (Ekynsmith 2002, McRobbie 2002)) and gaining industry 'know-how'. Grabher, when researching London's advertising industry noted how the area of Soho is critical:

> Rather than equating the agglomeration of creative projects in Soho simply with reduced costs of transaction, it provides a vibrant site for 'hanging out', training and thus, gaining access to networks at the peripheries of projects... Through processes of negotiating meaning, these networks act as local interpretive communities which filter noise into signals. (Grabher 2002: 258)

Essentially, the overall 'ambience' of Soho, with its bars, cafés and clubs provide the environment in which advertising professionals learn about the industry and the specific nature of current projects. The area of Soho is perhaps unique in its milieu and how it fosters creative talent in this way, but other cities have similar areas; the fashion industry in Faubourg Saint-Honoré in Paris or the jewellery quarter in Birmingham (Pollard 2004). The fundamental characteristic of these 'types' of clusters is that they have built up over time, gained a critical mass and inertia which has helped sustain the area as a key creative industrial location. Crucially, there has been a distinct lack of planning policy; the growth has been more 'organic' (Scott 2006).

Other examples of creative industry clustering phenomena can be seen in so-called incubator spaces (Turok 2003, Jayne 2004). These are more planned than a Soho-style cluster. They are often purposefully designed spaces that are rented out at relatively low-cost to small-scale creative industry workers (freelancers or small companies) with the specific intention of creating a vibrant, collaborative environment. Often (but not always) they are in re-commissioned older buildings that have been reconfigured. Note, that these are not the same as rentable office spaces in city centres (such as those offered by Regus and the like), in that they are tailored toward companies that require 'creative' spaces such as exhibition rooms for art shows or performance areas. One such example (that is relevant due to its proximity to MediaCityUK in Salford) is Islington Mill. It is located in an old cotton-spinning mill in Salford, and acts as an affordable office and exhibition space for local artists. It houses a number of permanent resident artists and has recording studios and a club facility. It is a privately run enterprise, opening in 2001. These incubator spaces are crucial to the creative industry landscape of a city as they provide the valuable (and affordable) space needed for freelancers and small-scale creative industry companies. These micro-creative clusters can often stimulate local auxiliary activity (cafés, retail etc.), and while remaining relatively small in scale provides that key ingredient, the creative milieu that is needed for micro-business to grow.

Hence, creative industry clusters have traditionally been viewed as small-scale, entrepreneurial and un-planned (by public interventions). Media cities however occupy a much different typology of creative industry cluster. Larger in geographic scale, investment levels and technological capability, they clearly cater for larger clients than ephemeral city centre locations or incubator spaces. Nevertheless, the clustering of creative industry companies in a media city represents another type of agglomerative activity that is changing the geographical characteristics of creative industry activity. To continue with example of MediaCityUK in Salford, since it officially opened, there has been a steady increase in commercial tenants. There is the obvious presence of the BBC, ITV and the School of Media, Music and Performance of the University of Salford, however, some of the peripheral buildings and locations have been taken up by national independent production companies, some of who rely heavily on commissioned work from the BBC. However, also on-site there is a facility known as The Greenhouse, which is designed as an incubator space similar to the Islington Mill. Housing small to medium offices and flexible leases, this space is designed to give the opportunity for smaller scale creative industry companies to locate in MediaCityUK.

Part of the rhetoric of media cities is to stimulate the creative environment which is so critical to the development of a vibrant industry. The way in which these media cities have developed however has created an environment that is qualitatively different to those in other types of creative clusters. As described in the previous section, media cities are typically characterized by high levels of private investment. The real estate company that owns the land demands much higher levels of rent that are found in other creative clusters, rent that is unaffordable to many local creative industry practitioners that wishing to relocate (However, office space targeted directly at this income bracket (such as The Greenhouse in MediaCityUK) temper this process somewhat). The development of MediaCityUK was highly predicated on the BBC's relocation of some of its high profile departments, and with the promise of the creation of over 2,300 jobs (BBC, 2011) for the region. To date however, of the 680 new jobs that have been created thus far, only 16 have gone to local residents of Salford (Hollingshead 2012). Other critiques include local community groups and representatives of the nearby estate of Orsdall who claim that the money spent by the local council to develop MediaCityUK has been diverted from other local services such as bus routes, libraries and schools (Hollingshead 2012).

While its 'success' can be debated and it has been controversial, there is little doubt that it has had a profound effect on the shifting geographies of creative industry production in the region, and the UK as a whole. Already there has been a concentration of the region's main television production companies to the area (BBC North and ITV), with many companies that provide editing, pre- and post-production services moving up from London to MediaCityUK. It is important to note however that television and associated digital media production is one facet of the creative industries. Definitions of the sector by the UK government's Department for Culture, Media and Sport (DCMS) and other politically-orientated bodies (such as NESTA and the Work Foundation) have been attempted in recent years, all with an element of contention (O'Connor 2007, Pratt 2005). However, the role of television and the BBC has always been considered a fundamental activity with the UK's creative industry landscape. As such, MediaCityUK as an institution is already having (and will no doubt continue to have) a pivotal role in national creative industry provisioning. Other media cities around the world that have a longer history have already influenced global and regional media production.

Global Media Hubs

The rise of the media city policy concept and its prominence as a creative industry cluster is clearly an important characteristic, but of equal merit is its relevance in the international network of globalized media production. Put crudely, while they arguably look 'down' (to the local networks of creative industry practitioners), they definitely look 'up' (to attracting international media activity). Previous research on the internationalization of creative industry activity has focused on how there is a global network of media companies, in much the same way as there is a global network of advanced producer service firms, so described by the work of the Globalization and World Cities group (GaWC) at Loughborough University (the most recent work of which is comprehensively detailed in Taylor et al. 2010). The media firms construct a concurrent city network with the 'traditional industries' involved in the world city network theorizations (law, accountancy, advertising etc.). Krätke (2003: 625–6) noted how 'the globally operating media firms are at least as influential as the global providers of corporate services, because they create a cultural market space of global dimension'.

The globalization of cultural goods hence has created a global city network of media providers. The research positing cities in a media industry urban network produces a hierarchy – with New York, London, Paris, Los Angeles, Berlin, Munich and Amsterdam occupying what Krätke (2003) labels as 'Alpha world media city' status. This list is similar to the Alpha cities that occur through the world city network of advanced producer service firms via the work of Taylor et al. (2010). Further research into the global urban network of media industries conducted by Watson and Hoyler (2010) indicates again how New York, London and Paris still occupy the top positions atop the hierarchy of global 'media cities'. Essentially, the previous work on the internationalization of the creative and media industries has painted a picture of a world city network that does not vary significantly from city networks based on other sectors. There are however nuances to this, with a high degree of regionalization, i.e. cities exporting predominately to domestic markets. As such, the media industry is characterized as less globalized than major corporations in other sectors (Flew 2007).

Given the preponderance of the global media urban network to closely align with that of other sectors, will the emergence of media cities have any effect? Will Dubai, Salford, Seoul, Copenhagen and other cities that have recently built a media city start to rise up the hierarchy as they attract more media and creative industry companies? Given the relative novelty of the media city concept, it is too early to fully assess and analyse their changing function to the global media production. However, some initial foundational observations can allude to how the geography is changing in the short to medium term. These observations can be generalized into three broad (and inter-related) changes, namely the rise of the cities from the Middle East and North African (MENA) region, so-called 'second-tier' cities and acute geographical concentration of internationalized production.

Rise of the MENA Cities

Dubai's media city, while perhaps the most prominent, was not the first in the region. There was Jordan Media City built in Amman in 2001 and before that in 1995, Cairo completed its Egyptian Media Production City (Quinn et al. 2004). Currently, Abu Dhabi and Fujairah are constructing similar sites in order to compete with Dubai for media talent. The rush for media cities in the MENA region is arguably a realization of the need for alternative income sources to the oil and gas industry, and the diversification of the industry base (Stanley 2003). Also, the construction and real estate industries in the Gulf States is colossal, with vast amounts of disposal income being funnelled into construction of leisure, hotel and conference facilities. Also, the alleged 'Arab entrepreneurialism', characterized by the CEO-like activity of Arabian royal governments, has predicated an increasingly service-based economy (Bassens et al. 2010). Dubai, therefore has been described by Pacione (2005: 264) as '[an] attractive 'sun–sand–sea' ecosystem [that] has become the leading tourist destination in the Middle East. In addition to hotel, entertainment and retail complexes the city has developed trade centres, conference facilities and theme parks in order to enhance its image as a major leisure-tourist destination'.

Dubai has been characterized by large-scale property developments. 'The World' and 'Palm Jumeirah' are two gargantuan real estate developments where reclaimed land in the Persian Gulf offshore from the main city has been shaped to form luxury housing estates. Also, the recent completion of the tallest building in the world, the Burj Dubai is emblematic of Dubai's wealth and ostentatiousness in the real estate market. Dubai Media City can be seen as an extension of these real estate developments, with the desire to create further facilities for international business and tourism. Another tactic used by Dubai Holdings to attract media companies is to make Dubai Media City a 'Free Zone' where tax credits are offered and 100 per cent foreign ownership is permitted (whereas outside Dubai Media City, foreign investors are required to have an Emiriti co-owner (Quinn et al. 2004, Davis 2006).

Given the contagion of many urban and economic development policies from one UAE city to another, and the intense competition within the region (Bagaeen 2007), is it no surprise that Abu Dhabi and other UAE cities are planning media cities of their own. And, the presence of Amman's and Cairo's offerings creates a MENA regional 'cluster' of media cities. The longevity of the region as a creative industry hub is questionable given two restrictive characteristics. First, there is a tempestuous relationship between media production companies in Dubai and the national governments censorship laws, and the freedom of expression that often characterizes international media production may not be as tolerated in Dubai as in other cities around the world (Quinn et al. 2004). Second, media cities require a mix of provisions for international, but also national and local markets. Watson and Hoyler (2010) have shown how media companies tend to export the majority of their cultural products to their local and regional markets. With only a limited population regionally (approximately 350 million people across all the Arab League countries (United Nations 2009)), there will be a limited demand for the potential over-supply of multiple media cities.

So the rapid pace of media city development in the Middle East region does have the potential to raise its stock as a global player in the media and creative industries. However, the over-supply of large-scale media-orientated real estate coupled with a lack of a vibrant local creative industry to sustain its employment base, the long-term sustainability is questionable.

Second-tier cities

As has been discussed, many of the world's global cities have vibrant creative industry clusters. London, New York, Paris, Los Angeles and Tokyo are all examples of global cities (Alpha cities in GaWC's rankings) that have vibrant creative industry sectors. The diversity of cultural provisions, and the embeddedness of creative professionals into the fabric of specific urban areas (such as London's Soho as described above) are factors in mediating these cities as global creative industry hubs. Many of these global cities will have primacy within their region or nation, and as such have a tendency to attract a disproportionate amount of creative talent from the hinterland. They have cultural and historical 'inertia', i.e. a vibrant milieu that has developed over the long-term, and offers a vibrancy that is not easily replicated in the short-term. London, for example, is often viewed as a magnet for UK creative industry talent (Higgs et al. 2008), leaving many other large cities in the UK implementing policies in order to maintain or attract talent of its own. MediaCityUK's development and the rhetoric of the BBC's move to Greater Manchester is a prime example, but other cities such as Sheffield, Leicester, Birmingham and most recently Cardiff have implemented media city (or the related cultural quarter urban regenerative tool) developments, reminiscent of initiatives outlined by Markusen (1999) as representative of 'second tier' cities. As such, media cities represent an attractive policy initiative for a city that is attempting to compete against another location with high cultural and historical inertia.

Therefore, many of these media cities are situated in (or just outside) these second tier cities. The debate about Salford's position as part of the Manchester city-region is far too complex to visit here, suffice to say that MediaCityUK has developed Manchester's prominence as a city that can boast of its access to creative industry activity. Since it opened, MediaCityUK has seen a steady stream of small and medium sized businesses relocate from other parts of the country (including London), which is slowly increasing the stock of creative, and media industry activity. Also, we have seen above how cities in the MENA region are constructing media cities; and if we utilize the GaWC classification of cities, many of them are classified as Beta and Gamma cities (Taylor et al. 2010). Therefore, they can be said to be located in the 'second tier' of the world's cities (the obvious exception to this is Dubai, which recently went from a Beta-city in 2008 to an Alpha+city in 2010).

It is clear then that there is a role played by media cities in developing a city's economic base and increasing its global competitiveness. The Global Cities of this world (London, New York, Tokyo etc.) will already have a diverse and developed creative industry base, and lack the affordable space to house large studio complexes within the city itself. So these second (or perhaps third) tier cities play host to media cities, but it is worth noting that cities of the Global South are seemingly by-passed by the media city policy phenomena. While Cairo has developed a media city, and Durban in South Africa has positioned itself as a 'film-friendly' city (Goldsmith et al. 2010), the media city policy initiative has not yet been implemented in Global South cities. The cost of developing such a site alone is a major obstacle in constructing a media city, with vast sunk costs including the technological capabilities and auxiliary facilities needed. As such, it seems that the cities with the impetus to build a media city are those with the financial resources to match the ambition to compete for international creative industry activity.

Concentrated Production

Media cities, through the diversity of facilities on offer and the high-speed virtual connectivity are beginning to concertina creative work into more geographically concentrated locations. In order to explain this process however, it is first necessary to understand the 'project-based' nature of creative industry work (Grabher and Ibert 2006). Cultural output from media and creative industries (such as feature films, television shows, digital content, computer games, music etc.) have a highly fragmented production system in all but a few exceptional circumstances. Once a commissioning agent has 'green lit' a project, then a network of creative professionals, ranging from freelancers to large established media firms will work together for the duration of the project, and the disband upon completion. The variety of companies and individuals will vary considerably depending on the project. With feature films a commissioning agents (often a large multinational media firm such as Universal or Time Warner) for example hiring a myriad of professionals such as freelance directors, carpenters, caterers, haulage companies, advertising firms, cinematographers, runners, automobile manufacturers – a whole range of companies and individuals hired to do a particular job temporarily.

Media cities, in their clamour to attract media companies are offering state-of-the-art technology and facilities that will not only attract permanent business residents, but also short-term, project-led work. Each media city clearly has nuances and their own specialized facilities, but as they become more homogenous in their creative industry provisioning, more of the equipment, skills and spaces that are needed to carry out the entire project on site will be available. The BBC's studios at MediaCityUK for example have very malleable features which allow for different parts of specific television with very different spatial and technological needs shows to be filmed in the same studio. Previously, a piece of film which needed to be edited using a particular piece of hardware or someone with a specific skill set may have been sent to another location. Media cities with their range of services allow for it to be sent somewhere else on site. Different companies that often work together that had had to locate in different parts of the city or even in different cities can now co-locate because of the facilities on offer. An example is the company Flix which often works closely with post-production on BBC shows. They relocated to MediaCityUK from Deansgate in Manchester in January 2012. Being on the same site as the BBC and having access to the same super-fast broadband networks clearly attracted Flix to MediaCityUK and with more of the BBC shows they work on being co-located at MediaCityUK, there has been an intense geographical concentration on this particular part of the project network.

This concentration of activity is redolent of creative clusters and the agglomeration of creative industry activity (that has been outlined above) more generally. However it is the level of production that is critical here as often, many large-scale productions (i.e. feature films, and high-budget episodic television dramas) have had to use companies and other agents that are dispersed geographically. Media cities offer the potential for a vast majority of a substantially funded project to be completed on-site, more so than a film studio or an incubator space. For example, the technological capabilities of more top-end computer generated imagery (CGI) companies are often located off-site to major film studios. One of Hollywood's major post-production studios, Industrial Light and Magic (ILM - the credits include the Star Wars films and the latest Transformers movies) is located in San Francisco, not Hollywood. Media cities offer the facilities for both filming and the post-production on the technological scale of ILM to be conducted onsite.

Of course, this is all dependent on commissioning agents choosing to shoot and produce a cultural product in a media city, rather than continue to use their original networks of companies; however, as they continue to develop they will increasingly see the concentration of high-end media production. In sum, they offer the geographical concentration of (national and international) corporatized media production.

Conclusion

There has been a surge recently in the popularity of 'creative city' policies in recent years (Evans 2009, Pratt 2010). Many of the these policies however have been criticized as ambiguous, self-serving and lacking any real understanding of creativity and its ability to rejuvenate struggling urban areas and depressed economies (Peck 2005, Atkinson and Easthorpe 2009). Through the popularization of creative class thesis (Florida 2002, 2005), specific city governments are using creativity as an excuse to develop and justify existing development strategies. Media cities then represent a more 'robust' creative city policy. In other words, those urban governments (Salford, Dubai, Copenhagen, Seoul etc) that have developed extremely expensive media cities have attempted to develop the economic base of their city via specific media and creative industry activity. In this respect, they can be identified as creative city policies that adhere to a more 'realistic' view of creativity. However, given the gargantuan amounts of sunk investment – the infrastructure, the real estate, branding, international advocacy – the (primarily private) owners have tailored these environments for a very specific market, i.e. the international, corporatized creative and media industry companies. Freelancers and SMEs are very prevalent in the creative industries (Higgs et al. 2008), and their importance in maintaining the vibrant and 'collegiate' atmosphere of a creative cluster cannot be overstated (McRobbie 2002, Ekynsmith 2002). By pricing these agents out of a media city environment, the long-term success of a media city as an incubator and stimulus for creative talent is highly questionable. The presence of large, international media companies clearly aids in the economic vibrancy of these areas, and creates an exciting atmosphere of international media production. However, it remains to be seen whether this will translate into the stimulation of local creative industry talent and the legacy of a sustainable creative workforce.

Moreover, many of these media cities, given the large amounts of finance needed to stimulate production, will follow the financialized contours of the world economy. The financial servicing of media production in these media cities is such that much of the revenue and profit streams will remain situated within the 'traditional' world city network articulated by Taylor et al. (2010). Therefore, by extricating a network of media cities from that of the advanced producer service firms network would be to limit the full understand of the complexities of the economic activity. As has been outlined in this chapter, media cities are having, and will continue to have a resounding effect on the international geographies of creative and media industry production. However, the creative industries thrive in areas that can offer a milieu that inspires, engages, conflicts and challenges the status quo. These environments are the imbued characteristics of many cities across the world – time will tell if they can be replicated in media cities.

References

Atkinson, R and Easthorpe, H. 2009. The consequences of the creative class: The pursuit of creativity strategies in Australia's cities. *International Journal of Urban and Regional Research*, 33(1), 64–79.

Bagaeen, S. 2007. Brand Dubai: The instant city; or the instantly recognizable city. *International Planning Studies*, 12(2), 173–97.

Bassens, D., Derudder, B. and Witlox, F. 2010. Searching for the Mecca of finance: Islamic financial services and the world city network. *Area*, 42(1), 35–46.

BBC 2011. *About the Move.* [Online]. Available at: http://www.bbc.co.uk/aboutthebbc/bbcnorth/about.shtml [accessed: 17 February 2012].

Cooke, P and Lazaeretti, L. 2008. Creative cities: An introduction, in *Creative Cities, Cultural Clusters and Local Economic Development*, edited by P. Cook and L. Lazaretti. London: Edward Elgar Publishing, 1–24.

Davis, M. 2006. Fear and money in Dubai. *New Left Review*, 41, 52–72.

Ekinsmyth, C. 2002. Project organization, embeddedness and risk in magazine publishing. *Regional Studies*, 36(3), 229–43.

Evans, G. 2009. Creative cities, creative spaces and urban policy. *Urban Studies*, 46(5–6), 1003–40.

Flew, T. 2007. *Understanding Global Media*. Basingstoke: Palgrave MacMillan.

Flew, T. 2011. *The Creative Industries: Culture and Policy*. London: Sage.

Florida, R. 2002. *The Rise of the Creative Class: and how it's transforming Work, Leisure, Community and Everyday Life*. New York: Basic Books.

Florida, R. 2005. *Cities and the Creative Class*. New York: Basic Books.

Goldsmith, B and O'Regan, T. 2003. *Cinema Cities, Media Cities: The Contemporary International Studio Complex*. Sydney: Australian Film Commission.

Goldsmith, B, Ward, S and O'Regan, T. 2010. *Local Hollywood: Global Film Production and the Gold Coast*. Queensland: University of Queensland Press.

Grabher G. 2002. The project ecology of advertising: Tasks, talents and teams. *Regional Studies*, 36(3), 245–63.

Grabher, G and Ibert, O. 2006. Bad company? The ambiguity of personal knowledge networks. *Journal of Economic Geography*. 6(3), 251–71.

Higgs, P, Cunningham, S and Bakhshi, H. 2008. *Beyond Creative Industries: Mapping the Creative Economy in the UK*. London: NESTA.

Hollingshead, I. 2012. *Media City: Can the BBC save Salford?* [Online: Telegraph]. Available at: http://www.telegraph.co.uk/culture/tvandradio/bbc/9031837/Media-City-Can-the-BBC-save-Salford.html [accessed: 17 February 2012].

Jayne, M. 2004 Culture that works? Creative industries development in a working-class city. Capital & Class, 28, 199–210.

Knell, J and Oakley, K. 2007. *London's Creative Economy: An Accidental Success?* London: Work Foundation.

Krätke, S. 2003. Global media cities in a worldwide urban network. *European Planning Studies*, 11(6), 605–28.

Krätke, S. and Taylor, P. 2004. A world geography of global media cities. *European Planning Studies*, 12(4), 459–77.

Landry, C. 2008. *The Creative City: a Toolkit for Urban Innovators*, 2nd edn. London: Earthscan.

Markusen, A. 1999. *Second Tier Cities: Rapid Growth beyond the Metropolis*. Minnesota: University of Minnesota.

McRobbie, A. 2002. Clubs to companies: notes on the decline of political culture in speeded up creative worlds. *Cultural Studies*, 16(4), 516–31.

Mould, O. 2008. Moving Images: world cities, connections and projects in Sydney's TV production industry. *Global Networks*, 8(4), 474–95.

Norcliffe, G, Bassett, K and Hoare, T. 1996. The emergence of postmodernism on the urban waterfront. *Journal of Transport Geography*, 4(2), 123–34.

O'Connor, J. 2004. "A special kind of city knowledge": Innovative clusters, tacit knowledge and the 'Creative City'. *Media International Australia*, 112, 131–49.

O'Connor, J. 2007. *The Cultural and Creative Industries: A Review of the Literature*. London: Arts Council.

Pacione, M. 2005. Dubai. *Cities*, 22(3), 255–65.

Peck, J. 2005. Struggling with the creative class. *International Journal of Urban and Regional Research*, 29(4), 740–70.

Pollard, J. 2004. From industrial district to 'Urban Village'? Manufacturing, money and consumption in Birmingham's jewellery quarter. *Urban Studies*. 41(1), 173–93.

Pratt A.C. 2005. Cultural industries and public policy: An oxymoron? *International Journal of Cultural Policy*, 11(1), 31–4.

Pratt, A.C. 2008. Creative Cities: the cultural industries and the creative class. *Geografiska Annaler B*, 90(2), 107–17.

Pratt, A.C. 2010. Creative cities: Tensions within and between social, cultural and economic development. A critical reading of the UK experience. *City, Culture and Society*, 1(1), 13–20.

Quinn, S, Walters, T and Whiteoak, J. 2004. A tale of three (media) cities. *Global Media Journal*. 3(5).

Scott, A. 2006. Creative cities: Conceptual issues and policy questions. *Journal of Urban Affairs*, 28(1), 1–17.

Stanley, B. 2003. 'Going global' and wannabe world cities: (Re)conceptualizing regionalism in the Middle East, in *Emerging issues in the 21st century world-system, Vol I: Crisis and resistance in the 21st century world-system*, edited by W. Dunaway. Westport: Praeger, 151–70.

Taylor, P, Ni, P and Derudder, B. 2010. Introduction: The GUCP/GaWC project, in *Global Urban Analysis: A Survey of Cities in Globalization*, edited by P.J. Taylor, P. Ni, B. Derudder, M. Hoyler and J. Huang. London: Earthscan, 1–16.

Turok, I. 2003. Cities, clusters and creative industries: The case of film and television in Scotland. *European Planning Studies*, 11(5), 549–65.

United Nations 2009. *World Population Ageing. Department of Economic and Social Affairs*. New York: United Nations.

Watson, A and Hoyler, M 2010. Media centres in the world economy, in *Global Urban Analysis: A Survey of Cities in Globalization*, edited by P.J. Taylor, P. Ni, B. Derudder, M. Hoyler and J. Huang. London: Earthscan, 40–47.

PART III

PART III

Chapter 9

Agglomeration and Knowledge in European Regional Growth

Teodora Dogaru, Frank van Oort, Dario Diodato and Mark Thissen

Introduction

The Treaty establishing the European Community sets economic and social cohesion as one of the main priorities of the Union. This priority is operationalized by the EU cohesion policy that should promote economic and social progress as well as a high level of employment, and to achieve balanced and sustainable development. Since its inception and the first programming period, the Treaty's text has very often been interpreted as the promotion of convergence among regions, as measured in terms of GDP per head. In a recent discussion, scholars argue that the perspective of per-capita income convergence is actually quite limited, for two reasons (Becker et al. 2010, Montfort 2009, Beugelsdijk and Eijffinger 2005, Magrini 2004, Ederveen et al. 2006). First, income captures only one of the several dimensions of economic development and well-being, especially from the point of view of measuring inequality. Second, regional convergence does not always adequately capture or reflect economic development opportunities. Especially the efficiency goal of cohesion policy is targeted at a full use of a region's potential and economic growth and does not necessarily result in convergence. Diverging growth trajectories and speeds on varying spatial scales due to the existence of agglomeration economies (i.e. advantages of larger urban regions or specialized regions), global urban network effects of spillovers stemming from professional relations, differing strategies for regional economic resilience and technology adaptation, or localized national or regional policies also contribute to these differences (Baldwin and Wyplosz 2009, Capello et al. 2008, Derudder et al. 2011).

The recent discussion on reforming cohesion policy (Barca 2009, Barca et al. 2012) is in line with other reports on place-based development policies in the context of agglomeration economies and economic growth (Worldbank 2009). The discussion highlights the importance of agglomeration for efficiency and economic growth due to an underutilization of potential resources, persistent social exclusion, and the possible detrimental effect if place-based policies inhibit agglomeration in an attempt to influence regional inequality (Thissen and Van Oort 2010). Insight in localized agglomeration economies for growth will contribute to our understanding of effective place-based policies in European regions, but should be complemented by the simultaneously important impact of economic networks on a global scale, especially concerning the knowledge economy (Bathelt and Glückler 2011).

In this chapter, we investigate the contribution of agglomeration economies to economic growth in European regions that received objective-one funds compared to regions that did not. We hypothesize that while employment growth is related to the opening up of new markets and product innovation in a diverse economy, productivity growth links to process improvements in existing markets in economies that are specialized in the production of certain goods and services. The knowledge economy, reflected in localized skills and a higher educated workforce, R&D-expenditures both public and private, and innovation (patent applications), as well as networks of knowledge in inventors and researchers collaboration patterns, is highly instrumental to localized patterns of development in Europe (Westeren 2012). To test this hypothesis, we conduct an empirical analysis on growth differentials over 235 European regions between 2000 and 2010. As our agglomeration hypothesis is confirmed, we argue that the type of agglomeration circumstances and knowledge economic positions in networks, related to the type of growth, is crucial for future long-term development prospects of regions. As we do not explicitly test the knowledge-hub hypothesis on central network locations of regions, we can only be suggestive on it. Relating our agglomeration findings to the existing knowledge network literature confirms the potential of a knowledge-hub hypothesis.

This chapter is structured as follows. The second section summarizes the main arguments for differences in regional growth given by modern agglomeration theories, like the New Economic Geography, Urban Economics and Endogenous Growth Theory. This section ends with our hypothesis on the relationship between agglomeration economies and economic growth in objective-one regions versus other regions in Europe. We pay attention to the hub-function of knowledge centres in Europe that benefit from agglomerated economies (being both specialized and diverse). The third section distils from the empirical literature the variables needed to test our hypothesis in a statistical model, and subsequently introduces and describes the data used. The fourth section presents econometric models for regional growth in Europe. We present models for both productivity growth and employment growth – two main variables of regional economic performance (Van Oort 2007, Henderson et al. 1995). The fifth section draws conclusions, and links the discussion to policy implications for the European Union, network versus locational (place) based development and future research opportunities.

Regional Growth Differentials, Agglomeration Economies and Knowledge Endowments

The recent regional economic development literature has shown a renewed interest in agglomeration economies from the New Economic Geography (NEG) and the related empirical literature on economic geography and urban economics (Puga 2002). Thissen and Van Oort (2010) argue that the main difference between the

NEG proper and related economic geography theories is that the former describes a distribution of economic activity and population resulting in different welfare effects while the latter concerns the implications of different spatial distributions of people and activity for productivity and GDP levels or growth. Both sets of theories share the recently observed trend towards increased urbanization as an outcome.

The new theoretical insights from NEG are in line with the empirical observation that inter-regional disparities in Europe, especially within countries, have grown since the 1980s. The evidence reviewed in Montfort (2009) leads to the conclusion that in the last ten to fifteen years disparities have diminished *among* countries and increased *within* countries. Theories on agglomeration advantages as an explanation for such observed spatial concentration of economic activities are increasingly used in economic geography (McCann and Van Oort 2009). The New Economic Geography describes agglomeration forces leading towards a dynamic and self-enforcing process of increased agglomeration, and higher levels of welfare of the population in these agglomerations. According to the NEG, these welfare effects are generated by a love of variety by consumers and a supply of varieties that increases with the economic size of a region.

The role of knowledge and human capital as a determinant of economic growth has gained greater appeal after its incorporation in economic growth models (Thissen and Van Oort 2010). In these models, knowledge spillovers between economic agents play a crucial role in the growth and innovation process and lead to external economies of scale in production. New technological knowledge is seen as tacit, meaning that its accessibility, as well as its growth spillovers, is bounded by geographic proximity of high-tech firms or knowledge institutions. Also in endogenous growth theory, the generation of new knowledge and innovations is explained by increased investment in knowledge, like research and development (R&D). In this view, it is possible to create a knowledge production function (KPF), with investments in R&D as input and knowledge, and patents as an output. Recent applications at the regional and urban level show that this line of thinking is fruitful for explaining urban growth differentials (Breschi and Lissoni 2009). Knowledge creation and diffusion becomes more global in character – but is attached to certain (top) regions. These regions function as knowledge hubs, as they connect international knowledge networks to regional ones, and provide learning opportunities for local firms (Bathelt and Glückler 2011). Cities can cumulatively specialize in certain kinds of knowledge connected to different economic specializations – serving both regional and international markets (Hoekman et al. 2009).

Regions can only function as knowledge hubs if they are able to capture knowledge and translate it locally in a productive manner. The spatial diffusion of knowledge and its effect on innovation is of major importance to ensure productivity and employment growth of firms and regions, and to improve the welfare of regions. As knowledge is hard to appropriate, it generates benefits to other agents through several spillover mechanisms. Understanding the geographical structures that underlie these spillover benefits is necessary for any evidence-based innovation policy to stimulate Europe's transformation towards a knowledge economy society (Hoekman et al. 2009). The strength of inter-regional knowledge flows is generally assumed to decrease rapidly with geographical distance (Acs 2002), but alternatively, a growing literature stresses that spillovers are embedded in international knowledge-based network relationships, like co-publications in science-based research, patent citations and research collaborations. It has been proven difficult to distinguish between different channels of knowledge spillovers despite the fact that previous research has produced a certain degree of coherence empirically (Fritsch and Slatchev 2007). This has led scholars to rely on specifications that are only suggestive of knowledge spillovers without explicitly modelling the mechanisms through which such spillovers occur in practice. In this chapter we stay close to the conceptualization of regional knowledge endowments that facilitate a good embedding of high-performance (international) firms and refer to the chapter of Bentlage and Thierstein in this volume for knowledge networks as spillover mechanisms.

Both the NEG and economic geography build on this concept of localized externalities or spillovers. Externalities or spillovers occur if the behaviour of a firm increases the performance of other firms without the latter having to pay compensation. Spatially bounded externalities are related to location decisions of firms or individuals within their network. The driving mechanism in agglomeration economies is then that increased size of (urban) agglomerations leads to increased productivity, which will attract more people to migrate to larger agglomerations (Fujita et al. 1999). This in turn will cumulatively cause higher productivity levels and higher economic growth. Naturally, there are also dispersion forces at work, but after a certain threshold of transport costs and freeness of trade has been reached, the strength of agglomeration economies outweighs the dispersion factors.

Most discussions of spatial externalities link to a twofold classification. First, external economies may exist within a group of local firms in a certain sector due to firm size or the existence of a large number of local firms: localization economies. These may occur due to labour pooling, specialized suppliers or (the aforementioned) knowledge spillovers (so-called Marshallian externalities). Second, external economies may be available to all local firms in dense urban areas, irrespective of the sector: so-called urbanization economies. Urbanization economies are often viewed as interchangeable with variety or Jacobs' externalities, but it is also argued that in addition to spillovers occurring between firms within a sector, spillovers can also occur between sectors, aside from urbanization per se (Frenken et al. 2007).

The empirical evidence of agglomeration economies is strong, and in an overview paper by Rosenthal and Strange (2004) it is shown that a doubling in the size of an agglomeration leads to an increase in productivity between 3 and 11 per cent. Melo et al. (2009), using a sample of 34 studies on agglomeration economies for 729 estimated values of elasticity, find a variation up to 29 per cent. In another meta-analysis considering 31 studies, de Groot et al. (2009) conclude that the theory provides 'strong indications for sectoral, temporal and spatial heterogeneity'. Beaudry and Schiffauerova (2009) confirm this view in their extensive - qualitative - overview of most recent agglomeration studies. Determining factors appear to include the spatial unit of analysis, the measurement of localized growth, the time frame of analysis, and the number and detail of economic sectors included in the analysis. This heterogeneity in research outcomes is not encouraging for agglomeration research. A renewed conceptual focus, on life-cycles of firms and industries, and on evolutionary economic development, may be a way out of this ambiguity (Van Oort and Lambooy 2012).

An interesting theoretical contribution to the specialization-variety debate has been provided by lifecycle theory, which holds that industry evolution is characterized by product innovation in the first stage and process innovation in a second stage (Saviotti 1996). Following this two-stage logic, Pasinetti (1993) explains growth as a combination of structural change caused by process innovation within existing sectors and product innovation leading to new sectors. Two consequences arise from this: growth in variety is a necessary requirement for long-term economic development; and growth in variety inducing productivity growth and new sectors, are endogenous aspects of economic development. This distinction does not imply that product innovation occurs exclusively at the time of birth of a new industry with process innovation taking only occurring thereafter. Rather, product lifecycle theory assumes product innovation peaks before process innovation peaks (Abernathy and Clark 1985). In a geographical framework this translates into new lifecycles starting in urban environments and which move to more rural environments over time (Vernon 1966). The knowledge of the urban labour force, capital services, and product markets in urban environments foster the incubator function for starting firms (Duranton and Puga 2006). In accordance with the economics of agglomeration, evolutionary economists also stress the important role of variety to create new varieties. In other words, Jacobs' externalities are assumed to play an important role in urban areas in creating new varieties, new sectors and employment growth. When firms survive and become mature, they tend to standardize production and become more capital-intensive and productive. The initial advantages of the urban agglomeration core can now become disadvantages: growth is difficult to realize *in situ* and physical movement becomes opportune when limited accessibility and high wages become disadvantageous. Growing firms are expected to 'filter down' towards more peripheral locations and regions where land, labour and transport costs are lower. This reasoning lies behind the notion of an 'urban product lifecycle' that new products are developed in large diverse metropolitan areas with a diversified skill base, but that mature firms eventually move to more peripheral regions.

In Europe, this filtering down process might have taken place on a larger scale: from the economic core regions to the peripheral objective-one regions. We will therefore test in our empirical analysis whether employment growth is related to a diverse economy in regions, while productivity growth positively relates to specialized regions. As objective-one regions are in general much more specialized than non-objective-one regions (Combes and Overman 2004), we expect the specialization-productivity thesis to especially hold in those regions, while the diversified-employment growth relation is expected to hold especially in non-objective-one regions. Simultaneously, we hypothesize that high levels of knowledge endowment enhance the network position of regions in knowledge networks. Given the unequal ('spiky') distribution of knowledge hubs in the world (Florida 2005), it can be hypothesized that larger Western-European knowledge cities (housing top universities and multinational corporations) as well as the capital cities of Eastern-European countries play a significant role in these networks. Besides the diversity/specialization-agglomeration debate, we therefore also explicitly look at the knowledge economy variables of R&D and higher education.

Data and Variables used in Modelling

According to the literature, many factors can contribute to employment and productivity growth in regions and cities. Overviews can be found in Capello et al. (2008), Combes and Overman (2004), Crespo-Cuaresma et al. (2009) and Rodrigues-Pose and Tselios (2010). Our empirical analysis uses data on 235 NUTS2-regions for Austria, Belgium, the Czech Republic, Germany, Denmark, Spain, Finland, France, Greece, Hungary, Ireland, Italy, The Netherlands, Poland, Portugal, Romania, Sweden, Slovakia and the United Kingdom.[1] 92 regions receive objective-one funding in the period 2000–2006, 135 regions do not. The 8 Romanian regions received pre-accession funds, which we treated as objective-one funding. The explanatory variables we introduce in our model are summarized in Table 9.1. This table presents summary statistics, and correlations between the variables. We will present and discuss them, together with their hypothesized sign, in more detail.

Employment and labour productivity[2] (output per employee) data are obtained from the Cambridge Econometrics statistical database on European regions. From the Cambridge Econometrics dataset, we took the data for 2000 and 2010. For this period we are able to link Objective-one funding to regions, including the pre-accession funds for Romania. Further research should also focus on other periods of analysis. Productivity growth and employment growth are defined as $\ln(emp_{2010}/emp_{2000})$ and $\ln(prod_{2010}/prod_{2000})$, in order to normalize its distributions. Figure 9.1 shows the distribution of productivity growth and employment growth respectively over the regions in our analysis.

The largest growth rates are in the eastern European regions, especially in Poland, Hungary, Slovakia and Romania. Also Greek regions show a considerable growth in productivity (due to a smaller decrease in output than the decrease in employment). Outside the eastern European countries, regions that show relative high productivity growth rates are Dublin, Bordeaux, Utrecht in the Netherlands, regions in southern Germany and Scandinavia.

---

1   For reasons of optimal data comparability, small modifications were made to the regional divisions in Belgium, Sweden and the UK (Scotland). Data from regions in Norway, Switzerland and Luxemburg are missing for the trade-related data.

2   Due to data limitations we cannot analyze total factor productivity growth.

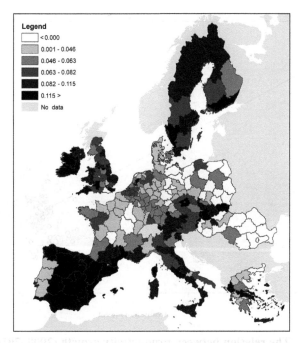

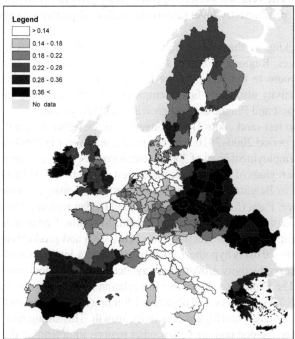

Figure 9.1 **Productivity growth and employment growth 2000–2010 in European regions**

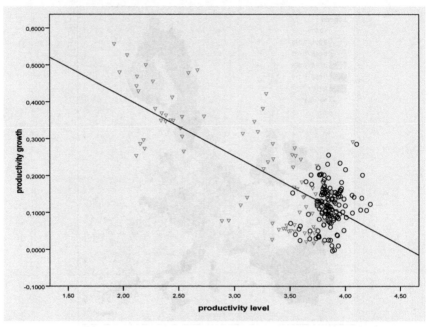

Figure 9.2   The relation between productivity growth (2000–2010) and productivity level (2000) (triangles: objective-one regions)

When looking at the growth figures in terms of employment, a different pattern emerges. Regions in Spain, Ireland, Italy, Austria and Scandinavia now particularly come to the fore. Only a few eastern European regions that grow fast in productivity also grow fast in employment. Especially the capital regions around Budapest and Prague are fast growing in employment.

In order to test (and control) for convergence, we relate regional productivity growth in the period 2000–2010 with the *productivity level* in 2000 (and similarly, we relate the employment level of 2000 to employment growth). In general, the 'old' economic core regions of Europe have the highest productivity levels: a band ranging from London to Belgium, the Netherlands, Western Germany, Northern Italy and Western France, Paris (Ile-de-France) and Scandinavian regions. The lowest score are in the eastern European regions of Poland, Slovakia, Romania and Hungary. The relationship between productivity level (in 2000) and productivity growth (in the period 2000–2010) is hypothesized to be negative: a lower level of productivity leads to higher productivity growth: convergence. Figure 9.2 confirms this negative relationship. The figure also shows that this relation is especially determined by the scores of the regions that received objective 1 funding in the period 2000–2006, with low productivity levels and high productivity growth. This strong relation confirms that using objective-one regions versus other regions to determine the relationship between the explanatory variables (among which the degree of specialization and sectoral diversity) and productivity growth is potentially useful.

The relation between employment level in 2000 in the 235 regions and employment growth in the period 2000–2010 in the same regions is less profoundly negative than that of productivity and productivity growth. Also, the distinction between objective-one region and non-objective-one regions is less clear for employment.

All other explanatory variables in our models for employment and productivity growth are measured for the year 2000, because of endogeneity reasons. The circumstance in 2000 can cause subsequent growth in the period 2000–2010, but the circumstances in 2010 cannot. Moreover, the growth in the period 2000–2010 may in turn affect the circumstances in all the years over the period 2000–2010. Therefore we measured all explanatory variables for the year 2000. *Investments in private and public research and development (R&D)* are calculated as percentages of GDP from Eurostat statistics. These investments in innovation are hypothesized to positively relate to economic growth (Moreno et al 2006). Private R&D investments (its regional pattern is shown in Figure 9.4, top left) mainly occurs in regions with larger multinational enterprises, like Eindhoven (Philips), Stockholm (Ericsson), Helsinki (Nokia), Leverkusen (Bayer), Stuttgart (Bosch, Porsche , Mercedes) and Toulouse (Airbus). Public R&D (also in Figure 9.4, top right) is more related to regions with technological universities and regions where universities and firms alliance, like Cambridge, Leiden, Braunschweig and Rome.

The *degree of sectoral specialization and diversity* is a crucial variable in our models, as it tests our central hypothesis (specialization is related to productivity growth, especially in objective-one regions; while sectoral diversity is related to employment growth, especially in non-objective-one regions). The degree of regional specialization is measured by the Theil index over the location quotients of 59 products including agriculture, manufacturing and services. This unique dataset has been collected by the Netherlands Environmental Assessment Agency (PBL) and is based on regionalized production and trade data for European NUTS2 regions, 14 sectors, and 59 product categories. Location quotients measure the relative specialization of a region in a certain sector as the percentage of employment accounted for by a sector in a region relative to the percentage of employment accounted for by that sector in Europe as a whole:

$$LQ_i = \frac{X_{i,j} / \sum_j X_{i,j}}{\sum_i X_{i,j} / \sum_{i,j} X_{i,j}}$$

in which X represents the production and i and j the location and product group respectively. This quotient measures whether a sector is over- or underrepresented in a region compared with its average representation in a larger area, and therefore is to comprise localization or specialization economies of agglomeration. The Theil coefficient then measures deviations from the European average distribution of production specializations in all sectors. A high score represents a large degree of sectoral specialization in a region, and a low score represents sectoral diversity.

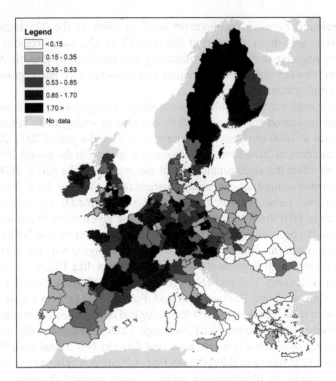

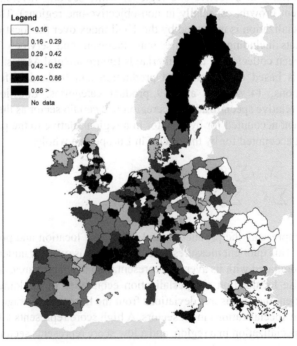

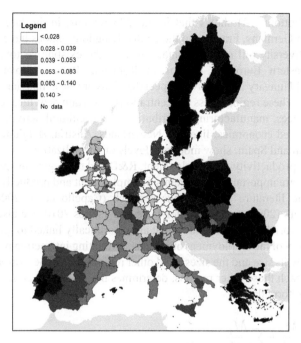

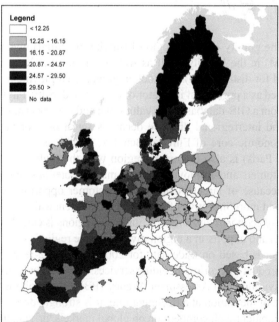

Figure 9.3 **Private R&D (top left), Public R&D (top right), degree of specialization (bottom left) and educational level (bottom right) in 235 European regions**

192 Hub Cities in the Knowledge Economy

Figure 9.3 (bottom left) shows that in our 235 regions, in the largest national economies of Germany, France and the United Kingdom regions have high levels of sectoral diversity (all regions contain most of the existing sectors, including services). Eastern European regions in Romania, Poland, Slovakia, Czech Republic and Hungary are relatively specialized, as are Scandinavian, Greek and Irish regions. These regions miss concentrations of certain activities, e.g. specific types of services, manufacturing, distribution or agricultural activities. A group of medium-sized economies, like The Netherlands, Austria, Belgium, Denmark, Italy, Portugal and Spain, show moderate levels of specialization.

Levels of productivity and employment, R&D and the degree of specialization and diversity are important determinants of employment and productivity growth. Based on the literature and previous research (Capello et al. 2008, Crespo-Cuaresma et al. (2009) and Rodriguez-Pose and Tselios 2010) we also introduce several other variables in our models that are theoretically linked to growth. First, a gravity model of the employment of regions, estimating interaction potentials for each region by its size and the sizes of all other regions in Europe, corrected for the distance to reach those other regions, determines the *market potential* of regions, following the formula:

$$P_i = \frac{M_i}{d_{ii}^\beta} + \sum_{i \neq j} \frac{M_j}{d_{ij}^\beta}$$

in which P is the gravity value of region I (market potential), measured by total employment (M) in the locality itself as well as in all other localities, the latter being corrected for distances (d). We took aggregated employment as a measure, for it is perceived as a prominent indicator of economic density. Physical distances are extracted from a GIS-database. The values of a and b, measuring the magnitude of the intra- and interregional distance decay, is set at one for national gravity values. The economic core of Europe (Benelux, South-east England, Germany, Northern Italy, Paris) is also the macro-region with the highest market potential (accessible customers and employees). Large market potential may lead to higher growth rates because of larger business and customer opportunities, potentially higher profits and more incentives for innovation and renewal.

The *degree of economic openness* of European regions is calculated as the total value of imports and exports in a region divided by the region's GDP. This volume of trade indicator is based on trade data for 2000 on NUTS2-level concerning 14 sectors and 59 product categories, including services. This dataset is developed by the Netherlands Environmental Assessment Agency (PBL). The volume of trade goes up with the size of the region at a declining rate. It is strongly dependent on global economic development with competition on global markets, driving up productivity and attracting new investments and collaborations. High potential may also spill over to nearby regions or in the regional network of specialized and subcontracting industries and regions. Some (but not all) larger regions score high on this indicator:

Table 9.1 Descriptive statistics and correlations of explanatory variables

	Descriptive statistics				Correlations										
	Min	Max	Mean	Std. Dev.	PR	PU	OE	MP	PD	EL	WA	SDI	EMP	PROD	OBJ1
Private R&D (PR)	0,008	5,008	0,844	0,938	1.000										
Public R&D (PU)	0,010	2,280	0,511	0,407	0,397	1,000									
Openness Economy (OE,ln)	-0,933	1,481	-0,349	0,392	-0,084	-0,160	1,000								
Market Potential (MP,ln)	8,284	10,413	9,467	0,459	0,375	0,200	-0,241	1,000							
Population Density (PD)	5	8494	358	850	0,053	0,236	-0,064	0,413	1,000						
Educational Level (EL)	5,488	45,818	20,467	7,886	0,423	0,443	-0,205	0,380	0,388	1,000					
Wage Level (WA)	1072	81838	20842	12380	0,501	0,344	-0,350	0,601	0,310	0,534	1,000				
Specialization – Diversity Index (SDI)	0,020	0,329	0,077	0,057	-0,211	-0,183	0,334	-0,592	-0,091	-0,279	-0,474	1,000			
Employment Level (EMP)	15816	5371400	852206	680388	0,191	0,178	-0,088	0,405	0,259	0,212	0,309	-0,170	1,000		
Productivity Level (PROD)	3,278	68,498	37,598	15,570	0,479	0,314	-0,474	0,613	0,233	0,497	0,777	-0,516	0,184	1,000	
Objective 1 regions (dummy) (OBJ1)	0	1	-	-	-0,402	-0,157	0,273	-0,663	-0,153	-0,331	-0,579	0,536	-0,167	-0,714	1,000

Barcelona, Madrid and Andalucia in Spain, The Low Countries (Belgium and The Netherlands), Dublin, Northern Italy, Paris and some internationally oriented trade-intensive regions in Germany (Thissen et al. 2012). *Density* (measured as population density) measures whether agglomeration (economic size) matters for economic growth. This dimension of agglomeration is not directly related to localization economies (specialization) and diversity economies, but to pure urban size effects (Frenken et al. 2007). The variable of density correlates strongly with an indicator of physical accessibility (by car and train) that we also constructed. The latter is therefore not included in the analyses. In general the literature suggests that higher density enables better interaction, enhancing growth (Puga 2002). We measured the *average educational level* of regions by the percentage of tertiary and higher educated in the total population (Figure 9.4, bottom-right). The hypothesized relationship with (employment and productivity) growth is positive, as more skilled people can be more productive, and agglomeration may attract more of these people. Remarkable low scores on this indicator are found in Greece, eastern European regions and Italian regions. The regional *wage level*, as an indicator of personal income, is hypothesized to positively relate to growth. The wage level variable correlates high with GDP per capita as an indicator. Higher wage levels and productivity levels are also highly correlated. In the productivity growth models, the wage level is therefore excluded from the analysis (and productivity level included). Finally, a dummy variable is introduced in the models: for those regions that received objective-one funding in the period 2000–2006. Although there is considerable debate on how the impact of these funds on productivity growth should actually be estimated (see Lopez-Roderiguez and Faina 2006), using time lags and controlling for the heterogeneity within the funds, we use this indicator to preliminary test for the relation of objective-one funds with growth – controlled for the many other possible factors influencing growth.

To avoid multicollinearity in our models, we tested for high correlations between all these explanatory variables, and we analysed variance inflation factors for each variable added to the models. None of the correlations are disturbingly high (above 0.65, see Table 9.1) – except for those mentioned above (wage and productivity level).

Models on Productivity Growth and Employment Growth

We present models for productivity growth (2000–2010) and employment growth (2000–2010) in Table 9.2. Reading from left to right, the first model in Table 9.2 explains productivity growth using explanatory variables according to Ordinary Least Squares (OLS) estimation. In the tables, positive and negative significant coefficients are indicated at the 5 per cent and 10 per cent level. The first model presented in Table 9.2, for productivity growth, confirms the regional convergence hypothesized, witnessed by the negative and significant parameter for the productivity level coefficient. Concerning the agglomeration variables, both density and degree of specialization are positively related to productivity growth in European regions. We hypothesized that for productivity growth, specialization and not diversification is important. The control variables mostly perform as expected. Investments in private R&D are positively related to productivity growth, but public R&D is negatively related. Public R&D may not have a positive effect because it seems to be (a less productive) substitute for private R&D (compare Guellec and van Pottelsberghe 2001). Higher educational levels significantly coincide with higher productivity. The openness indicator turns out to be not related to growth.

The next two columns in Table 9.2 show the same type of model of productivity growth where the sample is split in two regimes: those regions that received objective-one funds in the period 2000–2006 (including the eight Romanian regions), and those that did not. Regime analysis estimates the two equations simultaneously, and performs a spatial Chow-Wald test to determine the significance of the regime (see Van Oort 2004 for detailed explanation). The estimation software used also provides information on which variables especially cause the regimes to be different. In Table 9.2, those variables are pairwise marked by a box. The spatial Chow-Wald test for the total productivity growth equation (6.487, with high probability) shows that the two regimes significantly differ from each other. Concerning the most important variable, the relationship between productivity growth and the degree of specialization turns out to be relevant in the subset of objective-one regions, and not in the other regions. The convergence indicator (productivity level) is negatively related to productivity growth in both objective-one and non-objective-one regions. The openness indicator of trade has a positive effect in objective-one regions and is apparently leading to (international) growth externalities in these regions. Private R&D is especially important for productivity in non-objective-one regions, and higher educational levels are related to both types of regions.

The regime analysis shows that regions receiving objective-one funds perform fundamentally different on certain variables than other regions: on the specialization indicator (important in objective-one regions only), on the initial productivity level (having a much stronger convergence effect in objective-one regions), and on the public R&D indicator (negatively attached to growth in objective-one regions). We hypothesized especially the knowledge-economic variables to be important for growth. As policymakers specifically focus on these indicators for developing regional development policies (Barca et al. 2012), these outcomes are important. The insignificance of private R&D and the negative relation of public R&D with productivity growth suggest that investments in such knowledge sources do not warrant knowledge-outcomes or growth effects.

The regime analysis shows the complexity of regional productivity growth, and its determining factors. The heterogeneity found makes clear that policies and strategies for productivity improvement should be tailor-made on specific regions. Investments in the knowledge economy (educational level and business R&D) are in general the most promising factors to be stimulated – but only when focused on the specific sectoral specializations in (objective-one) regions.

Table 9.2   Regression results for productivity growth and employment growth in 235 European regions, 2000–2010

	Productivity growth			Employment growth		
	Total	Regimes		Total	Regimes	
		Obj.1	Non-obj.1		Obj.1	Non-obj.1
Constant	0,277	0,038	0,032	0,198	-0,612**	0,938**
	(1,441)	(0,152)	(0,124)	(0,974)	(-2,011)	(3,463)
Productivity level (ln)	-0,007**	-0,007**	-0,003**	-	-	-
	(-11,981)	(-10,270)	(-2,930)			
Employment level (ln)	-	-	-	-0,002	0,024**	0,005
				(-0,246)	(2,129)	(0,515)
Population density (ln)	0,014**	0,015*	0,009	0,003	-0,004	0,012*
	(2,459)	(1,703)	(1,235)	(0,634)	(-0,424)	(1,761)
Specialization – diversity (ln)	0,058**	0,097**	0,007	-0,013*	-0,002	-0,025**
	(5,384)	(6,024)	(0,445)	(-1,908)	(-0,129)	(-2,481)
Objective 1 (dummy)	-0,022	-	-	-0,009	-	-
	(-1,315)			(-0,643)		
Private R&D (ln)	0,015**	0,008	0,014*	-0,006	-0,004	-0,013*
	(2,383)	(0,991)	(1,890)	(-1,012)	(-0,543)	(-1,682)
Public R&D (ln)	-0,014**	-0,027**	-0,005	-0,006	-0,031**	0,002
	(-2,419)	(-2,655)	(-0,948)	(-0,687)	(-3,091)	(0,198)
Higher education (ln)	0,054**	0,097**	0,075**	0,027*	0,027	0,021
	(3,564)	(3,982)	(4,170)	(1,902)	(1,212)	(1,236)
Openness economy (ln)	0,017	0,033*	-0,007	0,033**	0,044**	0,037
	(1,019)	(1,794)	(-0,236)	(2,189)	(2,447)	(1,367)
Market potential (ln)	0,012	0,030	-0,002	-0,079**	-0,074**	-0,105**
	(0,527)	(1,073)	(-0,053)	(-3,909)	(-2,751)	(-3,789)
Wage level (ln)	-	-	-	0,054**	0,102**	-0,003
				(5,434)	(6,972)	(-0,227)
Adjusted R2	0,667	0,746		0,187	0,296	
Spatial Chow-Wald test		6,487	(0,000)		4,404	(0,000)

*$p<0.1$; **$p<0.05$; t-values in parentheses. Coefficients that significantly differ over regimes are boxed

The models 4–6 in Table 9.2 show similar models for employment growth across the European regions. In these models, the average wage level is included in the analysis (it was left out of the productivity growth analyses because of a high correlation with productivity level). Most importantly, and as hypothesized, the degree of diversity (and not the degree of specialization) is positively linked to growth, especially in non-objective-one regions (the economic core regions of Europe).[3] Private and public R&D are not as clearly (positively or negatively) linked to employment growth as to productivity growth. For employment, we also notice a limited process of 'convergence', as regions with a low level of employment do not show faster employment growth – in objective-one regions the relation is even positive (regions with a low level of employment have less employment growth). The trade openness and wage level indicators are positively related to employment growth, while market potential is negatively related – in both objective-one and other regions. The educational level is not significantly positive related to employment growth in both regimes.

Conclusions and Policy Implications

In this chapter, we investigated the contribution of agglomeration economies and knowledge endowments to economic growth in European regions that received objective-one funds as compared to regions that did not. We argue that the type of agglomeration economies in combination with the local knowledge structure of the economy is crucial for future long-term development prospects and competitiveness of regions. Regions with high knowledge potentials and a diverse economy are hypothetically able to absorb new knowledge typically for knowledge hubs or brainports in the European economy, creating new employment and raising productivity.

We found, in line with our hypothesis, that employment growth is primarily related to diverse economies in non-objective-one regions, while productivity growth is mainly the case in specialized (objective-one) regions. The type of agglomeration economies (specialization or diversity) related to the type of growth and embedded in knowledge-economic circumstances is important for regional economic growth. Our analysis suggests that at least the large (capital city, population-dense) objective-one regions should increasingly diversify their economy to reap long-term innovation and employment growth. The heterogeneity in significant results indicates, however, that policies for productivity growth as well as for employment growth should be tailor-made and region specific.

This outcome favours a focus on place-based development, as advocated recently by the European Union. Since its inception, European cohesion policy has been a subject of criticism (Bachtler and Wren 2006, Martin and Tyler 2006). Manzella (2009: 3–5) summarizes main criticisms and concludes that it has developed into a 'catch-all' policy without a clear mission and has an insufficient

---

3   Note that a negative relation between specialization and employment implies a positive relation between diversity and employment.

focus on growth. One of the biggest problems to proponents of Cohesion Policy is the difficulty in providing a credible economic case for the policy, which is based on conclusive evidence of effective results (Lopez-Rodriguez and Faiña 2006). In the recent discussion on the future of Cohesion policy, fuelled by Barca (2009), both critics and supporters have tended to agree on the need for a 'modernization' of the policy, in recognition of the weaknesses in the current approach and of the emerging challenges faced by the European economy, society and broader integration process. In this context of reform, it is of ever more importance to have insight in the relation between types of agglomeration economies, the economic structure of regions and regional economic development in regions with and without structural funds.

Besides the testing of this central hypothesis and its policy implications, this chapter particularly focused on the knowledge economic determinants of growth. We argued that especially regions endowed with public and private R&D initiatives and higher educational levels better link in with international knowledge networks of co-patenting, research collaboration, mobility of knowledge workers and patent citation (leading to innovation). The role of knowledge and human capital as a determinant of economic growth is more and more recognized in economic growth models. In these models, knowledge spillovers between economic agents play a crucial role in the growth and innovation process and lead to external economies of scale in production. New technological knowledge is seen as tacit, meaning that its accessibility as well as its growth spillovers are bounded by geographic proximity of high-tech firms or knowledge institutions. Our analysis shows the complexity of regional productivity growth in relation to these determining factors. Investments in the knowledge economy (educational level and business R&D) are in general the most promising factors for economic growth – but only when focused on the (objective-one) region specific sector specializations.

Our findings also urges for further research. Regional (place-based) specialization initiatives should be initiated and investigated intensively to learn from regional regularities and best-practices. We conclude that regions with high private knowledge potentials and a diverse economy are more able to absorb new knowledge typically for economic growth, also from knowledge networks. This hypothesis of knowledge hubs or brainports in the European economy should be tested more robustly by analysing firm networks, the knowledge content flowing through them and their actual contribution to growth.

References

Abernathy, W.J. and Clark, K.B. 1985. Innovation: mapping the winds of creative destruction. *Research Policy*, 14(1), 3–22.
Acs, Z.J. 2002. *Innovation and the Growth of Cities*. Cheltenham: Edward Elgar.
Bachtler, J. and Wren, C. 2006. Evaluation of European Union cohesion policy: Research questions and policy challenges. *Regional Studies*, 40(2), 143–54.

Baldwin, R. and Wyplosz, C. 2009. *The Economics of European Integration*, London: McGraw-Hill.

Barca, F. 2009. *An Agenda for a Reformed Cohesion Policy. A Place-Based Approach to meeting European Union Challenges and Expectations*. Brussels: Report for the EU.

Barca, F., McCann, P. and Rodriguez-Pose, A. 2012. The case for regional development intervention: Place-based versus place-neutral approaches. *Journal of Regional Science*, 52(1), 134–52.

Bathelt, H. and Glückler, J. 2011. *The Relational Economy: Geographies of Knowledge and Learning*. Oxford: Oxford University Press.

Beaudry, C. and Schiffauerova, A. 2009. Who's right, Marshall or Jacobs? The localization versus urbanization debate. *Research Policy*, 38(2), 318–37.

Becker, S.O., Egger, P.H. and von Ehrlich, M. 2010. Going NUTS: the effect of EU Structural Funds on regional performance. *Journal of Public Economics* 94(9–10), 578–90.

Beugelsdijk, M. and Eijffinger, S.C.W. 2005. The effectiveness of structural policy in the European Union: An empirical analysis for the EU-15 in 1995–2001. *Journal of Common Market Studies*, 43(1), 37–51.

Breschi, S. and Lissoni, F. 2009. Mobility of skilled workers and co-invention networks: An anatomy of localized knowledge flows. *Journal of Economic Geography*, 9(4), 439–68.

Capello, R., Camagni, R., Chizzolini, B. and Fratesi, U. 2008. *Modelling Regional Scenario's for the Enlarged Europe*. Berlin: Springer Verlag.

Combes, P.P. and Overman, H. 2004. The spatial distribution of economic activities in the European Union, in *Handbook of Regional and Urban Economics*, edited by J.V. Henderson and J. Thisse. Amsterdam: Elsevier, 2120–67.

Crespo-Cuaresma, J., Doppelhof, G. and Feldkircher, M. 2009. The determinants of economic growth in the European Union. CESifo Working Paper 2519. Munich.

de Groot H.F.L., Poot, J. and Smit, M.J. 2009. Agglomeration, innovation and regional development: Theoretical perspectives and meta-analysis, in *Handbook of Regional Growth and Development Theories*, edited by P. Nijkamp and R. Capello. Cheltenham: Edward Elgar, 256–81.

Derudder, B., Hoyler, M., Taylor, P.J. and Witlox, F. 2011. *International Handbook of Globalisation and World Cities*. Cheltenham: Edward Elgar.

Duranton, G. and Puga, D. 2001. Nursery cities: urban diversity, process innovation, and the life cycle of products. *American Economic Review*, 91(5), 1454–77.

Ederveen, S., de Groot, H. and Nahuis, R. 2006. Fertile soil for structural funds? A panel data analysis of the conditional effectiveness of European cohesion policy. *Kyklos*, 59(1), 17–42.

Florida, R. 2005. The world is spiky. *The Atlantic Monthly*, October 2005, 48–52.

Frenken, K., van Oort, F.G. and Verburg, T. 2007. Related variety, unrelated variety and regional economic growth. *Regional Studies*, 41(5), 685–97.

Fritsch, M. and Slavtchev, V. 2007. Universities and innovation in space. *Industry & Innovation*, 14(2), 201–18.

Fujita, M., Krugman, P. and Venables, A. 1999. *The Spatial Economy. Cities, Regions and International Trade*. Cambridge, MA: The MIT Press.

Glaeser, E.L., Kallal, H.D., Scheinkman, J.A. and Schleifer, A. 1992. Growth in cities. *Journal of Political Economy*, 100(1), 1126–52.

Guellec, D. and van Pottelsberghe, B. 2001. The impact of public R&D expenditure on business R&D. *Economics of Innovation and New Technology*, 12(3), 225–43.

Henderson, J.V., Kuncoro, A. and Turner, M. 1995. Industrial development in cities. *Journal of Political Economy*, 103(5), 1067–85.

Hoekman, J., Frenken, K. and van Oort, F. 2009. The geography of collaborative knowledge production in Europe. *The Annals of Regional Science*, 43(3), 721–38.

Lopez-Rodriguez, J. and Faiña A. 2006. Objective 1 regions versus non-Objective 1 regions: what does the Theil Index tell us? *Applied Economics Letters*, 13, 815–20.

Magrini, S. 2004. Regional (di)convergence, in *Handbook of Regional and Urban Economic: Cities and Geography*, edited by J.V. Henderson and J.F. Thisse. Dordrecht: Elsevier, 2741–96.

Manzella, G.P. 2009. *The Turning Points of EU Cohesion Policy*. Glasgow: University of Strathclyde.

Martin, R. and Tyler, P. 2006. Evaluating the impact of the Structural Funds on Objective 1 regions: An exploratory discussion. *Regional Studies*, 40(2), 201–10.

McCann, P. and van Oort, F.G. 2009. Theories of agglomeration and regional economic growth: A historical review, in *Handbook of Regional Growth and Development Theories*, edited by R. Capello and P. Nijkamp. Cheltenham: Edward Elgar, 19–32.

Melo, P.C., Graham, D.J. and Noland, R.B. 2009. A meta-analysis of estimates of urban agglomeration economies. *Regional Science and Urban Economics*, 39(3), 332–42.

Montfort, P. 2009. Regional convergence, growth and interpersonal inequalities across the EU. DG Regional Policy, European Commission.

Moreno, R., Paci, R. and Usai, S. 2005. Spatial spillovers and innovation activity in European regions. *Environment and Planning A*, 37(10), 1793–812.

Pasinetti, L.L. 1993. *Structural Economic Dynamics*. Cambridge: Cambridge University Press.

Puga, D. 2002. European regional policies in light of recent location theories. *Journal of Economic Geography*, 2(4), 373–406.

Rodrigues-Pose, A. and Tselios, V. 2010. Inequalities in income and education and regional economic growth in Western Europe. *The Annals of Regional Science*, 44(2), 349–75.

Rosenthal, S.S. and Strange, W.C. 2004. Evidence on the nature and sources of agglomeration economies, in *Handbook of Regional and Urban Economics*, edited by J.V. Henderson and J.F. Thisse. Amsterdam: Elsevier, 2119–71.

Saviotti, P.P. 1996. *Technological Evolution, Variety and the Economy*. Cheltenham: Edward Elgar.

Thissen, M. and van Oort, F. 2010. European place-based development policy and sustainable economic agglomeration. *Journal of Economic and Social Geography*, 101(4), 473–80.

Thissen, M., Burger, M., van Oort, F. and Diodato, D. 2012. The magnitude and distance decay of trade in goods and services: new evidence for European countries. *Review of World Economics*.

Van Oort, F.G. 2004. *Urban Growth and Innovation. Spatially Bounded Externalities in the Netherlands*. Alsderhot: Ashgate.

Van Oort, F.G. 2007. Spatial and sectoral composition effects of agglomeration economies in the Netherlands. *Papers in Regional Science*, 86(1), 5–30.

Van Oort, F.G. and Lambooy, J.G. 2012. Cities, knowledge and innovation. In: Fischer, M. and Nijkamp, P. (eds.), *Handbook of Regional Science*. Springer, Berlin.

Vernon, R. 1966. International investment and international trade in the product lifecycle. *Quarterly Journal of Economics*, 80(2), 190–207.

Westeren, K.I. 2012. *Foundations of the Kknowledge Economy. Innovation, Learning and Clusters*. Cheltenham: Edward Elgar.

World Bank. 2009. *Reshaping Economic Geography*, Washington.

Chapter 10

Types of Hub Cities and their Effects on Urban Creative Economies

Zachary P. Neal

Introduction

At least since the 2002 publication of Richard Florida's *Rise of the Creative Class*, and even more intensely following the global economic crisis in 2008, cities and their leaders have been looking to the creative and knowledge economies for solutions to a wide range of social and economic problems. At about the same time, a short paper by physicists Albert-László Barabási and Réka Albert (1999) altered the course of an emerging new science by demonstrating that most networks contain a few actors with an unusually large number of connections: hubs. To be sure, the conventional language of urban economic development had already told us that hubs are important. Regional economic development strategies often explicitly focus on creating 'Hubs of Innovation and Opportunity' (see http://www.development.ohio.gov/urban/ohiohubs.html), while more generally all civic leaders want their city to be a 'hub of activity'. However, a decade after these insights transformed their respective fields, we still know little about how hubs are important for creative economies. What does it mean for a city to be a hub, and how is being a hub important for cities' creative economies?

In this chapter, I aim to provide some preliminary answers to these questions. As an intrinsically relational concept, thinking about cities as hubs requires also thinking about cities as nodes in urban networks. Thus, I begin by considering the role that urban networks play in urban economies generally; and in their creative economies specifically. While cities that serve as focal points in these networks are commonly described as hub cities, and are viewed as economically advantaged, I argue that multiple types of hub city are possible. Paralleling Freeman's (1979) three conceptions of centrality in networks, at least three types of a hub city are possible: degree, closeness, and betweenness. Examining data on airline traffic among 128 US metropolitan areas in 2010 reveals that these different types define different rankings of hub cities, and that when it comes to their effects on urban creative economies, not all types of hubs are created equal (see also Graham and Goetz, 2005). The number of creative jobs in a city is strongly associated with the extent to which the city serves as a degree hub, weakly with the extent to which it serves as a betweenness hub, and not at all with its role as a closeness hub. These findings suggest that while hub cities are typically viewed as a key to the creative

economy and as a promising strategy for economic development, a more nuanced
view of hubs and their economic effects is necessary.

Networks and Urban Economics

Claims that urban networks play an important role in structuring urban economies
have a long history. As early as 1927, McKenzie argued that cities, not nation-states,
were key foci because 'the world is fast becoming a closed region [...] in which
centres and routes are gaining precedence over boundaries and political areas as
points of interest in spatial distribution' (p. 28). More contemporary investigations
into the relationship between urban networks and economies trace to one element
of Friedmann's world city hypothesis, namely, that 'key cities throughout the world
are used by global capital as 'basing points' [whereby] the resulting linkages make
it possible to arrange world cities into a complex spatial hierarchy' (1986: 71).
In the vast literature that has emerged from these early paradigmatic statements,
there is now general consensus that a city's position within networks of human
(e.g. migration), informational (e.g. Internet), and material (e.g. trade) exchanges
shapes its economic development in the region, and indeed the world.

Among the many positional characteristics of cities in urban networks,
centrality is perhaps most frequently identified as economically significant. Unlike
spatial conceptions of centrality that focus on a city's location in the middle of a
geographic territory (e.g. central place theory; see Christaller 1966), centrality
in the network context focuses on a city's location in the middle of a series of
exchanges with other cities. However, network centrality is not a single concept,
but rather a family of related concepts that provide slightly different ways of
operationalizing the inherently ambiguous notion of being 'in the middle.' Freeman
(1979) distinguished three forms of centrality: (1) degree centrality focuses on a
node's sheer number of connections, (2) betweenness centrality focuses on the
importance of a given node for moving from one part of the network to another,
and (3) closeness centrality focuses on a node's accessibility to other nodes.

When applied in the context of urban economies, more central cities are
generally presumed to be more economically dominant.[1] Three foundational
theories of regional economic dynamics serve to illustrate, however, that different
forms of centrality underlie different forms of economic dominance (see Figure
10.1; Irwin and Hughes 1992). First, economic base theory contends that a
city's economic dominance depends on its production of basic versus non-basic
goods, and thus on its level of exporting activity. Cities that export many goods
and services to many other places are more dominant because these other places
are dependent upon it (Andrews 1953, Alexander 1954, Mayer 1954). Recast in
network terms, economic base theory views centrality as critical for economic

---

1   It is important not to conflate centrality with power, which Neal (2011a) has argued
elsewhere are distinct concepts associated with different network positions.

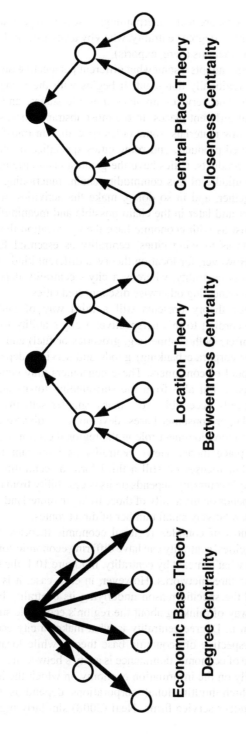

Economic Base Theory   **Location Theory**   **Central Place Theory**

Degree Centrality   **Betweenness Centrality**   **Closeness Centrality**

Figure 10.1 Conceptions of centrality and theories of regional economics

dominance. However, its theoretical underpinnings rest not on just any form of centrality, but specifically on degree centrality, whereby a city's centrality depends on its total volume of interactions (here, exports).

Second, location theory adopts a somewhat different perspective on the factors that make a given city regionally dominant. It begins with the recognition that the production of goods and services involves multiple stages, and that these stages may be located in different places. In the most abstract sense, some cities specialize in supplying raw materials, some cities specialize in transforming the raw materials into finished products, and some cities specialize in marketing or consuming the finished products. Cities have the greatest economic power when they are located in the middle of this commodity chain, functioning as bridges that hold the chain together, and in so doing, make the activities of cities and industries located earlier and later in the chain possible and meaningful (Cooley 1894, Cronon 1991). Just as with economic base theory, location theory can be recast in network terms as viewing cities' centrality as essential for regional economic dominance. However, for location theory, a different kind of centrality is important: betweenness centrality, whereby a city's centrality depends on its lying between and thus connecting otherwise disconnected cities.

Finally, central place theory presents still a third way of understanding regional economies. According to this perspective, a city's ability to develop a diverse economy that offers both routine (e.g. groceries or fuel) and specialized (e.g. couture fashion or corporate banking) goods and services depends on the availability of a large pool of consumers. These consumers may come not only from within the city itself, but also from the surrounding towns and villages. Thus, cities that are readily accessible from many smaller settlements in their hinterlands will enjoy larger consumer bases, develop more diverse economies, and subsequently play a more dominant role in the regional economy (Christaller 1966). Again, central place theory views centrality as important for a city's economic dominance, but focuses on still a third form of centrality: closeness centrality, whereby a city's centrality depends on its accessibility from other cities. More specifically, it depends on the ability of those living in hinterland settlements to reach the city using a relatively small number of direct routes.

While only caricatures of complex regional economic theories, these three examples illustrate that cities' centrality can have differing economic consequences depending on precisely what is meant by centrality. In Figure 10.1, the shaded city is central in each of the three networks. However, in each case, it is central for a different reason, and the specific reason underlying its centrality highlights a distinctively different way of thinking about the region's economic structure and of the city's role within it. Degree centrality is what makes a city economically dominant from the perspective of economic base theory, while location theory contends that the source of economic dominance is a city's betweenness centrality.

Focusing specifically on the information economy, in which the information and services upon which multinational corporations depend is transmitted through advanced producer service firms, Neal (2008) similarly highlights the differing consequences of cities' degree, closeness, and betweenness centrality. Cities with a high level of degree centrality in corporate information and services networks offer their local businesses more direct and immediate access to the global economy. In contrast, cities with a high level of closeness centrality offer their businesses less direct access, but also offer access to a wider slice of the global economy through indirect connections. Finally, and perhaps most significantly, cities with a high level of betweenness centrality offer their businesses the power to strategically block or facilitate the flow of information, which must pass through them en route to other cities and firms.

When the focus is on urban networks of economic exchange, notions of city centrality can appear abstract at best. However, when considered in the context of interurban transportation networks, cities' centrality takes on a particularly tangible meaning, captured in the commonsense notion of hubs. Indeed, we regularly speak of downtown bus depots and train stations as transportation hubs. Moreover, we recognize that easy access to these transportation hubs provides a range of practical benefits, including greater travel options at lower costs (see Conventz and Thierstein, this volume). In the case of airline travel in the United States, transportation hubs have taken on particular significance following the Airline Deregulation Act of 1978. This legislation prompted nearly all commercial airlines to replace their former point-to-point route structures with hub-and-spoke structures, which not only provided greater efficiency, but also catapulted certain cities – the hubs – into an entirely different strata of economic significance. As a result, much effort has been devoted to understanding the structure and evolution of transportation networks generally, and of airline networks in particular (Shaw 1993, Bania et al. 1998, O'Kelly 1998).

Studies of the economic consequences of a given city serving as airline hubs typically focus on such places offering greater levels of service and accessibility to local businesses and business travellers, and thus being associated with higher levels of employment (Brueckner 1985, Goetz 1992, Debbage and Delk 2001, Neal 2010). However, the finding that cities with busy airports also tend to have more jobs is relatively unsurprising. Thus, other investigations have turned to uncovering the causal relationship between hubs and economic growth. Across studies using differing methods and examining data from different time periods, there is remarkable consensus that economic growth, and specifically employment growth, is a consequence rather than a cause of cities' roles as hubs in the airline transportation network (Irwin and Kasarda 1991, Ivy et al. 1995, Brueckner 2003, Neal 2011b). Moreover, hubs seem to have these stimulative effects even for employment in specific sectors, leading to growth in high-tech (Button and Lall 1999) and creative jobs (Neal 2012).

Three Conceptions of a Hub City

These past studies highlight the economic importance of hub cities. However, they fail to take account of the fact that a city's hubness, like its centrality, is not a unidimensional concept. Just as the regional economic theories illustrate that there are multiple ways for a city to be central in a network, similarly there are multiple ways for a city to be a hub. Button (2002) identifies the multiplicity of definitions as one reason that the role of hubs, and their advantages and disadvantages, are difficult to assess. However, drawing on Freeman's (1979) three conceptions of centrality, which have been widely adopted in the social network literature, offers one way out of this conceptual confusion. While different hub types have been distinguished in the past (Fleming and Hayuth 1994, Derudder et al. 2007), situating these types within a common framework of centrality highlights their commonalities and provides a more consistent language for comparing their effects.

Fleming and Hayuth (1994) use 'centrality' to refer to the volume of terminally inbound passengers to a city, that is, the volume of passengers for whom the city is a final destination rather than a connecting stop. Similarly, Derudder et al. (2007) use 'relative hub intensity' to refer to the proportion of a city's passengers that are terminally inbound, that is, the proportion of passengers for whom the city is a final destination. While the former focuses on absolute volumes and the latter on relative volumes, these two concepts aim to capture the same characteristic as contributing to city hubness: the extent to which it serves as a destination for people. Because this characteristic is focused on capturing a city's total volume of interactions, it closely parallels degree centrality, and thus can be viewed as capturing a specific kind of hub: a *degree hub*.

The importance of degree hubs in the transportation context mirrors the importance of cities with degree centrality for export base theory: they participate in large numbers of interactions and thus are sites of concentration. Being a degree hub is potentially significant for a city's creative economies because, as a place that attracts large numbers of people, it is a place with greater concentrations of demand and information. Specifically, the large number of inbound passengers found in degree hubs can serve as consumers for the products of creative workers, and bring with them not only their spending power, but also new tastes and perspectives, which are essential for supporting creative work that is exciting rather than stale (Neal 2012). Past studies of hub cities have focused almost exclusively on degree hubs, and have found that such places have more robust and faster growing economies, both generally (Brueckner, 1985, Irwin and Kasarda 1991, Goetz, 1992, Ivy et al. 1995, Debbage and Delk 2001, Brueckner 2003, Neal 2011b) and within the creative sector (Neal 2012).

In contrast to their notions of centrality and relative hub intensity, Fleming and Hayuth (1994) use 'intermediacy' and Derudder et al. (2007) use 'absolute hub intensity' to refer to the volume of inbound but non-terminal passengers. That is, these concepts both aim to capture the volume of passengers for whom the city is a connecting or intermediate stop rather than a final destination.

Because this characteristic is focused on capturing a city's role lying between and thus linking otherwise disconnected origin and destination cities, it closely parallels betweenness centrality, and can be viewed as capturing a different kind of hub: a *betweenness hub*.

The importance of betweenness hubs in the transportation context mirrors the importance of cities with betweenness centrality for location theory: they are key connecting points in larger processes of exchange. However, betweenness hubs likely have little impact on creative employment because they merely identify places that connect passengers from one leg of a flight to the next. These connecting passengers do not engage with a city's economy in a meaningful way because they rarely even step outside the airport. Indeed, as Fleming and Hayuth (1994: 18, emphasis added) note, being a betweenness hub can 'be quite a transitory and artificial characteristic [...] that generates great *operational* significance to airports'. That is, the locations of betweenness hubs are driven primarily by individual airlines' routing strategies, and their economic impact is restricted primarily to the operational aspects of the transportation sector (Neal 2010). Empirical investigations of betweenness hubs are much more limited, but consistent with Fleming and Hayuth's (1994) expectation, Neal (2010) has found that their economic effects are concentrated in air transportation-related employment (e.g. baggage handlers, air traffic controllers, etc.).

Although not present in Fleming and Hayuth's (1994) discussion, Derudder et al. (2007) identify still a third characteristic of hubs. They use 'city hub intensity' to refer to the number of places to which a given city provides direct (i.e. nonstop) service. That is, it captures the number of places from which a given city is accessible without requiring a connecting flight. Because this characteristic is focused on a city's accessibility to and from other cities, it closely parallels closeness centrality, and can be viewed as capturing a final kind of hub: a *closeness hub*.

The importance of closeness hubs in the transportation context mirrors the importance of cities with closeness centrality for central place theory: they are the most convenient locations for consumers. The primary virtue of a closeness hub is the increased flexibility and convenience it offers those for whom it is their point of departure. For example, one need not worry about missing a connecting flight when departing from a city that offers direct, nonstop service to a large number of places. Few studies have directly examined the economic impact of closeness hubs. However, it seems unlikely that flexibility and convenience alone can drive creative economic growth.

Table 10.1 summarizes these three conceptions of hub cities, their relationships to existing terminology, and their previously demonstrated economic effects.[2] As this table and the preceding discussion illustrate, there has been little consistency in

---

2   Preston (1971), working within a central place theory framework, offers a similar set of concepts. Airline passengers can be viewed as a type of resource that cities either consume locally (i.e. because it serves as their final destination) or export (i.e. because it serves as a connecting stop). What Preston calls 'L' or local consumption mirrors the

Table 10.1   Three conceptions of a Hub City

Centrality-Based Terminology	Related Terminology[a]	Definition	Economic Effects
Degree	Centrality (FH) Relative Hub Intensity (DDW) Local Consumption (P)	City serves as a final destination for many passengers.	Positive, generally and in the creative sector (e.g. Brueckner 2003; Neal 2011b; Neal 2012).
Betweenness	Intermediacy (FH) Absolute Hub Intensity (DDW) Centrality (P)	City serves as an intermediate stop for many passengers en route to other destinations.	Restricted to the air transportation sector (Neal 2010).
Closeness	City Hub Intensity (DDW)	City provides direct service to/ from many other cities.	Previously unstudied

[a] FH = Fleming and Hayuth (1994); DDW = Derudder, Devriendt, and Witlox (2007); P = Preston (1971, see footnote 2)

the terminology used to describe the various conceptions of hub cities. Adopting a centrality-based terminology provides a more structured framework for discussing hub cities because it links notions of hubs to both established measures of network centrality (Freeman 1979) and longstanding theories of regional economics (see Figure 10.1). The table also illustrates that there are varying levels of evidence concerning the economic effects of each type of hub. First, much is known about the economic effects of degree hubs, while relatively little is known about the effects of closeness hubs. Second, those few studies that have investigated hub cities' economic effects generally do not focus on their effects for the creative or knowledge economies (Neal 2012 is an exception). Finally, each past study has focused on only one conception of a hub city, and thus has been unable to compare the relative economic effects of each type of hub city.

Measuring Hubness

These gaps in the literature have been driven in part by methodological challenges. Measuring the extent to which cities serve as each type of hub requires a specific

---

concept of a degree hub. Similarly, what he calls 'C' or centrality mirrors the concept of a betweenness hub.

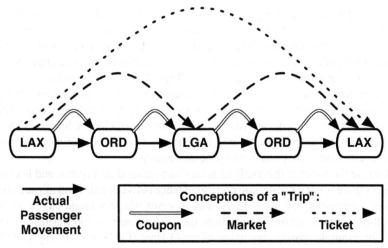

Figure 10.2   Conceptions of trip in the Origin and Destination Survey

kind of data. Thus, the specific conception(s) of hub cities investigated in past studies may not by theoretically driven, but instead as Button (2002: 179) notes, 'often reflects practical limitations of the quality of the data and information available'. However, using data from the U.S. Bureau of Transportation Statistics' Airline Origin and Destination Survey (ODS), it is possible to examine and compare each type of hub city. The ODS contains a range of information – origins and destinations, but also layovers and fares – about a 10 per cent random sample of all commercial passenger air traffic wholly between US cities. It has been released in quarterly intervals for several decades, and is available electronically since 1993 at http://www.transtats.bts.gov.

A key strength of these data is their organization according to three nested conceptions of a 'trip': coupon, market, and ticket (see Figure 10.2). The boxes and solid arrows illustrate the movements of an individual flying round-trip from Los Angeles (LAX) to New York City (LGA), with a layover in Chicago (ORD) in each direction. This journey can be deconstructed in several different ways. First, it is composed of four separate 'coupons' or nonstop service with a single takeoff and landing, so-called because each movement requires a separate boarding pass or coupon (hollow arrows). Second, it is composed of two 'markets' or combinations of an initial origin and final destination, so-called because the two cities are the markets in which the passenger meaningfully engages (dashed arrows). Finally, it is composed of one 'ticket' or complete itinerary from start to finish, so-called because it reflects the total movement of the passenger on a given airline ticket (dotted arrow).

By combining data on these different types of trip, it is possible to measure different types of hubness among cities. Degree hubs are the termini of markets, or cities that serve as passengers' final, rather than intermediate, destination.[3] In this example, New York City is a degree hub because it serves as the terminus of a market (i.e. it is the passenger's final destination).[4] In contrast, betweenness hubs are the termini of coupons but not markets; they are cities that serve as passengers' intermediate, rather than final, destination. Thus, Chicago is a betweenness hub because it serves as the terminus for a coupon but not a market, and indeed Chicago is clearly 'between' Los Angeles and New York. Finally, closeness hubs offer coupons (i.e. nonstop service) to a large number of cities. Chicago is also a closeness hub in this example because it offers coupons to two destinations, while the other cities offer coupons to only one destination.

Because the focus of this analysis is on cities rather than airports, and because in the US there is not a one-to-one correspondence between cities and airports, two types of aggregation are necessary.[5] First, in cases where a single city is served by multiple airports, all traffic to or from the city's airports is combined (N = 11). Thus, for example, passengers using either O'Hare (ORD) or Midway (MDW) airports are simply treated as Chicago passengers. Second, in cases where multiple cities are served by a single airport, the two cities are treated as one (N = 10). For example, because the Raleigh-Durham International Airport (RDU) serves both the Raleigh-Cary Metropolitan Area and the Durham Metropolitan Area, these two places are combined. Following these aggregations, it is possible to examine the hub roles of 128 cities, served by 145 airports.[6]

Not all Hubs are Created Equal

Comparing the extent to which US cities serve as degree, closeness, and betweenness hubs, it is clear that not all hubs are created equal. Table 10.2 lists the top 10 hub cities of each type in the US in 2010, with the corresponding measure of its hubness. For example, in 2010 Atlanta was the final destination for 11,469,230 passengers

---

3　In formal network terms, this corresponds to in-degree centrality because it focuses on inbound passengers. A slightly different approach might conceptualize a degree hub as the *origins* of markets, which corresponds to out-degree centrality because it focuses on outbound passengers. Here I concentrate only on the former conceptualization of degree hub/centrality because nearly all past investigations of hub cities have focused on cities where passengers are *going to*, rather than cities where passengers are *coming from*.

4　Los Angeles might also be viewed as a degree hub because it serves as the terminus of a market. However, it lies at the terminal end of a market that is merely the return leg of a round-trip. To avoid double counting, it is useful to focus only on the outbound coupons and markets of a round-trip ticket.

5　Throughout, I use 'city' to refer to metropolitan statistical areas, as defined by the US Census Bureau in 2010.

6　A complete list of the sample cities is provided in Neal (2012), table 1. Notably, although they both have major airports, Anchorage, AK and Honolulu, HI are excluded from these analyses as geographically outliers that are practically accessible only by air travel.

Table 10.2   Top 10 U.S. Hub Cities in 2010, by type of hub

Degree (Gini = 0.661)[a]		Betweenness (Gini = 0.866)		Closeness (Gini = 0.471)	
New York	26,503,070	Atlanta	18,366,780	Chicago	108
Los Angeles	21,166,460	Chicago	12,507,880	Atlanta	105
Chicago	17,271,180	Dallas	11,298,840	Detroit	102
Miami	14,896,710	Charlotte	10,086,900	Orlando	99
San Francisco	14,546,780	Denver	8,373,880	Dallas	98
Las Vegas	12,816,180	Houston	7,053,900	Houston	87
Orlando	12,681,740	Phoenix	6,053,630	New York	86
Dallas	12,006,540	Detroit	5,038,850	Minneapolis	83
Atlanta	11,469,230	Washington	3,813,680	Washington	83
Denver	11,194,100	Minneapolis	3,563,560	Denver	81

[a] Gini coefficients are computed for the complete sample (N = 128)

(degree), the intermediate destination for 18,366,780 passengers (betweenness), and provided nonstop service to 105 of the 128 cities in the sample (closeness). Far from an abstract quantification, these data exhibit much face validity for anyone who has flown in the US. The degree hub rankings clearly highlight the largest and most economically dominant US cities, focusing on what some have called America's global cities (Abu-Lughod 1999). The closeness hub rankings focus on places from which one can find a direct, nonstop flight to virtually any destination. Finally, the betweenness hub rankings list cities in which nearly any US air passenger has spent some time waiting for a connecting flight.

But, these simple rankings call attention to two important patterns. First, and most obviously, each ranking is unique, composed of different cities in a different order. Some cities – Atlanta, Dallas, and Denver – appear on all three lists, but many appear on only one. For example, while there is evidence that Miami serves as a degree hub, there is no indication that it serves as a betweenness or closeness hub. Looking beyond rankings to the actual measures of cities' hubness, correlations similarly indicate that there is only moderate association between the extent to which a city is, for example, a betweenness hub and degree hub ($r = 0.575$) or closeness hub ($r = 0.693$). The differences in the three lists presented in Table 10.2 highlight not only that there are multiple types of hub city, but also that being a hub of one type does not imply being a hub of another type.

These data also illustrate a second pattern, which is less obvious in the rank ordering, but is captured by the gini coefficient. The gini coefficient is a measure of inequality in a distribution, and here measures the extent to which there is inequality in cities' hubness. Values near zero indicate that all cities serve as

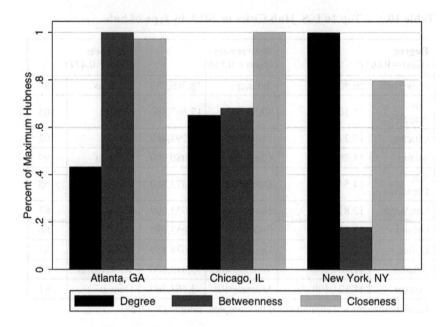

Figure 10.3   Hub profiles for three cities

hubs to an equal extent, while values near one indicate that only a small set of cities serve as hubs. Mirroring Neal's (2008) findings for cities' centrality in a network of corporate information and services, there is relative equality among closeness hubs and relative inequality among betweenness hubs. Thus, in the case of closeness hubs, although Chicago is a prime example with nonstop service to 85 per cent of the system, most other cities are not far behind. The second-ranked Atlanta offers nonstop service to 83 per cent of the system, while the tenth-ranked Denver still offers direct flights to 64 per cent of other cities. In contrast, Atlanta best exemplifies the role of a betweenness hub, and does so by a wide margin. The second-ranked Chicago serves 32 per cent fewer connecting passengers, while the tenth-ranked Minneapolis serves a striking 81 per cent fewer such passengers. Because there is little to distinguish one closeness hub from the next, whether a city serves as a closeness hub likely has little impact on its economy. Conversely, the greater levels of inequality observed among degree hubs or betweenness hubs suggest that these roles may be more consequential for economic outcomes.

Figure 10.3 presents a slightly different view of these data by focusing on the three cities that best exemplify each type of hub: Atlanta as a betweenness hub, Chicago as a closeness hub, and New York as a degree hub. Considering a city's three levels of hubness together – its hub profile – reveals its distinctive and multidimensional role as a hub in the urban system. These cities' hub profiles cannot be distinguished in terms of closeness; indeed, as noted above, most cities are closeness hubs. However, they can clearly be differentiated in terms of their

Table 10.3   Effects of hubness on creative employment (N = 128)

	(1)	(2)	(3)	(4)
Degree	0.719**			– 0.663**
Betweenness		0.446**		– 0.197**
Closeness			0.951**	– 0.327**
Constant	0.084**	4.478**	5.589**	– 0.036**
R^2	0.776**	0.723**	0.680**	– 0.801**

** $p < .01$; * $p < .05$ (using heteroskedasticity robust standard errors)

Note: All variables are logged; estimates represent elasticities

degree and betweenness. Atlanta serves as a betweenness hub, but not as a degree hub, highlighting its role in facilitating the movement of air passengers (and, by extension, their money and ideas), and thus its role as an *operations centre* for the airline industry. In contrast, New York serves as a degree hub, but not as a betweenness hub, highlighting its role as a *destination* for air passengers, information, and capital. Finally, Chicago lies between these two extremes, acting as both operations centre and destination.

How, then, do these different types of hubs impact the creative economy? Table 10.3 reports the results of a series of regressions that use cities' levels of hubness to predict the size of their creative economies. Here, the size of a city's creative economy is measured by the number of individuals employed in 'Arts, Design, Entertainment, Sports, and Media Occupations' (SOC 27-0000) in 2010, using the US Department of Labor's Occupational Employment Statistics Survey (2010). Models 1–3 examine the relationship between hub city status and creative employment at the bivariate level (i.e. for each type of hub separately). In contrast, model 4 uses all three forms of hubness simultaneously to predict cities' levels of creative employment, thereby isolating the unique effect of each type of hub. Preliminary data screening indicated that the relationship between creative employment and each type of hubness is nonlinear. To accurately capture these nonlinearities, all variables were log transformed. Thus, the coefficients in all models may be interpreted as elasticities (i.e. a 1 per cent change in the independent variable is associated with a <coefficient> per cent change in the dependent variable).

The results of models 1–3 largely confirm commonsense expectations that being a hub city of any kind has a significantly positive effect on creative employment. Doubling a city's degree hubness (i.e. its number of terminally inbound passengers) is associated with a 72 per cent increase in the number of creative jobs, doubling its betweenness (i.e. its number of connecting passengers) with a 45 per cent increase, and doubling its closeness (i.e. its number of nonstop destinations) with a striking 95 per cent increase. It is at this point that most past studies have stopped, concluding that being a hub city is good for creative economic development. To be sure, some forms of hubness (e.g. closeness) appear to be better than others (e.g. betweenness), but all appear to confer at least some economic advantage. However, focusing on only one form of hubness at a time, as these bivariate models and many past studies have done, potentially masks a more complex story about the economic effects of hub cities. Indeed, model 4, which considers all three forms of hubness simultaneously, yields results that differ from those of the simpler bivariate models.

The estimates in model 4 demonstrate, first, that the extent to which a city serves as a degree hub has a significantly positive effect on its number of creative jobs. This lends additional support to existing claims that degree hubs are economically significant (e.g. Brueckner 2003, Neal 2011b, 2012) by finding that terminally inbound passengers have a unique and strong economic impact that cannot be attributed to other factors like the city's number of nonstop destinations. Second, the extent to which a city serves as a betweenness hub has a significant, but relatively weak, positive effect on its number of creative jobs. This is consistent with Neal's (2010) earlier finding that the economic advantages enjoyed by betweenness hubs are primarily restricted to the transportation sector. Finally, the extent to which a city serves as a closeness hub has no significant effect on its number of creative jobs. Notably, being a closeness hub appears to have a strong effect on creative economies at the bivariate level (model 3), but once other forms of hubness are considered, its effect disappears. This is more consistent with the observation – highlighted previously by the low gini coefficient in Table 10.2 and bars of near-identical height in Figure 10.3 – that there is little variation among closeness hubs.

Geography Still Matters

Despite overblown claims about the 'death of distance' in a globalizing and networked world, geography still matters. In this analysis, geography is particularly important to consider as a potential source of location effects and boundary effects.

Location effects describe the effect that a city's location, relative to other cities, plays in its potential to serve as a hub. For example, Chicago's and Atlanta's locations in the middle of the country and near its population centre of gravity make them ideal cities to serve as closeness and betweenness hubs. In contrast, Seattle's or Miami's locations at the geographic extremes of the continental United States make them impractical hub sites. Providing nonstop service from Seattle or Miami to a large number of destinations (i.e. closeness), or requiring the passengers pass through these locations en route to their final destinations (i.e. betweenness), would be cost prohibitive and inefficient, at least given the country's current population distribution. Thus, in virtue of their location, some cities are more likely to be closeness or betweenness hubs than others. Notably, however, degree hubs are not subject to location effects in the same way because passengers' final destinations depend on their reason for travelling, and not on the destination's convenience. If one wishes to swim in the Atlantic Ocean, or must attend a business meeting at Microsoft Headquarters, one must fly to Miami or Seattle, no matter how locationally inconvenient these destinations might be.

Also driven by geography, boundary effects describe the effect that an artificial geographic boundary plays on a city's apparent hub status. The data analysed above include only air traffic wholly between US cities, but do not include traffic that begins or ends in a non-US city. Thus, these data include the relatively rare traffic between Lincoln, NE and Miami, but do not include the significantly more frequent and economically significant traffic between Miami and Rio de Janiero. Imposing a US boundary on these data provides a US-focused assessment of cities' hub status, but may yield an under- or over-estimate of their hub status at the global scale. For example, Table 10.2 illustrates that Miami is a major degree hub, but not a betweenness or closeness hub *with respect to air traffic in the United States*. However, with respect to global air travel, Miami likely does serve as a betweenness hub given its role as the primary transportation (and cultural) gateway linking North and South America. Conversely, while Orlando is a closeness hub in the US by offering nonstop service to and from many other US cities, its lack of nonstop service to non-US cities means it is not a closeness hub globally.

The Hub as an Economic Development Strategy

Bearing in mind the potential distortions introduced by location and boundary effects, these results provide a more complete portrait of the multiple types of hub city, precisely specifying the defining feature of three different concepts of a hub, and identifying the US cities that serve as a hub city in one or more ways. But more practically, they also illustrate that viewing hubs as a development strategy in the creative economy is not as straightforward as the standard policy rhetoric might suggest. Specifically, they illustrate that not all types of hubs are created equal, and thus that whether or not transforming a city into a hub will translate into creative economic growth depends on the specific form of hubness that is cultivated.

Political and business leaders frequently trumpet the addition of new nonstop flights as a driver of urban economic growth. Commenting on Japan Airlines' addition of nonstop service between Boston and Tokyo, Massachusetts governor Deval Patrick noted that 'a direct flight [...] is an invaluable economic partnership for the Commonwealth [of Massachusetts], and we look forward to the increased [...] economic development with Japan that it will bring' (Japan Airlines 2011). Similarly, on announcing the creation of nonstop service between Detroit and Beijing, Delta vice president Vinay Dube argued that 'our new flight to Beijing will mean even more opportunities for economic development and job growth in the city' (Delta Airlines 2011). Moreover, such gains are believed to come not only from international nonstop service, but also from domestic routes, with Lansing, Michigan and Madison, Wisconsin both adding service to Washington, DC in 2011. These added flights will certainly enhance cities' roles as closeness hubs.

However, as the findings above demonstrate, by itself this is likely to have no impact on the growth of their creative economy.

Similarly, attracting airlines to use a city as an intermediate destination for connecting flights is often viewed as a path toward regional economic growth. In the early 1990s, the Oklahoma Transportation Commission spent $156,000 to study the feasibility of attracting an airline operations hub (May 1990), while more recently Destin, Florida has successfully attracted leisure-focused Vision Airlines' operational hub (Yamanouchi 2011). Even in small markets like South Bend, Indiana, conventional wisdom holds that airports focusing on connecting flights are not only 'a place that you pass through in order to get from one destination to another. But in the grand scheme of things [...] play a central role as a driver of regional economic development' (Barger 2011). Attracting airlines' connecting and layover operations will certainly enhance cities' status as betweenness hubs. But again, as the findings above demonstrate, this is likely to have at most a modest effect on their creative economic growth.

Ultimately, only enhancing a city's status as a degree hub is likely to yield any significant growth in its creative economy. That is, while adding nonstop flights or attracting major airline operations are frequently adopted strategies for urban economic development, the real benefit comes from having a large number of terminally inbound passengers, who can infuse the local creative scene with new information and spending potential. That degree hubs, not closeness or betweenness hubs, are the key to creative economic growth is significant because it clarifies that creative economic growth is not the result of the structural features of airlines' route networks. For example, Los Angeles does not offer nonstop flights to many cities (i.e. it is not a closeness hub) and does not serve as a connecting point for many passengers (i.e. it is not a betweenness hub). It is, nonetheless, a destination for large numbers of people (i.e. a degree hub), and consequently the location of one of the largest urban creative economies. Simply modifying the structural arrangement of airline routes, by adding nonstop service or connecting flights, would likely have little impact on the city's creative scene because it is the incoming passengers – their ideas and capital – and not the airline routes themselves that are critical.

Conclusion

This analysis has provided a new and more precise language for discussing the role of hub cities in the creative economy, and more importantly has clarified that when it comes to creative economic development, not all (types of) hubs are created equal. While on a superficial level, being a hub appears to be economically beneficial, only certain forms of hubness offer real economic advantage. Specifically, closeness hubs that offer nonstop service to a range of destinations and betweenness hubs that serve as intermediate destinations hold little promise for creative economic growth. Instead, degree hubs that are terminal destinations for large numbers of passengers are the key to such growth. This finding makes possible the formulation of more targeted economic development strategies that are focused narrowly on the most beneficial types of hub cities.

References

Abu-Lughod, J.L. 1999. *New York, Chicago, Los Angeles: America's Global Cities*. Minneapolis: University of Minnesota Press.
Alexander, J.W. 1954. The basic-nonbasic concept of urban economic function. *Economic Geography*, 30(3), 246–61.
Andrews, R.B. 1953. Mechanics of the urban economic base. *Land Economics*, 29(2–4), 161–167, 263–268, 343–350.
Bania, N., Bauer, P.W. and Zlatoper, T.J. 1998. U.S. air passenger service: a taxonomy of route networks, hub locations, and competition. *Transportation Research E*, 34(1), 53–74.
Barabási, A.-L. and Albert, R. 1999. Emergence of scaling in random networks. *Science*, 286(5439), 509–12.
Barger, R. 2011. The South Bend regional airport: Michiana's landing zone for economic development. *South Bend Tribune*, April 26.
Brueckner, J.K. 1985. A note on the determinants of metropolitan airline traffic. *International Journal of Transport Economics*, 12(2), 175–84.
Brueckner, J.K. 2003. Airline traffic and urban economic development. *Urban Studies*, 40(8), 1455–69.
Button, K. 2002. Debunking some common myths about airport hubs. *Journal of Air Transport Management*, 8(3), 177–88.
Button, K. and Lall, S. 1999. The economics of being an airport hub city. *Research in Transportation Economics*, 5, 75–105.
Christaller, W. 1966. *Central Places in Southern Germany*. Englewood Cliffs, NJ: Prentice-Hall.
Cooley, C.H. 1894. *The Theory of Transportation*. Baltimore, MD: American Economic Association.
Cronon, W. 1991. *Nature's Metropolis:Chicago and the Great West*. New York: W.W. Norton.
Debbage, K.G. and Delk, D. 2001. The geography of air passenger volume and local employment patterns by US metropolitan core area: 1973–1996. *Journal of Air Transport Management*, 7(3), 159–67.
Delta Airlines. 2011. *Delta launches Nonstop Service between Detroit, Beijing*. Press Release, July 1.
Derudder, B., Devriendt, L. and Witlox, F. 2007. Flying where you don't want to go: Empirical analysis of hubs in the global airline network. *Tijdschrift voor Economische en Sociale Geografie*, 98(3), 307–24.
Fleming, D.K. and Hayuth, Y. 1994. Spatial characteristics of transportation hubs: centrality and intermediacy. *Journal of Transport Geography*, 2(1), 3–18.

Florida, R. 2002. *The Rise of the Creative Class: And How It's Transforming Work, Leisure, Community, and Everyday Life*. Basic Books: New York.

Freeman, L.C. 1979. Centrality in social networks: conceptual clarification. *Social Networks*, 1(3), 215–39.

Friedmann, J. 1986. The world city hypothesis. *Development and Change*, 17(1), 69–83.

Goetz, A.R. 1992. Air passenger transportation and growth in the U.S. urban system, 1950–1987. *Growth and Change*, 23(2), 217–38.

Graham, B. and Goetz, A. (2005) Global air transport, in *Transport Geographies: Mobilities, Flows and Spaces*, edited by R. Knowles, J. Shaw and I. Docherty. Oxford: Blackwell, 137–55.

Irwin, M.D. and Kasarda, J.D. 1991. Air passenger linkages and employment growth in U.S. metropolitan areas. *American Sociological Review*, 56(4), 524–37.

Irwin, M.D. and Hughes, H.L. 1992. Centrality and the structure of urban interaction: measures, concepts, and applications. *Social Forces*, 71(1), 17–51.

Ivy, R.L., Fik, T.J. and Malecki, E.J. 1995. Changes in air service connectivity and employment. *Environment and Planning A*, 27(2), 165–79.

Japan Airlines. 2011. *Japan Airlines to launch Nonstop Service between Boston and Tokyo in 2012*. Press Release, May 27.

May, B. 1990. Commission to study attracting airline hub. *The Journal Record* (Oklahoma City, OK), June 5.

Mayer, H.M. 1954. Urban nodality and the economic base. *Journal of the American Planning Association*, 20(3), 117–21.

McKenzie, R.D. 1927. The concept of dominance and world-organization. *American Journal of Sociology*, 33(1), 28–42.

Neal, Z. 2008. The duality of world cities and firms: Comparing networks, hierarchies, and inequalities in the global economy. *Global Networks*, 8(1), 94–115.

Neal, Z. 2010. Refining the air traffic approach to city networks. *Urban Studies*, 47(10), 2195–215.

Neal, Z. 2011a. Differentiating centrality and power in the world city network. *Urban Studies*, 48(13), 2733–48.

Neal, Z. 2011b. The causal relationship between employment and business networks in U.S. cities. *Journal of Urban Affairs*, 33(2), 167–84.

Neal, Z. 2012. Creative employment and jet set cities: Disentangling causal effects. *Urban Studies*, 49, 2693–709.

O'Kelly, M.E. 1998. A geographer's analysis of hub-and-spoke networks. *Journal of Transport Geography*, 6(3), 171–86.

Preston, R.E. 1971. The structure of central place systems. *Economic Geography*, 47(2), 136–55.

Shaw, S.-L. 1993. Hub structures of major US passenger airlines. *Journal of Transport Geography*, 1(1), 47–58.

U.S. Department of Labor. 2010. *Occupational Employment Statistics Survey.* Washington, DC: US Bureau of Labor Statistics.

U.S. Department of Transportation. 2010. *Airline Origin and Destination Survey (DB1B).* Washington, DC: US Bureau of Transportation Statistics.

Yamanouchi, K. 2011. Vision airlines sees hub in Destin. *Atlanta Journal Constitution*, May 17.

Chapter 11

Capital Cities as Knowledge Hubs: The Economic Geography of Homeland Security Contracting

Heike Mayer and Margaret Cowell

Introduction

This chapter examines the economic geography of federal procurement for homeland security products and services from 2001 to 2004. We argue that homeland security procurement acts as a powerful economic development force and its spatial distribution mirrors the geography of defence contracting. Homeland security contracting is disproportionately concentrated in states that make up the gunbelt, which stretches down the East Coast and along the South and the West of the United States. Furthermore, the data shows that the Washington D.C. capital region captured more than half of all procurement contracts and has become the most important location in the gunbelt and can thus be considered the knowledge hub of this industry. Examination of industry activity in the homeland security sectors shows that the tertiarization of the defence and homeland security industry facilitates strong agglomeration economies in the Washington D.C. region.

Capital cities play an important role in the formation and consolidation of the cultural, social and political identity of a nation. Capital cities like Washington D.C. are a nation's command and control centres and their power is not only reflected in their representative urban morphology but also in the ways in which knowledge that is essential for the functioning of a nation is formed. We argue that Washington D.C, like many capital cities, hosts a very specific type of economy that benefits from close interactions between government, administration, nonprofits and the private sector. Through these interactions, the capital city economy creates a unique economic geography. Yet, it is not only the physical infrastructure (e.g. airports, government quarters, etc.) that ensures the functioning of a capital city as a knowledge hub. In addition it is the – often immaterial – institutional, political and economic infrastructure that is created in such a capital city economy that is of interest here (Cooke 2012, Hoekman et al. 2012). Capital cities function as knowledge hubs because they are the centres of political decision-making and the execution of political power. It is in these capitals where the intersection of politics and economy seems to be most evident, particularly when it comes to private sector-government interactions. The homeland security industry – a sector that deftly walks the line between private and public entities – is an interesting lens through which these interactions can be studied. We are particularly interested in the role of the private sector and specifically the role of new types of industries that have emerged in the capital city economy.

In the United States, the tragic terrorist attacks in 2001 set in motion a variety of government reforms such as the creation of the Department of Homeland Security (DHS) in 2002 and the formulation of various legislations governing domestic protection and security (Kettl 2004). Along with these reforms, federal government significantly increased its contracting activities with the private sector for products and services designed to make the nation safer. This research shows that between 2001 and 2004 more than $18 billion were spent on airport and border screening equipment, electronic sensors and detectors that could discover explosive devices, modernization of the Coast Guard's fleet, tools for infrastructure protection, electronic tracking, information technology services, and strategy consulting among other advanced products and services. Total Federal contracting to private firms far exceeded the amount that was appropriated to state and local governments. For example, from 2003 to 2005, federal government appropriations to governmental entities totalled about $11.22 billion with an average of about $3.7 billion per year (Reese 2005). Moreover, local and state government agencies are facing continued reductions in federal appropriations while procurement from the private sector remains comparatively strong.

Procurement of these products and services from the private sector is a significant component of DHS' budget. In 2004, for example, homeland security contracts represented 15 per cent of the DHS' enacted budget (Department of Homeland Security 2005). Even though DHS' procurement activities only accounted for 1.7 per cent of total federal procurement in 2004, the investments by the federal government in the private sector, totalling $18 billion, warrants a closer look at the economic geography of homeland security investments, specifically as they relate to knowledge hubs and capital cities like Washington, D.C.

Capital cities can be conceptualized as knowledge hubs because they can be conceptualized as 'public information capitals' (Abbott 1999: 156). Particularly Washington D.C. shows characteristics of a knowledge hub: Abbott (1999: 148) argues that the shift towards information and service industries in the U.S. capital and the economy's specialization in defence, information industries, administration, research, education, culture and tourism reveals D.C.'s role as an 'information capital'. Associated with this development is, according to Abbott (1999) the rise of private idea brokers and information specialists. Against this background, capital cities could also be described as 'transactional cities' (Gottman 1977, 1985), which produce and disseminate information. In this sense, capitals can be called hubs because they mediate information, they are at a crossroads between local, state and federal interests, and they bundle actors who are genuinely interested in connections for the purpose of information sharing.

In this paper, we examine the geographic distribution of contracting activity with particular reference to the Washington D.C. region. We place this analysis in the context of the discussion about the geographic concentration of defence spending in the perimeter of the United States, the so-called 'gunbelt' (Markusen et al. 1991). The data suggest that the Washington D.C. region continues to be not only an important capital city region but also an emerging centre for defence services and a knowledge hub in the increasingly complex defence and homeland security industries. We argue that federal procurement for homeland security products acts as a powerful economic development force and that the Washington D.C. region has solidified and expanded its importance as a central knowledge hub in the gunbelt. This is illustrated by the increased spatial concentration of government procurement activity in defence and homeland security (Cowell et al. 2012).

Background

During the late 1980s and early 1990s, the regional development literature discussed extensively the economic geography of government contracting. Then and now, researchers were primarily interested in the spatial distribution of prime contracts with the Department of Defense (Enders and Sandler 2012). They argue that defence spending heavily influenced regional economic performance and the location of economic activity in the United States. In their seminal publication, Markusen et al. (1991) found that the majority of defence contracts were concentrated in an area called the 'gunbelt'. The gunbelt connected the two Coasts through the Southern part of the country and included 'New England, New York, the Washington, D.C., area, Florida, the central states from Missouri to Utah, Texas, Arizona, California, and Washington' (Markusen et al. 1991: 21). Defence-related activities contributed heavily to this region's economic growth and were among the factors responsible for the increased disparities between the Rust- or Frostbelt and the Sunbelt (Markusen et al. 1991, Atkinson 1993, Rundquist and Carsey 2002). The gunbelt's rise to prominence was reinforced by the immigration of labour (Campbell 1993), growing geographic concentration of defence research and development spending (Atkinson 1993), and an increase in subcontracting activities (Scott 1993). Research has shown that states that receive military procurement tend to have higher economic growth, which suggests that such spending fosters local economic development (Rundquist and Carsey 2002). Within the gunbelt, various regions developed certain specializations: Los Angeles and Seattle received most of the aerospace contracts, the New England area around Boston and New York specialized in aircraft, missile and spacecraft, and the Washington D.C. area emerged as a location for technology service providers (Malecki 2011; Markusen et al. 1991). Driving this development were firms that were new to the industry such as Northrop Grumman, Lockheed Martin, or TRW. These firms became leading government contractors and began to represent the so-called 'modern military industrial firm' (Ettlinger 1992).

Washington D.C. in particular captured the attention of scholars because it illustrated the emergence of a new organizational paradigm for government contracting activity: The region benefited from increased government outsourcing of tertiary activities that were not linked to manufacturing. Markusen et al. (1991: 213) called this development the 'tertiarization of the defence industry'. These tertiary activities were mostly associated with business, engineering and management services that involved advanced technologies and systems requirements (Stough et al. 1998). Often contracting for these services required close face-to-face interaction between the contractor and the government agency from the time contract requirements were written to when the product or service was delivered. Such close collaboration in turn meant that the contracting firm needed to be near the decision makers in the Pentagon or other federal agencies (Markusen et al. 1991). The requirement for information exchange facilitated the emergence of a critical mass of contractors in the Washington D.C. region, a knowledge hub that benefits from close interactions between government, administration, nonprofits and the private sector.

Additional research supported the claim that Washington D.C. specialized in defence services and government contracting (Fuller 2003, 2004a, 2004b, 2005, Stough et al. 1998). Moreover, other studies found that the region diversified and matured as a result of increased government outsourcing (Cowell et al. 2012). New firms emerged and built a vibrant industry cluster of biotech, information, and communication technology firms (Feldman 2001). This firm formation was spurred by exogenous events such as government downsizing, ability to provide services to government agencies, and the passage of various legislative acts that supported innovative and entrepreneurial activities (examples include the Stevenson-Wydler Technology Innovation Act, the Bayh-Dole University and Small Business Act, the Cooperative Research and Development Agreements, and the Small Business Innovation Research program) (Feldman and Francis 2004, Feldman et al. 2005).

In sum, the Washington D.C. region emerged as the defence-services centre of the gunbelt and was able to diversify its economy into industry sectors that are ancillary but less dependent on government contracting (Cowell et al. 2012). However, assessments of the continued importance of the D.C. region as a location for tertiary defence activities are missing and this chapter attempts to examine the gunbelt and knowledge hub hypotheses by using data on homeland security contracting. Previous research shows that the region's economy developed as a 'state-anchored industrial district' (Markusen 1996) and that there was economic diversification. Established military industrial firms, but also new firms are in place to take advantage of new opportunities the government may present. The emergence of the Department of Homeland Security and the need for developing products and services that would improve domestic safety could be seen as a new opportunity for Washington-based firms.

The present analysis can provide some insights as to whether the D.C. region has retained or even expanded its central position in the gunbelt and whether the region has taken advantage of additional contracting activity in the homeland security sector. The emergence of the homeland security industry is not just tied to the tragic terrorist attacks in 2001 and the establishment of DHS. Rather, the economic geography analysis suggests that many established defence firms and actors took advantage of this opportunity, essentially creating a new market within the emerging homeland security field. The evolution of the homeland security industry can largely be seen as an offshoot of the defence industry whereby existing players were able to take advantage of established networks and resources. Like the defence industry, these networks and actors are often called upon to develop products under very short deadlines. It can be hypothesized that because of the urgent need for a timely response, the development of requirements and the procurement of homeland security products and services may involve close interaction between private firms and the agencies that constitute the Department of Homeland Security, a process that likely facilitates agglomeration economies. The economic geography of homeland security contracting may thus be significantly tilted towards the D.C. region and towards established government contractors. Thus, homeland security contracting may display the same geographic patterns as defence contracting. In addition to analysing national patterns, we also examine the role of Washington D.C. as a knowledge hub and centre for government procurement in homeland security.

Methodology and Data

Many studies have utilized data on federal procurement to analyse the geographic and economic impact of federal spending activity (Cowell et al. 2012, Fuller 2003, 2004b, Markusen et al. 1991, Rundquist and Carsey 2002, Warf 1993). Federal government agencies and departments generally contract for products and services with the private sector. These activities are considered federal procurement. Traditionally, the Federal Procurement Data Center[1] provided information on government contracting activity. Beginning October 2004, a private company (Global Computer Enterprises[2]) began to operate the Federal Procurement Data System and called it *FPDS-Next Generation* (FPDS-NG). We gathered the data online from the Federal Procurement Data System Next Generation website (https://fpds.gov). Contracting information for all federal agencies is stored in a free but password-protected area of the website. The FPDS system is a significant upgrade from previous federal data systems because it allows government agency users to revise contract information that is either incorrect or revised at a future date.

For the purpose of this chapter, we utilized several criteria to gather the homeland security procurement data. First, data were collected for each fiscal year from 2001 to 2004. Fiscal year data was identified in the database by the 'Date signed' of the contract, per instructions from FPDS-NG consultants. The first year, 2001, constitutes the 'pre-9/11' year. That year reflects federal procurement activity prior to the increase in attention to domestic protection and the formation of the

---

1   For more information see http://www.fpdc.gov/fpdc/fpdc_home.htm.
2   GCE's website is http://www.gce2000.com/

Table 11.1   Agencies with independent contracting authority

DHS agencies with independent contracting authority
Animal and Plant Health Inspection Service
Federal Emergency Management Agency
Federal Law Enforcement Training Center
Immigration and Naturalization Service
Transportation Security Administration
U.S. Coast Guard
U.S. Customs Service
U.S. Export Administration
U.S. Secret Service

Source: Adapted from Fuller (2004b)

Department of Homeland Security. Second, data were gathered by both vendor (i.e. government contractor) and place of performance. The vendor allowed for an analysis of different companies and their role in homeland security contracting across time. Information on place of performance formed the basis for analysing data at the level of States and Metropolitan Statistical Areas (MSA).[3] Finally, data were gathered for the agencies that had independent contracting authority and comprised the Department of Homeland Security (DHS) after its formation. Independent contracting authority is important, for without that it is impossible to tell if a department within an agency was the source for a contract or not. For instance, the Office of Domestic Preparedness was established by the Department of Justice after 11 September, 2001. The Office eventually became part of the DHS, but it did not have independent contracting authority and consequently any contracts that it issued were issued by the Department of Justice. Its contracting data is not possible to disaggregate from the remainder of the Department of Justice using the FPDS database. The nine agencies that had independent contracting authority prior to the formation of the DHS and that were incorporated into the DHS are illustrated in Table 11.1.

Additionally, DHS itself has independent contracting authority and their procurement was also included in our analysis. However, DHS did not begin contracting until 2004. We did not include agencies such as the Central Intelligence Agency (CIA) or the National Security Administration (NSA) because they are exempt from reporting their contracts to FDPS. The selection of these nine agencies is in line with prior studies on the impact of federal spending in homeland security. In particular, Fuller (2004b) has utilized the same set of agencies to determine federal spending in homeland security.

The data was gathered from the FPDS Next Generation website. We prepared online reports in which we identified each of the above agencies by their 'Agency

---

3   The U.S. Census provides definitions for metropolitan statistical areas and lists each MSA's components on the following website: http://www.census.gov/population/estimates/metro-city/List1.txt.

ID' number and then ran a query for all information from each agency for the years 2001 to 2004. A total of just over 25,000 records were collected for four years of Homeland Security contracting. We geo-coded the data and identified only MSAs within the domestic United States for the analysis. All foreign contracts or contracts to United States territories were excluded from analysis. While this reduced the total records analysed to just over 24,000 in total, its impact on procurement was minimal as the vast majority of Homeland Security expenditures (99 per cent in 2004) took place within the domestic United States.

It should be noted that exact replication of this data analysis is difficult. The FPDS Next Generation online system has an open interface whereby contractors or government procurement agents can, at any time, go into the contracting record and change information related to the contract. While this should, in the long run, serve to make the database more accurate than a one-time entry, it also means that the data may be subject to review and change at any time. Our data was collected between 1 and 13 March, 2005. For an exact replication, the database would have to be retrieved from FPDS-NG that corresponds to those dates; whether this is possible or not is unknown.

Additionally, the data has a number of limitations. First, the data does not provide information on multiple contractors. Contracts that involved the cooperation of two companies on a larger project are always assigned to one corporation or the other. Qualitative analysis of the contract in question is required in both of these situations to better ascertain where the contracting dollars will ultimately procured. Second, especially for the year 2004, a significant part of the data had missing information about the industry sectors (NAICS codes). Therefore, some of the high-tech analyses could not be performed for the year 2004 and we limited our analysis of procurement by sectors to 2001 to 2003 (see Table 11.5).

Homeland Security Contracts: A National Overview

In 2001, federal agencies that were combined in 2002 to constitute the Department of Homeland Security, awarded contracts valued at $2.447 billion. This increased in the post 9/11 years to $5.345 billion in 2004 (see Table 11.2). Compared to the Department of Defense, DHS' contracting activity is modest, though in absolute terms and with regard to the geographic distribution of $18 billion dollars over a four year period it can be considered a significant economic force.

After an intense investment period during 2002 and 2003, it appears that procurement for homeland security products and services has slowed down: During 2004, there was a slight decrease (−2.2 per cent) in activity compared to the year before (see Table 11.2 and Figure 11.1). The spike in procurement does not come as a surprise since federal security activities increased after September 11, 2002. The government invested in particular in aviation security after the 2001 passage of the Aviation and Transportation Act and the associated creation of the Transportation Security Administration (TSA). TSA had to fulfil mandates for

Table 11.2   Total Homeland Security Spending, 2001–2004

Year	Actions	Dollars	Homeland Security	Portion of Total Federal Procurement	Change (Year to Year)
2001	624,253	$221,324,866,589	$2,447,014,703	1.1%	
2002	806,650	$260,029,932,077	$4,758,836,507	1.8%	94.5%
2003	1,136,445	$309,090,683,308	$5,463,435,326	1.8%	14.8%
2004	1,706,874	$314,973,729,928	$5,345,844,348	1.7%	−2.2%
Total	4,274,222	$1,105,419,211,902	$18,015,130,885	1.6%	

Source: FDPS-NG (2005)

tighter and safer procedures in baggage screening set forth in the Act. Thus, major investments in equipment (e.g. screening technology) and services (e.g. TSA personnel at airports) primarily occurred during the fiscal year 2002.

Figure 11.1 illustrates Washington D.C.'s share in procurement activity and illustrates the growth trends in domestic homeland security procurement relative to the nation's capital share and the share of other metropolitan statistical areas. We will discuss the Washington D.C. case in more detail below.

Most interesting is the geographic concentration of procurement activity at the level of states. From 2001 to 2004, Virginia received 26.96 per cent ($4.857 billion) of the nation's contract activity. The District of Columbia captured 20.76 per cent ($3.740 billion). These two geographies received almost half (45.72 per cent) of all contracting activity. Texas (10.65 per cent or $1.918 billion), Maryland (7.07 per cent or $1.273 billion), and California (6.46 per cent or $1.163 billion) follow distantly. Other states that received a significant amount of homeland security procurement from 2001 to 2004 are Georgia ($481 million), Florida ($336 million), New York ($319 million), Washington ($315 million), and Arizona ($312 million). Except for Georgia, these states were all classified as the gunbelt by Markusen et al. (1991). Georgia's high level of contracting activity can be explained by the headquarter location of the Federal Law Enforcement Training Center in Glynco, Georgia (Federal Law Enforcement Training Center 2005). The Center spends more than half of its budget on procurements from the private sector (in 2004, this amounted to $112 million or 59 per cent of its enacted budget). From 2001 to 2004, the Center contracted for more than $257 million in Georgia, explaining the state's high ranking in overall contract activity.

Figure 11.2 and 11.3 illustrate at the national level the geographic patterns of homeland security and defence procurement. The maps visualize the correlation between the two types of procurements. States that received high levels of defence procurements from 2001 to 2004 also received high levels of homeland security procurement. The top three states that received the most procurement in both

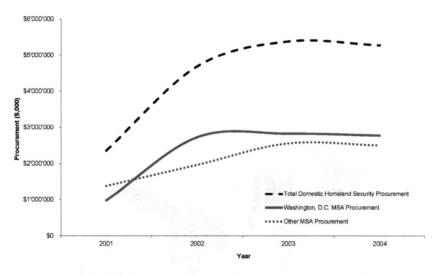

Figure 11.1   Homeland security procurement trends, 2001 to 2004

Source: FDPS-NG (2005)

categories – defence and homeland security – are: California, Texas, and Virginia. These three states anchor the gunbelt and illustrate that the

> new military-industrial regions do indeed resemble the belt around the hips of the solitary sheriff in pursuit of the bad guys in an old western movie. The southwestern states, Texas, and the Great Plains make up the holster; Florida represents the handcuffs ready to be slipped on the wrists of the villains; New England is the bullet clip. (Markusen et al. 1991: 4)

In the homeland security procurement map the holster is slimmer, but the overall geographic pattern of the gunbelt remains.

Metropolitan Investment Patterns in Homeland Security

A strong geographic concentration becomes apparent when analysing the metropolitan patterns of homeland security investments. In each year from 2001 to 2004, the Washington MSA has topped the list of metropolitan areas receiving homeland security contracts. In 2001, its share of total homeland security procurement was about 39 per cent. This rose to 51.9 per cent in 2004 indicating further concentration of economic activity in the homeland security sector. From 2001 to 2004, a total of $9,302,058,483 was spent on work performed in the Washington D.C. metropolitan region. When compared to venture capital

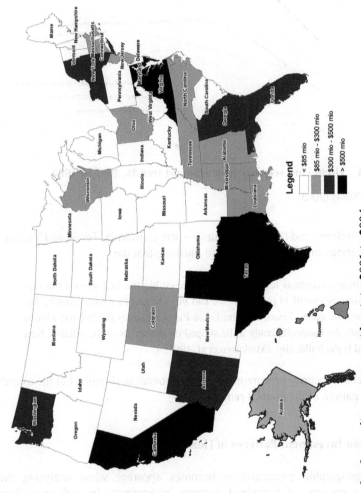

Figure 11.2 Homeland security procurement by state, 2001 to 2004

Source: FDPS-NG (2005)

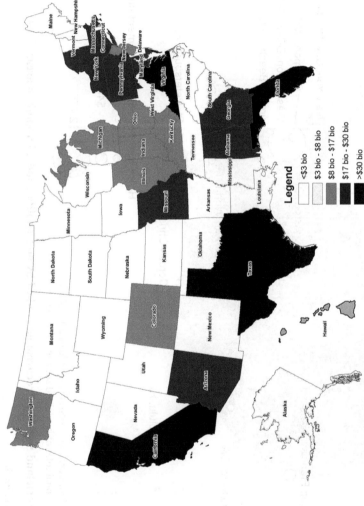

Figure 11.3 Department of Defense procurement, 2001 to 2004

Source: FDPS-NG (2005)

Legend

<$3 bio

$3 bio - $8 bio

$8 bio - $17 bio

$17 bio - $30 bio

>$30 bio

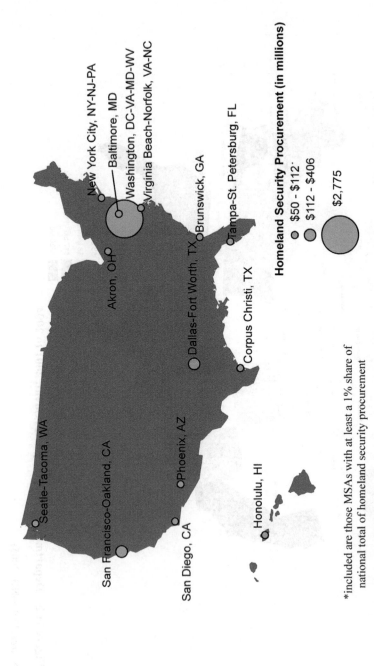

New York City, NY-NJ-PA

Baltimore, MD

Washington, DC-VA-MD-WV

Virginia Beach-Norfolk, VA-NC

Brunswick, GA

Tampa-St. Petersburg, FL

Akron, OH

Dallas-Fort Worth, TX

Corpus Christi, TX

Seatle-Tacoma, WA

San Francisco-Oakland, CA

Phoenix, AZ

San Diego, CA

Honolulu, HI

Homeland Security Procurement (in millions)

○ $50 - $112

○ $112 - $406

$2,775

*included are those MSAs with at least a 1% share of
national total of homeland security procurement

Figure 11.4   Homeland Security Procurement ranked by metropolitan and micropolitan areas, 2004

Source: FDPS-NG (2005)

investment, it becomes clear how much of an economic force government procurement can be: The investments in homeland security products and services were almost twice as high as the amount of venture capital invested in the region during the same time frame. From 2001 to 2004, 772 Washington D.C.-based firms received a total of $5,007,400,000 in venture investments (Ventureeconomics 2005). Though these venture capital investments certainly contribute to the Washington D.C. economy, homeland security procurement dollars fuelled more of the growth in the Washington D.C. metropolitan economy over these five years.

The Dallas-Fort Worth and the San Francisco metropolitan areas are a distant second and third to the Washington, D.C. region. Both regions captured less than 8 per cent in procurement in 2004. In Dallas-Fort Worth, Boeing received a total of $336 million in 2004. Other contractors in the Dallas metropolitan area included (in order of the amount of contracting activity they received):

- American Eurocopter (a helicopter manufacturer based in Grand Prairie),
- Godwin Corporation (a health care service firm providing contract services to the U.S. Coast Guard in Miller, Texas),
- Halff Associates (a civil engineering firm located in Texas that contracts with Federal Emergency Management Agency),
- Murillo Modular Group (working primarily worked with FEMA on modular buildings),
- Hayes, Seay, Mattern & Mattern (HSMM is headquartered in Roanoke, Virginia, and provided architectural and engineering services primarily for FEMA),
- Security Consultants Group (headquartered in Oakridge, Tennessee, the firm provides security services for the Bureau of Immigration and Customs Reinforcement),
- Superior Protection (headquartered in Arkansas, this company provides security services to the Bureau of Immigration and Customs Enforcement),
- Coastal International Security (headquartered in North Carolina, the firm provides security services to the Bureau of Immigration and Customs Enforcement), and
- Comprehensive Flood Risk Resources (provided services to FEMA).

The list of contractors illustrates that homeland security work performed in the Dallas-Fort Worth primarily concentrated on border security and protection as well as emergency management.

The major contractors in San Francisco included:

- Invision Technologies (based in Newark, California, the company develops detection equipment and contracted with TSA),
- Covenant Aviation Security (headquartered in Illinois the company provides aviation security services at San Francisco airport),
- BI Incorporated (headquartered in Boulder, Colorado, the company

provided services to the Bureau of Immigration and Customs Enforcement),
- Puglia Engineering (a shipbuilding firm based in Alameda, California, worked with the U.S. Coast Guard),
- All Star Services Corporation (provided housing construction and maintenance services to the U.S. Coast Guard),
- Oakwood Worldwide (housing services primarily for the U.S. Coast Guard),
- San Francisco Drydock (ship repair services for U.S. Coast Guard),
- Columbia Healthcare/Arora Group (health care services to U.S. Coast Guard),
- King Security Services (security and patrol services to U.S. Coast Guard), and
- Tandberg (video communication service provider headquarter in New York).

This list illustrates that in the San Francisco region, the U.S. Coast Guard and the San Francisco airports were the major drivers of homeland security contracting. Other metropolitan areas did not receive particularly large shares of homeland security contracts. In general, they received less than 2 per cent of contract activity and such a small share pales in contrast to the Washington D.C. region.

The Case of Washington D.C.

Homeland security contracting activity in the Washington, D.C. region more than tripled from $974 million in 2001 to more than $2.77 billion in 2004. Since 11 September 2001, the D.C. region captured a steadily high amount of contracting activity in homeland security. The region's share of total contracting increased from almost 40 per cent to 51.9 per cent in 2004 indicating further concentration in homeland security industry activity in the Washington, D.C. metropolitan area. In general, homeland security procurement seems to follow the spatial distribution patterns of defence procurement with high concentrations across the gunbelt; however, homeland security procurement tends to concentrate in the Washington, D.C. region.

Within the D.C. region, the data shows that homeland security contracting activity has become more concentrated in suburban Virginia. Almost two thirds (62.8 per cent) of all contracting activity in 2004 was performed in suburban Virginia counties such as Arlington, Fairfax, and Loudoun (as illustrated in Figure 11.5). While the Northern Virginia region gained contracting activity, the District of Columbia has seen a significant decline from 2003 to 2004. This seems to support the argument several scholars have made about the importance of suburban locations of government contractors (Harrington and Campbell 1997, Markusen et al. 1991) in what Garreau (1992) termed 'edge cities' like Tysons Corner, Virginia. These suburban locations may offer government contractors lower costs than downtown D.C. could offer. While close interactions with federal government agencies are important, suburban locations in the same metropolitan area seems to

Table 11.3 Homeland security contracting in Washington, D.C.

	2001	2002	2003	2004	Share of regional or national Procurement		
					2001	2004	Annual Change 01-04
District of Columbia	$ 349,794,547	$ 1,373,094,534	$ 1,312,082,319	$ 705,557,628	35.9%	25.4%	25.4%
Suburban Virginia	$ 481,548,602	$ 942,922,194	$ 1,307,771,123	$ 1,742,862,955	49.4%	62.8%	65.5%
Suburban Maryland	$ 143,245,000	$ 387,316,166	$ 205,259,221	$ 321,620,471	14.7%	11.6%	31.1%
Suburban WV	$ 376,000	$ 22,529,000	$ 788,341	$ 5,290,382	0.0%	0.2%	326.8%
Metropolitan D.C.	**$ 974,964,149**	**$ 2,725,861,894**	**$ 2,825,901,004**	**$ 2,775,331,436**	**39.8%**	**51.9%**	**46.2%**
Total United States	**$ 2,447,014,703**	**$ 4,758,836,507**	**$ 5,463,435,326**	**$ 5,345,844,348**			**29.6%**

Source: FDPS-NG (2005)

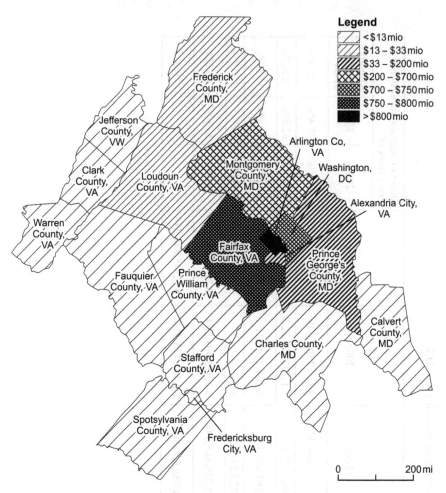

Figure 11.5   Homeland security procurement in the Washington D.C. metropolitan region, 2001 to 2004

Source: FDPS-NG (2005)

be sufficient. One suburban location in the D.C. region is Arlington County, which received more than $818 million or 29.5 per cent of the total procurement in the Washington, D.C. region. Arlington's share exceeded the metropolitan areas of Dallas-Fort Worth and San Francisco combined (see Figure 11.4). Agglomeration economies have emerged in large part because Arlington County is close to the Pentagon and is home to several other federal agencies such as the Defense Advanced Research Projects Agency (DARPA), the National Science Foundation, Office of Naval Research, the Transportation Security Administration (TSA) among others (Mayer 2005, Mayer et al. 2005). Furthermore, several think tanks and research groups such as the federally funded Homeland Security Institute (Homeland Security Institute 2005), the public-service research institute ANSER, and the Homeland Security Advanced Research Projects Agency (HSARPA) (Homeland Security Advanced Research Projects Agency 2005) call Arlington their home. The spatial concentration of such important institutions may explain the co-location of government contractors as they are able to be part of the policymaking process. Figure 11.5 illustrates the spatial distribution of homeland security contracting in 2004 in the Washington D.C. metropolitan region.

Markusen et al. (1991) have argued that the Washington D.C. region has benefited from a process of tertiarization of the defence industry. They have shown that rather than manufacturing products for government purposes, firms in the D.C. region have specialized in providing value-added services, often very knowledge intensive services. Such tertiary procurement concentrates on high-technology products and services without associated manufacturing. Firms contracting with government agencies function as conduits and integrators of systems, technologies, services and products utilized for homeland security and defence purposes but produced somewhere else. These firms employ specialized knowledge about existing products and apply it to specific government purposes. This so-called systems integration does not rely on adjacent manufacturing because the production is done elsewhere. Rather, government contractors depend on the availability and access to information about the latest products and services, a highly educated workforce, close interaction with procuring government agencies, and an ability to quickly react in flexible ways to government demands. These requirements facilitate spatial co-location of military industrial firms and government agencies. They also explain Washington D.C.'s growing share of highly educated workers that function as 'symbolic analysts' in this knowledge hub (Reich 1991). Markusen et al. (1991: 229) note that '[t]he result has been the establishment of an information complex similar, in many ways, to the cluster of financial institutions on Wall Street or the concentration of industrial headquarters offices in midtown Manhattan'.

Within homeland security contracting, Washington D.C.-based contractors have taken advantage of this process of tertiarization. To illustrate the concentration on tertiary activities, Table 11.5 presents the percentage share of high-tech and non-high-tech procurement for the D.C. region.[4] Government contractors located in the suburban Virginia part of the D.C. region specialize to a high degree in high-tech related procurement (especially high tech services such as computer systems integration, research and development, etc.). While other parts of the D.C. region are less specialized in high-tech, suburban Virginia has a location quotient of 1.28,

---

4   The high-tech industry classifications are defined by NAICS codes and are only complete for the 2001 to 2003 time period. Data with associated NAICS information for 2004 is very incomplete and could therefore not be used for this analysis. High technology procurement was defined using the high tech definitions developed by Chappel et al. (2004) and Paytas and Berglund (2004).

Table 11.4　　High-tech and non-high-tech homeland security procurement, 2001–2003

	Homeland Security Procurement		LQ for High Tech Procurement
	High Tech	Other	
District of Columbia	26 %	74 %	0.68
Suburban Maryland	19 %	81 %	0.48
Suburban Virginia	50 %	50 %	1.28
Suburban West Virginia	13 %	87 %	0.33

Source: FDPS-NG (2005)

which demonstrates that the region has a higher concentration in high technology procurement as compared to the national average.[5]

Ettlinger (1992) describes firms performing work for federal government agencies such as the Department of Defense and the Department of Homeland Security as military industrial firms (MIFs). These firms emerged after WWII and are characterized by a substantive commitment to innovation and research and development, a highly specialized workforce, the production of small quantities of goods, and a high degree of spatial concentration (primarily in the gunbelt region of the Southwest, along the Pacific Coast and New England). Ettlinger further notes that MIFs operate in an oligopolistic market that often is guaranteed (by the federal government) and has significant financial support. Markusen et al. (1991: 33) further elaborate on the nature of these firms and argue that the military industrial complex is a 'new form of continual industrial innovation, even if its market spin-offs may be minimal'. They continue to say that these firms have a high degree of concentrated market power and are very dependent on the federal government as a buyer.

Firms contracting with the Department of Homeland Security fit this category of military industrial firms. Often these firms are the 'usual suspects' that have been contracting with the Department of Defense for a long time and can be regarded as the pioneering MIFs. Examples include Lockheed Martin and

---

5　The location quotient (LQ) analysis is used to determine the relative concentration of a certain industry in a region compared to the national average. Typically the measure is used for employment and a location quotient for a particular industry is a ratio that compares the percentage of overall employment constituted by one particular industry in a local economy to the percentage of employment the same industry constitutes in a reference economy (i.e. the national economy). Location quotients, however, can also be used to calculate the concentration of other kinds of economic activity such as venture capital investments, patent registrations, or like in this paper, for government procurement contracts.

Table 11.5   Top 10 contractors in the Washington, D.C. MSA, 2001–2004

Rank	Company Name	Total in Washington D.C.	Total in 2004	Portion of Procurement in D.C. MSA
1	Integrated Coast Guard Systems	$550,196,658	$550,196,658	100.0%
2	Unisys Corp	$372,464,769	$372,464,769	100.0%
3	Cooperative Personnel Services	$138,857,727	$138,857,727	100.0%
4	Lockheed Martin	$126,648,248	$156,226,846	81.1%
5	Accenture	$90,683,948	$91,008,948	99.6%
6	Dewberry & Davis LLC	$80,808,946	$80,868,946	99.9%
7	Michael Baker Corporation	$76,655,094	$78,353,921	97.8%
8	Chenega Management LLC	$70,549,236	$71,693,943	98.4%
9	Computer Sciences Corporation	$69,268,055	$69,268,055	100.0%
10	EG&G Technical Services	$62,748,365	$62,748,365	100.0%
All other companies		$1,136,450,390		

Source: FDPS-NG (2005)

Northrop Grumman. They regard homeland security as a new market and have established distinct departments to cater to governmental needs for domestic protection, terrorism detection and prevention. In many cases these firms employ former DHS senior executives and thereby take advantage of their expertise and network connections. They can be considered the central actors in Washington's knowledge hub economy.

Table 11.5 outlines the top ten contractors that perform work in the Washington D.C. metropolitan region for the Department of Homeland Security. Common to these firms is their focus on professional service delivery to DHS agencies such as the U.S. Coast Guard, FEMA, Immigration and Naturalization Service, and the Transportation Security Administration. Unisys for example provides services for border control. The firm was enlisted to develop biometric systems to register travellers coming to the United States. Cooperative Personnel Services has been a major contractor for the Transportation Security Administration and has provided them with workforce recruiting, assessment and selection services. Lockheed Martin and Northrop Gumman operate the joint venture called Integrated Coast Guard Systems. Their venture is widely known as the Deepwater project and involves a $550 million grant to modernize the Coast Guard's fleet. Their work in the Washington D.C. region is primarily related to the coordination and logistics of this contract, again a tertiary activity. Dewberry & Davis, Michael Baker, EG&G Technical Services, and Chenega Management are firms that specialize in engineering services, computer facilities management, and telecommunication services. Most of these firms serve primarily the government market and they receive contracts from various DHS agencies. These firms also have a track record in working with the Department of Defense, which helps them in entering the homeland security market because they are already familiar with the government procurement bureaucracy and the special needs government agencies may have. Most of these firms that are headquartered outside of the D.C. region, have established local offices. In some cases, they even have multiple offices in the D.C. region such as Michael Baker Corporation which has two locations in Virginia (Alexandria and Manassas) and one in Maryland (Frederick). In many cases these firms also have a permanent presence inside government agencies. This is primarily the case when the firms work on internal service delivery such as updating an agency's information and communication technologies. The emphasis of these firms on delivering services as diverse as information technology, personnel, and engineering services, corroborates the notion of tertiarization of governmental activities in the D.C. region. Within the homeland security sector, this process has contributed to the emergence of a dense agglomeration in the region of service-oriented military industrial firms and in the continued economic and political significance of this capital city.

Conclusion

The region around the nation's capital has emerged as the most important location for homeland security contract activity. Washington D.C. is not merely a capital city that relies on political functions. Rather it has emerged as an important knowledge hub for the defence and homeland security industries. The increased tertiarization of defence and homeland security contracting facilitated the rise of the D.C. region as a central location on the gunbelt. In fact, as the data show, the nation's capital has become the most important bullet on the gunbelt, while states like California and Texas held their central position as the gunbelt's holster and buckle. New England is still important as the bullet clip, but is now more prominently anchored by Washington D.C. Within the Washington D.C. region, the Northern Virginia suburbs have emerged as central locations of private sector contractors. At a more detailed geographic level, high tech corridors have developed that symbolize the post-Fordist nature of Washington D.C. regional economy (Knox 1991).

Scholars have called the Washington D.C. capital region the 'national information broker' (Abbott 1999), illustrating how it functions as a knowledge hub. Abbott further argues that 'state power and public information are centralized forces that attract a complex of private sector activities in ways similar to the attractions of concentrated financial power. In this light, the federal government can be understood as a producer service that is an important input for domestic and foreign corporations' (Abbott 1999: 156). This type of central coordination is a powerful force for spatial agglomeration. For homeland security procurement, governmental needs to coordinate outsourcing and the acquisition of advanced services necessitated co-location of private contractors. In addition, the service nature of procurement activities contributed to increased tertiarization. Washington D.C.'s military industrial complex might be more similar to New York's financial service industry, which is clustered in and around Manhattan, than to the military industrial complexes in Southern California. While the Southern California military industrial complex drew heavily on traditional location factors such as lower labour cost and lower cost of living, which many Sunbelt locations were able to offer, the Washington D.C. region offers defence and homeland security firms a different environment. Firms in the Washington area benefit from spatial and relational proximity to government agencies and are able to draw on their resources. The question, however, is whether firms in the Washington D.C. region are innovative or whether they just fulfil specifications they co-develop with government agencies. We have not answered this question but think that this topic warrants much closer examination to tell us more about the nature of the economic milieu and whether the capital city as a knowledge hub is innovative and creative or whether it is highly protected and lethargic regarding innovation.

This research is especially significant for economic development practitioners because state and local government agencies are beginning to target the homeland security industry. States like Illinois, Michigan, and New York are focusing on the homeland security sector and are using traditional economic development incentives to attract firms (Empire State Development 2005, Illinois Department of Commerce and Economic Opportunity 2005, Michigan Economic Development Corporation 2005). In most cases, economic development practitioners also provide assistance with government procurement contracting to firms. Often, policymakers see the opportunity to attract jobs that can't be outsourced to countries like China and India. At the local level, several business incubators across the country are beginning to focus on entrepreneurial support for homeland security firms. From these observations, it seems that economic development practitioners are beginning to see the homeland security industry as a target sector much like it has been the case with biotechnology, life science, or nanotechnology. Still, there are large differences between these industries when it comes to capital needs, market exposure and international competition, all important distinctions that practitioners would be wise to consider. Like we see in so many gunbelt locales, this research presents evidence of powerful agglomeration forces that benefit locations that already have a significant advantage. Though in the case of the Washington, D.C. region it is a government town that acts as a knowledge and information hub. In that sense, the homeland security industry might follow the general patterns of spatial concentration of high technology industries (Cortright and Mayer 2000, 2002).

References

Abbott, C. 1999. *Political Terrain: Washington D.C., from Tidewater Town to Global Metropolis*. Chapel Hill: The University of North Carolina Press.

Atkinson, R.D. 1993. Defense spending cuts and regional economic impact: An overview. *Economic Geography*, 69(2), 107–22.

Campbell, S. 1993. Interregional migration of defense scientists and engineers to the Gunbelt during the 1980s. *Economic geography*, 69(2), 204–23.

Chapple, K., Markusen, A., Schrock, G., Yamamoto, D. and Yu, P. 2004. Gauging metropolitan "High-Tech" and "I-Tech" activity. *Economic Development Quarterly*, 18(1), 10–29.

Cooke, P. 2012. Knowledge economy spillovers, proximity, and specilization, in *Interactive learning for innovation: A key driver within clusters and innovation*, edited by B.T. Asheim and M.D. Parrilli. New York, NY: Palgrave Macmillan, 100–111.

Cortright, J. and Mayer, H. 2000. *A Comparison of High Technology Centers*. Portland, OR: Institute for Portland Metropolitan Studies, Portland State University.

Cortright, J. and Mayer, H. 2002. *Signs of life: The Growth of Biotechnology Centers in the U.S.* Washington D.C.: The Brookings Institution.

Cowell, M., Gabriel, C., Khan, S., Mayer, H., and O'Brien, P. 2012. *DC Innovation Strategy for Saint Elizabeths: Final Report*. Washington D.C.: District of Columbia, Office of Planning.

Department of Homeland Security 2005. *Budget-in-Brief: Fiscal Year 2006* [Online]. Available at: http://www.dhs.gov/interweb/assetlibrary/Budget_BIB-FY2006.pdf [accessed: 9 April 2005].

Empire State Development 2005. *New York State Homeland Security Initiative* [Online]. Available at: http://www.nylovesbiz.com/HomelandSecurity/default.asp [accessed: 5 December 2005].

Enders, W. and Sandler, T. 2012. *The Political Economy of Terrorism*. New York: Cambridge University Press.

Ettlinger, N. 1992. Development theory and the military industrial firm, in *The Pentagon and the Cities*, edited by A.M. Kirby. Newbury Park, CA: SAGE Publications, 23–52.

Federal Law Enforcement Training Center 2005. *About FLETC* [Online]. Available at: http://www.fletc.gov/pao/about_fletc.htm [accessed: 26 July 2005].

Federal Procurement Data Center 2005. *FPDS-NG Procurement Data* [Online]. Available at: https://www.fpds.gov/.

Feldman, M. 2001. The entrepreneurial event revisited: Firm formation in a regional context. *Industrial and Corporate Change*, 10(4), 861–91.

Feldman, M. and Francis, J. 2004. Homegrown solutions: Fostering cluster formation. *Economic Development Quarterly*, 18(2), 114–27.

Feldman, M., Francis, J. and Bercovitz, J. 2005. Creating a cluster while building a firm: Entrepreneurs and the formation of industrial clusters. *Regional Studies*, 39(1), 129–41.

Fuller, S. 2003. *Federal Spending, especially on Security, kept Washington Economy Growing in 2002.* Washington D.C.: The Brookings Institution Center on Urban and Metropolitan Policy.

Fuller, S. 2004a. *The Emerging Shape of the Expansion* [Online]. Available at: http://www.cra-gmu.org/forecastreports/12thAnnualFuller.doc [accessed: 3 December 2007].

Fuller, S. 2004b. *FY 2003 Federal Procurement Spending and its Impact on the Washington Economy in 2004 and Beyond* [Online]. Available at: http://www.cra-gmu.org/forecastreports/ProcurementReport.pdf [accessed: 3 December 2007].

Fuller, S. 2005. *Federal Procurement Spending in the Washington Area Increases by $7.8 Billion in 2004, Up 18.4 Percent, To a Total of $50.0 Billion* [Online]. Available at: http://www.cra-gmu.org/forecastreports/FederalProcurement2004Report.pdf [accessed: 15 July 2005].

Garreau, J. 1992. *Edge City: Life on the New Frontier*. New York: Doubleday.

Gottman, J. 1977. The role of capital cities. *Ekistics*, 44(264), 240–43.

Gottman, J. 1985. The coming of the transactional city. *Annals of the Association of American Geographers*, 75(3), 450–52.

Harrington, J.W. and Campbell, H.S. 1997. The suburbanization of producer service employment. *Growth and Change*, 28(3), 335–59.

Hoekman, J., Frenken, K., and van Ort, F. 2009. The geography of collaboratve knowledge production in Europe. *Annals of Regional Science*, 43, 721–38.

Homeland Security Advanced Research Projects Agency 2005. *Homeland Security Advanced Research Projects Agency Solicitation and Teaming Portal* [Online]. Available at: http://www.hsarpabaa.com/ [accessed: 29 July 2005].

Homeland Security Institute 2005. *What is HSI?* [Online]. Available at: http://www.homelandsecurity.org/about.asp [accessed: 29 July 2005].

Illinois Department of Commerce and Economic Opportunity 2005. *Homeland Security Market Development* [Online] [accessed: 5 December 2005].

Kettl, D. 2004. Overview, in *The Department of Homeland Security's first year: a report card*, edited by D. Kettle. New York: The Century Foundation, 1–29.

Knox, P. 1991. The restless urban landscape: Economic and sociocultural change in the transformation of metropolitan Washington D.C. *Annals of the Association of American Geographers*, 81(2), 181–209.

Malecki, E.J. 2011. Internet networks of world cities: Agglomeration and dispersion, in *International handbook of globalization and world cities*. Edited by B. Derudder, M. Hoyler, P.J. Taylor, and F. Witlox. Northampton, MA: Edward Elgar, 117–25.

Markusen, A. 1996. Sticky places in slippery space: a typology of industrial districts. *Economic Geography*, 72(3), 293–313.

Markusen, A., Hall, P., Campbell, S. and Deitrick, S. 1991. *The Rise of the Gunbelt: the Military Remapping of Industrial America.* New York: Oxford University Press.

Mayer, H. 2005. *The Homeland Security Industry and its Impact on the Arlington, Virginia, Economy* [Online]. Available at: http://www.arlingtonvirginiausa. com/docs/homeland_security_short.pdf [accessed: 21 November 2005].

Mayer, H., Holzheimer, T. and Glidden, H. 2005. Fostering emerging technology sectors in Arlington County: An economic development strategy for knowledge creation and innovation. *Economic Development Journal*, 4(1), 7–17.

Michigan Economic Development Corporation 2005. *Granholm Touts Michigan to Defense, Homeland Security Companies* [Online] Available at: http:// medc.michigan.org/news/major/combo.asp?ContentId=B377D5C7-4E40- 40F8-A454-F707BE0EC3C4&QueueId=1&ContentTypeId=7 [accessed: 5 December 2005].

Paytas, J. and Berglund, D. 2004. *Technology Industries and Occupations for NAICS Industry Data* [Online]. Available at: http://www.ssti.org/Publications/ Onlinepubs/NAICS_Tech1.pdf [accessed: 3 December 2007].

Reese, S. 2005. *State and Local Homeland Security: Unresolved Issues for the 109th Congress* [Online]. Available at: http://fas.org/sgp/crs/homesec/ RL32941.pdf [accessed: 2 December 2005].

Reich, R. 1991. *The Work of Nations: Preparing Ourselves for 21st Century Capitalism.* New York: Knopf.

Rundquist, B. and Carsey, T. 2002. *Congress and Defense Spending: The Distributive Politics of Military Procurement.* Norman: University of Oklahoma Press.

Scott, A. 1993. Interregional subcontracting patterns in the aerospace industry: The Southern California nexus. *Economic Geography*, 69(2), 142–56.

Stough, R., Haynes, K. and Campbell, H.S. 1998. Small business entrepreneurship in the high technology services sector: An assessment for the edge cities of the U.S. National Capital region. *Small Business Economics*, 10(1), 61–74.

Ventureeconomics 2005. *MoneyTree Venture Capital Profile for Washington Metroplex* [Online]. Available at: http://www.ventureeconomics.com/vec/ stats/2005q2/metro_2100.html [accessed: 25 July 2005].

Warf, B. 1993. The Pentagon and the Service Sector. *Economic Geography*, 69(2), 123–41.

Index

mimicking 98
Minneapolis 28, 213, 214
Mitchell, W.J. 145
mobile internet 125
mobile phones 125, 132, 151
    data analysis 152–4
mobility 79, 153, 198
models 11, 14, 15, 16, 38ff, 62, 85, 91,
    131, 152ff
    interaction 16, 152
    multi-linear 18
    productivity growth 182, 186ff, 194
    regression 18, 20ff, 154, 215
modules 111, 114, 154
mono-centric city 86
Montfort, P. 181, 183
Montgomery, J. 100, 101
Moreno, R. et al. 189
morphogenesis 77, 78
morphology 16, 95, 99, 100, 106
Moscow 27, 129, 133, 134, 135
Moss, M.L. 146
Mould, O. 5, 164
multi-layered spaces 77, 79, 97
multi-location firms 58
multiple hub types 203, 208ff
multi-port gateway 104–5, 107
Mumbai 23, 28, 135, 139
Munich 28, 43, 47, 48, 49, 64ff, 72, 133ff,
    170
    Airport 77, 80
Myrdal, G. 37, 59, 100

national scale 4, 13–14, 19, 20, 22, 23, 45,
    49
Neal, Z.P. 5, 13, 31, 204n, 206ff, 210
Neef, D. 148
neighbours 43, 73
neoclassical theory 59
Netherlands 16, 17, 28, 86, 87, 129, 133,
    153, 186ff, 192, 194
Netherlands Environmental Assessment
    Agency (PBL) 192
network access points (NAPs) 126, 131
network analysis 151
network data 62–4
network economies 32, 36, 38–9, 49, 83–4,
    99

network science 146, 153
'network society' 57, 149
networks 2, 3, 15, 31, 32ff, 55–73, 91, 98,
    104, 227
    and cities 55–6ff, 203ff
        and centrality types 206–7ff
    connectivities 41–2
    changes in 62–4ff
    functional 31, 37, 57
    integration 43, 45
    office 11, 15, 41ff
    scale-free 152
    and territory 57–8
    types of 56
    urban 204
New Economic Geography (NEG) 182–3
new firms 185, 226
new knowledge 33, 59, 70, 78, 83, 84, 98,
    183, 197, 198
New York 12, 28, 124, 129, 131, 132,
    134ff, 225, 230, 236, 243
New York City airport (LGA) 211, 212,
    213
Newman, M.E. 111
Niederrad 89
Niedersachsen 107
Nigeria 27, 134
Nijkamp, P. and Jonkhoff, W. 148
nodes 31, 38, 56, 57, 77, 81ff, 85, 95, 98,
    99, 149, 203, 204
    Internet 124
Nohria, N. and Eccles, R. 98
Nonaka, I. and Takeuchi, H. 56
non-aviation sector 80
non-material knowledge 56, 59, 62, 100,
    223
non-objective-one regions 185, 189, 195,
    197
non-physical flows 98
nonstop service (airline) 209, 211ff
non-tariff barriers 3
non-verbal communication 98
Nooteboom, B. 55
Norcliffe, G. et al. 166
North Germany 96, 101–3, 105–15
    collaboration in 107, 111, 114, 115
        data 113
    knowledge spillovers 108

For Product Safety Concerns and Information please contact our
EU representative GPSR@taylorandfrancis.com Taylor & Francis
Verlag GmbH, Kaufingerstraße 24, 80331 München, Germany